HISTORICAL DEVELOPMENT OF LEGAL LITERATURE ON CUSTOMARY LAWS IN ASSAM

HISTORICAL DEVELOPMENT OF LEGAL LITERATURE ON CUSTOMARY LAWS IN ASSAM
A Critical Study

Wakidur Rohman

Publications

KALPAZ PUBLICATIONS

DELHI-110052

Historical Development of Legal Literature on Customary Laws in Assam

Rs. 750

ISBN: 81-7835-428-4

Published in 2005 in India by
Kalpaz Publications
C-30, Satyawati Nagar, Delhi-110052
E-mail : Kalpaz@hotmail.com

Laser Typesetting at : Master Computers, Delhi
Printed at : Salasar Imaging System, Delhi

Dedicated To My Father

Contents

Preface

The people in Assam are found at different stages of development, basically who are living in the inner and hill areas. The situation is that either the village chief or the village panchayat dispenses justice according to the customary rules obtained till recently in varying degrees depending on the stage of development. While the British government extended its administration to these areas, it framed special rules for administration of civil and criminal justice among the tribes and races. But within the framework of these rules, customary practices in respect of crimes and imposition of punishment continued and are still continuing to a considerable extent. The traditional practices and beliefs have been well depicted in their behavioural and administrative pattern. Many of the general communities have also been practising their customs in respect of their culture, socio-religious aspect, etc. The customs have great influences on the personal laws of Islam. The customary practices of the tribal groups and other communities have been followed since long. The fact is that the basic factors for intervening in their all-round development are some of these traditional practices and beliefs. But the role of these customs and customary laws in the system of legal administration have a historical perspective and the sources of many of these have been embeded in the religio-legal or historical literature since ancient to modern age.

This research work includes the analysis of the literature which have been embracing lots of customs and which serve as the sources of legal information of the tribal and non tribal groups scattered in Assam. In this work an emphasis is given to furnish a comprehensive bibiliography which will depict the historical development of legal literature on customary laws in Assam. Instances of some adoptable or non adoptable customs practised by the local inhabitants and the various tribal groups have also been brought out on which government and social interference, codification or modifications are utmostly essential.

To make the complete report, the whole work has been divided into five chapters. The first three chapters are dealing with the related fields with that of fourth, which is the main chapter of the present study, basically done through historico-survey method. Notwithstanding that the third chapter depicts the chain of the inferences of literature which are much involved with this research topic. The first chapter is the introductory chapter and includes a general description of customs, problem of investigative report, its scope, hypothesis, methodology etc. The second chapter deals with the 'History of legal system' of India including Assam since ancient period to the modern age. A historical description has been made on the legal literature in respective periods of India and Assam in the third chapter of this report. A survey on the literature of few selected tribal groups along with general communities has been in the fourth chapter which includes their customary practices and law prevailing in their respective societies. It also caters to the analysis upon these surveyed customary literature. A general survey has also been made here upon the religious literature which are meant to be the sources of customs and personal laws of those religious groups. Inferences of adoptable, noticeable, repealable customs and the customs deserving codification have been described in this chapter. A chart showing the development of legal literature embracing the customs of the people of India as well as of tribal and non tribal groups of Assam has been furnished as a part of findings of this research work. The fifth i.e., the last chapter has been dedicated as 'Conclusion' of this work, which highlights the findings of the report with interpretations and provided suggestions.

Acknowledgements

My first and deepest acknowledgement in this regard is to my respected joint guides i.e., Dr. Alaka Buragohain, Prof and Ex Head, Department of Library and Information Science, Gauhati University and Dr. Aftab Hussain, Principal of University Law Collage, Gauhati University, who have taken all possible care and pain to guide me in preparing this thesis, without their valuable suggestions the work would not have taken this proper shape.

I am also grateful to the Director of Law Research Institute, Director of Tribal Research Institute, Director of Department of Historical and Antiquirian Studies, Assam, Director of Assam State Achieves, for their invaluable help and suggestions.

I express my sincere thanks to the staff of K.K. Handique Library, Gauhati University; Lakhminath Bezbaruah Library, Dibrugarh University; Kamrup Anusandhan Samiti, Guwahati; Directorate of Library Services, Guwahati; National Library, Calcutta; along with the District Libraries of Sibsagar, Jorhat, Golaghat, Dibrugarh, Kamrup, etc. I also express my sincere thanks to those elderly people and chiefs of the tribal villages and other places surveyed for their help.

Last but not the least, I take the opportunity to express my heartful thanks to the staff of the printing press 'G.N. Offset Printer', Demow, for their restless effort and my family members for giving inspiration and suggestions in preparing the thesis.

(Md. Wakidur Rohman)

Acknowledgements

1

Introduction

Introductory Concept of Human Conduct, Culture and Custom

All societies have some socio-cultural mechanisms for the maintenance of equilibrium, social order, tranquility and peace among the members composing unit. These socio-cultural mechanisms are taboos and sanctions. The folk culture of the time comprises of these social, ritual and supernatural public opinion, good sense and ethics in common possession of each adult group.

Human culture is unique in the sense that it is a product of human ingenuity, invention and man's accumulated experience over generations. But at the same time it is dynamic in character; it undergoes modifications, refinements, changes and alterations to suit the changing social needs over generations. These are the unseen socio-ritual forces which generally restrain the patterns of conduct of behaviour of individuals. The ways of living and the patterns of behaviour differ from group to group. What is considered to be a normal pattern of behaviour may be considered as an abnormal one in another society or in the same society at different point of time and space.

The natural instinct of all human beings is to respond quickly to the situations in which they find themselves. In his daily life he comes across a number of situations and if he is allowed to face the situations according to his own whims and to satisfy his urges and ego, he is apt to hurt the sentiments and feelings of some other individuals. The popular mind, therefore prescribes a limit within which actions and wishes of an individual are restrained. So the wishes and actions of an individual living within the framework of organisation are largely controlled and determined by the common likes and dislikes of other fellow individuals and their relations with each other as also by their membership in groups. An individual living with a homogenous group receives not only help and advice from the rest but also gains much from his association and involvement in social organisation. Accordingly, as soon as individuals become part of a social organisation, they become dependent on each other and bound by a distinctive set of social relations. The said act of social relations calls for social control and curbing some of his personal actions and wishes for the greater good of the entire organisation. They limit actions and restrain impulses that might threaten the orderly arrangement of independent lives. The individual, thus in order to earn membership in the social organisation has to pay a price- the price of the acceptance of restrain and of limitations on the freedom to do as he pleases. This curb is put by the common sense of the popular mind of the organisation so that one of them cannot become in instrument in disturbing the equilibrium of the organisation and the society at large of which he is only a member.

These restraints and limitations on the freedom to do whatever one pleases are evolved out of spontenous feeling of the popular mind of the organised group. They set-down the restraints and limitations in the nature of norms and conducts themselves for regulating their day-to-day life and generation after generation regarded themselves bound by the same and followed them with utmost devotion and sincerity. These gradually built up traditions and in course of time the said spontaneous evolutions of the common sense of the popular mind of an organised group because of their long and uninterrupted observance and on fulfilment of other necessary conditions become customs of that particular group.

The courts have come to recognise customs as valid rules of law codifying the same because justice demands that unless there is good reason to the contrary, people's common hopes and aspirations are to be fulfilled as far as possible rather than frustrated. Thus if the people of a particular society have for a long time continued a practice which reflects their common desires and wishes and which is not opposed to public policy or reason then there is no reason for disturbing or removing the same. These customary rules which possess certain qualifications and fulfil certain other requirements come to obtain force of law having binding authority.

With the origin of the conception of state many of the customary rules still continued to be followed and recognised. Later, on the customary rules come to be enforced by the agency of the state through its political organisation. They were unwritten and now written literature to some extent. They were well-known opinion of the community regarding right and wrong. They become laws and are doubtless for the time-being, the only law known. And the literature in this field whether it is written or unwritten may take a voluminous portion in different regions of our country which are beyond from our knowledge.

Problem to be Investigated

The historical development of the legal literature (which we merged with religion in ancient time) and literature relating to customs, traditions, ways of life and the cultural patterns of local inhabitants along with various tribes inhabiting Assam which are not well known to the outside world have become the subject matter of research in the recent times.

The local inhabitants and the tribal societies in the state of Assam have their age-old customary rules and usages which regulate their day-to-day life and their conduct in their internal affairs. These customary practices have survived through many centuries and are in a high degree conducive to the happiness of the inhabitants there. And an increasing quantity of literature with information relating to law which also embraces the traditional customs in the state have come into existence.

Few known institutes and departments in the state of Assam have investigated the customary laws and practices in North East Region of India, but a large portion of this area even in Assam have remained univestigated. Apart from this they did not concern with literature relating to customary laws of local inhabitants and the tribal peoples of Assam. So, it is high time to think about these sources and bring them out to the light for the benefit of its users and critically study their worth in different contexts. That is why, it has been tried to furnish a model study report on 'The Historical Development of Legal Literature on Customary Laws in Assam: A Critical Study.'

There is no systematic list of literature regarding laws including the customary practices in North-Eastern Region of India which will acquaint the common men and women of the country about the prevailling legal system. Therefore, it has become imperative to prepare such a list which may become a handy tool in this aspect. It will enable the future research workers to supplement or compliment this model study. Morever, I would like to find out the factors that justifies in codification of some of the social customs and traditions into customary laws like Hindu and Muslim personal laws. I would like to find out the customs and traditions which deserve to be codified but still remains uncodified. Thus, the fields which are still to be covered by legal literature also would be identified for future research work.

The present work of study has been selected so that it may guide the students, scholars, aspirants along with those of legal professionals who lack the proper information in this field. It will be humble venture to prepare a list of legal documents, specially embodied with customary laws at different periods of time in the state of Assam. It is expected to an exhaustive and clear guide to the users or researchers for further investigating work as well as to authors, publishers, vendors and librarians who might be inspired to select, procure and organise the literature in legal affairs. It is humbly hoped that it be a property to the library world.

Methodology and Literature Survey Adopted in the Research Work

In this work, the investigative study is made basically on the basis of historico-survey method; besides, the case-study method, citation indexing method and personal interview method are being followed.

The historical survey of legal literature in the country including Assam has been performed through searching different authoritative documents in the state as well as outside the state.

A survey of tribal groups of different tribal areas in different districts of Assam has also been done and thereby collected the information relating to their customary practices and literature.

The cited works by different authors at different points of time and places dealing with the concerned topic have been studied. Various case-studies regarding customary practices in different tribal areas of Assam have been consulted. Questionnairs provided to the adequate number of persons/personnels have also been discussed and analysed so as to meet the goal of this investigative work.

Regarding the research work entitled the aforesaid topic, literature and related materials collected from different libraries and information centres of Assam like, the Law Research Institute, High Court, Guwahati; the Judges

Library, High Court, Guwahati; Department of Historical and Antiquirian Studies, Guwahati; Assam Legislative Assembly Library, Dispur; Assam State Archives, Dispur; Kamrupa Anusandhan Samiti, Guwahati; Lakshminath Bezbaruah Library, Dibrugarh University; K.K. Handique Library, Gauhati University; District libraries of Dibrugarh, Jorhat, Golaghat, Sibsagar, Kamrup; Research and Reference Library, Directorate of Library Services, Guwahati; along with National Library, Calcutta, have been discussed.

Studies upon the customary laws and literature basically those of Deories, Mishing, Karbis, Sonowal-Kacharis, Dimasa-Kacharis have been done for the purpose of present investigative work as it is assumed to help in the study on the tribal legal systems and their literature.

Conclusion

The proliferation of information has created the problem of increasingly uncontrollable literature in different interdisciplinary or multidisciplinary subjects in the world at present. The researchers are getting much more difficulties to do research over them causing no effective control and organisation of these literature. It is humbly hoped that this work is to be a guide for the people specially those who are the frequent users of the law documents of the country. The present work of study is expected to guide the students, scholars, aspirants etc who lack the knowledges about the sources of present legal literature in the field of personal laws based on customs. The existing work is a critical study along with a bibliography with abstracts which depicts the chain of legal system, literature and its development throughout the ages and expected to be a source for work in the line in future as the list would identify the gaps as well on the field drawing attention of youths and researchers in the legal profession.

2

History of Legal System

Introduction

The evolution of human society clearly shows that man cannot, as a general rule live in isolation, but likes to associate himself with his fellow-men to satisfy his instinct of self preservation. In the early stages of society, these groups existed in the form of family, clans and tribes which eventually gave shape to the organised state. The state like the preceeding tribal organisations, also aims to secure peace and security for its people. It is therefore imperative that it must be ordained with certain power, authority, body of rules and procedure to ensure the continuance of the legal order. The state prescribes a certain uniformity of human action for the welfare and progress of the community and the individuals which is called law. The legal system of a state is the sum total of laws, on the legal materials or the objects with other beings with which law is enforced, present and its interaction with each other. The legal system of a country at a given time is not the creation of one man or of one day; it represents cumulative fruit of the endeavour, experience, thoughtful planning and patient labour of a large number of people through generations; somtimes it is based on the traditions and customs accepted by the respective societies through generations. India, has a known history of over 5000 years. Assam has also legal system of its own, developed through ancient time. Following is the historical perspective of legal system of India and Assam respectively in different periods of the time.

Legal System of India

"Uttaram yat Samudrasya

Himadreschaiva dakshinam

Varsham tad Bharatam nama

Bharati yatra santatih"

-Vishnu Purana

This means that the country that lies north of the ocean and south of the snowy mountains is called Bharata.[1] Any anecdote of religious sources has the indication that India in ancient days was a vast country situated geographically in a convenient place.

At present India measures 3214 km from north to south and 2933 km from east to west with a total land area of 3,287,263 sq km.[2] India shares its political borders with Pakistan and Afghanistan on the west and Bangladesh and Myanmar on the east. The northern boundary is made up of the Sinkiang province of China, Tibet, Nepal and Bhutan. Her isolation from others helped India to develop into a distinctive political and cultural unit. The vast dimensions of India, her varied physical features and variety of climate have resulted in different racial and linguistic peculiarities.

The Early History of Social and Political Institutions in India

The social structure and political institutions which were in existence in the early days give the basic understanding of legal system that prevailed in ancient India. In determining, the legal system involved with the social order two concepts i.e., the cast and joint family system are important. A caste in ancient time was a social group consisting solely of persons born in it.[3] Whole society was divided into four main castes. The four castes were precisely and clearly defined and rules pertaining to their lawful activities and functions dominated all social activities. The Brahmins were considered to be the most superior caste. The scholars and priests of the Hindus belonged to this caste. They had in law and in fact privileges and prerogatives not held by other sections of Hindu society. The Kshatriyas were the nobles and warriors and to this caste rulers of various states and kingdoms mostly belonged. The Vaishyas were the merchants and traders. The Sudras were the workers and ranked lowest. Although the caste was determine by birth in course of time, it was depended on merit, status of their activities etc. at the earliest time. Brahmins, Kshatriyas and Vaisyas were the elite of Hindu society. Caste determined the pattern of life amongst Hindus relating to their status of living, marriage, profession and social obligations. The caste association diluted political loyalities. In later centuries, caste exclusiveness became absolute and reached its peak in caste panchayats. Each caste panchayat was regarded as a supreme authority for a particular caste in each village. It gave stability to the Indian society.[4]

Another important institution amongst Hindus in ancient India was joint family system. It was regarded as a unit of the Hindu social system.[5] This joint family included parents, children, grand-children, uncles and their descendants and their collaterals on the male side. This social group had common dwelling and enjoyed their estate in common. The head of the family was the patriarch, whose authority was absolute over the members of his family. He represented all the members of his family before the law and claimed absolute obedience from them. A number of families constituted a sect, gram or village which became an administrative unit also. The concept of family led to private property which in turn led to disputes and strugles which necessitated law and a controlling authority. In later centuries problems concerning the division of land and inheritance came in for special attention. Two systems of family law namely, Mitakshara and Dayabhaga became the basis of civil law.[6]

India was divided into various independant states, some monarchies and the rest tribal republics. Rama Jois says in his book, *Seeds of Modern Public Law in Ancient Indian Jurisprudence*—

> In the context of the Dharmashastras (or Hindu political science) the word dharma came to mean 'the privileges, duties and obligations of a man, his standard of conduct' as a member of the Aryan community, as a member of one of the castes, as a person in a particular stage of life.[7]

Then society was the duty based society. It was not only the duty of individual towards the society but also the duty of the ruler towards the individuals and the society. The legal system which was the same for the whole of India, not withstanding the existence of large number of kingdoms, some larger in size and others smaller indicates that the concept of absolutist monarchies had always been rejected and the supremacy of 'dharma' (law) over the kings was respected.

The English doctrine of King can do no wrong was not accepted and the king himself was subject to law. Dharma or law constituted the master-plan for all round development of the individual and different sections of the society. Dharma is mostly misunderstood as religion. It is a word having no corresponding word in any other language.[8] Dharma was promulgated in the form of positive and negative commands (Vidhi and nishedha).

A few other important concepts were Vidatha, Sabha, Samiti & Parisada of early Hindu society. The term Vidatha has its equivalent in Gothic, an important Indo-European language. According to the rules of philology the term Vidatha can be reduced to the Gothic word vitoth, which means law.[9] Vidatha was an assembly of adult male and female meant for legal purpose along with other purposes such as secular, religious and military. It was a family council. A portion of the Vidatha may have been to conduct the tribal war against the hostile tribes. It also acted as a council of wise or a spiritual body.

The term Sabha is mentioned several times in the *Rig Veda* and denotes both the people in conclave and the hall which was the venue of their meeting. The Sabha performed judicial functions along with political and administrative functions. The judicial functions of the Sabha were exercised not by the whole assembly but by a standing committee of the same. It is a court or judicial assembly presided over by the king as Chief Judge and only the councillors, judges and police officers take part as men of authority over witnesses and accused.

The Samiti was a folk assembly in which people of the tribe gathered for transacting tribal business. It was a conference including not only all the common people (visah) but also the Brahmanas and the rich patrons known as Maghavan.[10] The Samiti was concerned with religious ceremonies, prayers made for reaching common agreements, military functions and political functions, those of which led to legal affairs through customs and practices.

The Parisada stabilised during the Pre-Maurya period. In the early Brahmanical law-books the Parisada took on the character of a body of legal experts. The Parisada as known to the *Dharmasutras* was an institution engaged in teaching and intellectual discussions, but its learned members were inclined towards law than teaching. On the otherhand it was essentially a council of the priests and named legal parisada.

All these institutions mentioned above acted as the courts of legal experts which were the sources and paved the way for early legal system in India.

Constitution of Courts in the Early Hindu Period

The king was regarded as the fountain-head of justice in this Hindu period. The king was honoured as the lord of dharma and was entrusted with the supreme authority of administration of justice in his kingdom. The king's court was the highest court of appeal as well as original court in cases of vital importance to the state. In the king's court the king was advised by learned Brahmins, the chief justice and other judges, ministers, elders and representatives of the trading community. Next to the king was the court of chief justice (pradvivaka). Apart from the chief justice, the court consisted of a board of judges to assist him. Sometimes some of the judges constituted separate tribunals having specified territorial jurisdiction. There were four kings of tribunals namely stationary, movable courts held under the royal signet in the absence of king, and commissions under the king's presidency.[11]

In villages the local village councils or Kulani, similar to modern panchayats, consisted of a board of five or more members to dispense justice to villagers. It was concerned with all matters relating to endowments, irrigation, cultivable land, punishment of crime, etc. Village councils dealt with simple civil and criminal cases. At a higher level in towns like Patliputra at the end of fourth century B.C. village councils were presided over by the government officers under the authority of the king to administer justice. The link between the village assembly and the official administration was the headman of the village. In each village a local headman was holding hereditary office and was required to maintain order and administer justice. He was also a member of the village council. He acted both as the leader of the village and the mediator with the government.[12] Various corporations, trade-guilds were authorised to exercise an effective jurisdiction over the members of guilds, associations of traders while dealing with the disputes. These tribunals consisting of a president and three or five co-adjudicators were allowed to decide their civil cases regularly just like the other courts. It was possible to go in appeal from the tribunal of the guild to local court, then to royal judges and from them finally to the king. Due to the prevailing institution of the joint family system, family courts were established. Radhakumud Mukherji in his *Local Government in Ancient India* describes –

> "First come the family arbitrators; the chief justice (Adhyaksha) is superior to the judges; the king is superior to all of them and his decision becomes law."[13]

The central court or the courts held under the Royal authority decided the cases of criminal aspects. At the village level the smaller judicial assembly was allowed to hear only the minor cases.

Judicial Procedure in the Early Legal Court

A suit (Vyavahara) consisted of four parts: (i) the plaint (poorvapaksha); (ii) the reply (oottar); (iii) the trial and investigation of dispute by the court (kriyaa) and (iv) the verdict or decision (nirnaya).[14] Filling of poorvapaksha before the court meant that the plaintiff as per existing procedure submitted himself to the jurisdiction of the court.

The court then was entitled to issue an order to the defendant to submit his reply on the basis of allegations made in the plaint. If the defendant admitted the allegations levelled against him in the plaint, the business of the court was to decide the case. Where the defendant contested the case before the court, it was the duty of the court to provide full opportunity to both the parties to prove their cases. After the trial was over, final decision was given by the court. During the course of proceedings both parties were required to prove their respective stand taken by them by producing evidence. Ordinarily, evidence was based on any or all the three sources, namely, documents, witnesses, and the possession of incriminating objects.[15]

Another method to determine the guilt of a person was trial by ordeal. The ancient Indian society which was largely dominated by religion and faith in God, considered the trial by ordeal as a valid method of proof. The ordeals were –

(a) Ordeal of balance

(b) Ordeal of fire

(c) Ordeal by water

(d) Ordeal of poison

(e) Ordeal of lot

(f) Ordeal of rice-grains

(g) Ordeal of fountain-cheese.

In ordeal of balance the accused was made to sit in a balance and weighed. He was then made to pray to God. If his part of balance was lowered after prayer he was deemed guilty. There is a reference to the ordeal of fire in *the Ramayana* where Sita had to prove her chastity during her captivity by Ravana by walking through fire. Accused was made to walk through fire. If he suffered no harm, he was held innocent. In ordeal by water the accused was made to drink water used in bathing the idol. If within14 days he had no harmful effect he was considered innocent. In ordeal of poison the accused was to drink poison. If no harm came to him, he was held innocent. In ordeal of lot he was to draw from two lots. If he drew the lot of dharma, he was held innocent. In ordeal of Rice-grains if the accused chewed unhusked rice and if no blood appeared in his mouth he was held innocent. In ordeal of fountain-cheese the accused was to drink some special type of water. If he becomes delirious and confesses his misdeeds he was held guilty.[16]

J.N. Das in his report *A study of Administration of Justice among the Tribes and Races of North-Eastern Region* describes that in the North-East Region in case of tribal areas oaths and ordeals were prevalent till Independence, and are even now prevalent in certain interior places. In Arunachal Pradesh among the Sherdukpens, an accused may prove his innocence by offering a scarf in the name of the deity and swearing that if he is responsible for the crime, blood will come out of his nose within three days. Among the Adis, a person accused of theft has to bring out an egg from boiling water contained in bamboo tube. Among the Nishis, an accused person has to pick up a stone from the bottom of a bamboo tube filled with boiling water and then to scratch his hand with a knife. If the skin does not peel off his innocence is proved. The ordeal of boiling water and egg is found among the Garos too. Another ordeal of the Garos, which continued till recently, was to tie up the accused to a tree in a jungle and leave him there alone for the night. He was supposed to be innocent if he was not davoured by a tiger. The ordeal of living longest under water was found among the Khasis and Manipuris.

Crimes and Punishments in the Early Hindu Legal System

In ancient Hindu period punishment was considered to be a sort of expiation which removed impurities from the man of sinful promptings and reformed his character. Men who are guilty of crimes and have been punished by the king go to heaven, becoming pure like those who perform meritorious deeds.[17] The punishments served four main purposes, namely to meet the urge of the person who suffered for revenge or retaliation, as deterent and preventive measures, and for reformation or redemption of the evil doer.[18] Manu states that there were four methods of punishment, by gentle reproof, by severe reproof, by fine, by corporal punishment; and these punishments inflicted separately or together according to the nature of offence.[19] Kautilya lays down that judges always considered the relevant circumstances before diciding the actual punishment.[20] Manu states that as a general rule a Brahmin offender was not to be sentenced to death or corporal punishment for any offence deserving a death sentence. An old man over eighty, a boy below sixteen, women and persons suffering from diseases are to be given half prayaschitta and a child less than five commits no crime nor sin by any act and is not to suffer any punishment.[21] In adultery and rape, punishment was awarded on the basis of the caste considerations of the offenders and of the woman. In abuse or contempt cases every care was taken to see that each higher caste got due respect from persons of the lower caste. A Kshatriya or a Vaisya abusing or defaming a Brahmin was to be punished respectively with a fine of 100 panas and 150 panas.[22] A Sudra was punished by corporal punishment (cutting off the tongue). While a Brahmin defaming a Kshatriya or Vaishya was to be fined 50, 25 or 12 panas respectively. If a person of a lower caste sat on the same bench with a man of a higher caste, the man of the lower caste was branded on the breech.[23] Kautilya prescribes death penalty for the murder, even if it occurred in a quarrel or duel. Capital punishment was given in varied forms namely roasting alive, drawning, trampling by elephants, devouring by dogs, cutting into pieces, impalement. Mutilation, torture and imprisonment, were the common penalties.[24]

It has been observed from the above discussion that the rules and justices followed in the courts were based not upon a written constitution or had a strong foundation but on practices accepted by the kings of ancient Hindu societies based on the judgement made by the king and the learned Brahmin or Puruhita considered as laws. In the present context of law those are practices only so far the nature of procedure and system were concerned. Division of the caste system, the practices and beliefs belonging to respective castes were entitled to continuance activities or tradition of then societies resulting in the fall of those caste based family system. This was the Vedic as well as the Smritikar's age which is related to ancient law literature (discussion is being made in the later chapter.), customs and traditions embodied the law, religious acts and justices.

Legal System in Muslim Period

During the period when the Muslims ruled over India, many significant changes were introduced by them in the Indian legal system from time to time. The Islamic jurisprudence was introduced in India by Muslim Sultans and later on adopted by the Mughals with certain modifications to suit the circumstances of the age and to satisfy the needs of the people of the time.[25]

The Muslim rulers while ruling over India regarded themselves as the servants of the God. As laid down in the Fat we-Alamgiri, the courts in India were to be guided by the following authorities while deciding the disputes.[26]

(i) ***Qur'an :*** This is the sacred and believed to be divined Book of Muslims. It contains collected verses revealed to Mohammed, the Prophet. This religious Book contains few of the law by which the Mohammedans were governed and are still governed. It is the basic source for Islam in guiding religious as well as legal aspects. This Book is regarded as legal literature, discussed in the later chapter.

(ii) ***Sunna :*** Mohammed, the Prophet of Islam decided during his life time many questions from case to case and the collections of his words and deeds and silent approval in such cases were reduced in writing at a later stage and came to be termed as Sunna or Traditions. These traditions of what Prophet said and did gradually laid the foundations of what is now called Ahadis. So, the Islamic law founded on religious tradition and in this regard the law and religion had an interrelationship.

(iii) ***Concurrent opinion of the Prophet's Companions:*** Acceptance of the opinion of the Prophet's companions resulted the formation of Islamic tradition and laws. By three steps it was adopted viz., Companion's of the Companions, Companions of the Companions' Companions', Companions of the Companions' Companions' Companions.

(iv) ***Isjma :*** The literal meaning of it is agreeing upon. Those disputed points of law for which no direct solution could be found either in *the Qur'an* or Sunna and which were resolved by the agreement of the juristic persons who have a right in nature of knowledge, to form a judgement of their own after the death of Prophet came to be regarded as a valid source of law, which was traditionally accepted and supplemented the Islamic law.

(v) ***Judgement according to individual discretion of the Judge:*** This was based on the doctrine of justice, equity and good conscience. According to Abu Hanifa, the Qazi could act on the principles of istihsan (public good), istihlah (public policy) or istihab (concordance).[27]

(vi) ***Qyas (Analogical deduction):*** According to this principle a solution of a new problem could be found by analogy. This has provided dynamism to Islamic law. Apart from these sources of Islamic law, custom (urf) and legislation at a later stage served as a source of Islamic law.

By the end of twelfth century Muhammad of Ghor established a Muslim sultanate at Delhi. From 1206 till 1526 Delhi belonged to the Sultans. Babor the Mughal emperor founded the Mughal empire in 1526 and lasted for nearly two centuries until the British took over. The judicial system of India during the mediaeval period may therefore be divided and studied under two separate periods—the Sultanate of Delhi and the Mughal period.

The civil administration of the Sultanate was headed by the Sultan and his Chief Minister (Wazir). The Sultanate was divided into the administrative divisions from the province to the village level. The sultanate was divided into provinces (Subahs). The province was composed of districts

(Sarkars). Each district was further divided into paraganahs. A group of villages constituted a paraganah.

The Administration of Justice: Constitution of Court

(a) Sultan Period

In mediaeval India the Sultan being head of the state was the supreme authority to administer justice in his kingdom. The judicial system under the Sultan was organised on the basis of administrative divisions of the kingdom. A systematic graduation of the courts existed at the seat of the capital, in provinces, districts, paraganahs and villages [28] discussed below.

(a) (i) *Central capital :* Six courts which were established at the capital of the Sultanate may be stated as follows -

(a) The Kings court (b) Diwan-e-Muzalim (c) Dewan-e-Risalat (d) Sadre-e-Jehan's court (e) Chief justice's court and (f) Diwan-e-Siyasat.

The King's court presided over by the Sultan exercised both original and appellate jurisdiction on all kinds of cases. It was the highest court of appeal in the realm. The Sultan was assisted by two reputed Muftis highly qualified in law. The court of Diwan-e- Muzalim was the highest court of criminal appeal and the court of Dian-e-Risalat was the highest court of civil appeal. Though the Sultan nominally presided over these two courts, he seldom sat in them. The Chief Justice (Qazi-ul- Quzat) was the highest judicial officer next to the Sultan. From 1206 to 1248 in the absence of the Sultan, the Chief Justice presided over these courts. In 1248 Sultan Nusir-Ud-Din, being disatisfied with the then Chief Justice, created a superior post of Sodre-Jahan. Since then Sadre Jahan became de-facto head of the judiciary. The court of Diwan-e-Siyasat was constituted to deal with the case of rebels and those charged with high treason. Its main purpose was to deal with criminal prosecutions. It was established by Muhammad Tughlaq and continued up to 1351. The Chief Justice's court dealt with all kinds of cases. Four officers, namely, Mufti[29], Pandit[30], Mohtasib[31] and Dadbak[32] were attached to the court of Chief Justice.

(ii) *Provinces :* In each province (Subah) at the provincial head quarters five courts were established namely, Adalat Nazim Subah, Adalat Qazi-e-Subah, Governor's Bench (Nazin-e-Subah's Bench), Diwan-e-Subah and Sadre-e-Subah.

Adalat Nazim Subah was the Subehdar's (Governor's) court. In the provinces the Sultan was represented by him and like the Sultan he exercised original and appellate jurisdiction. Adalat Qazi-e-Subah was presided over by the chief provincial Qazi. He was empowered to try civil and criminal cases of any description and to hear appeals from the courts of District Qazis. Apeals from this court were allowed to be made to the Adalat Nazim-e-subah. The court of Diwan-e-Subah was the final authority in the province in all cases concerning land revenue. The Sadre-e-Subah was the chief ecclesiastical officer in the province. He repesented Sadre-e-Jahan, in Subah in matters relating to grant of stipend, lands, etc.

(iii) *Districts :* In each district (sarkar), at the district headquarter, six courts were established namely, Qazi, Dadbaks or Mir Adils, Faujdars, Sadre, Amils, Kotwals.

The court of Sarkar Qazi[33] was empowered to hear all original civil and criminal cases. Appeals were also filed before this court from the judgements of the parganah Qazis, Kotwals and village Panchayats. The same four officers-Mufti, Pandit, Mohtasib and Dadbak were attached to this court. The court of the Faujdar tried petty criminal cases concerning security and suspected criminals. The court of Sadre dealt with cases concerning grant of land and registration of land. Appeals were allowed to be filed before the Sadr-e-Subah. Court of Amils dealt with the land revenue cases. Kotwals were authorised to decide petty criminal cases and police cases.

(iv) *Parganah :* At each parganah headquarter two courts were established, namely, Qazi-e-parganah and Kotwal. The court of Qazi-e-parganah had all the powers of a District Qazi in all civil and criminal cases except hearing appeals. Petty criminal cases were filed before the Kotwal. He was the Principal Executive Officer in towns.

(v) *Villages :* A parganah was divided into a group of villages. For each group of villages there was a village assembly or panchayat, a body of five leading men to look after the executive and judicial affairs. The panchayats decided civil and criminal cases of local character. Though the decrees given by the panchayats were based on local customs and traditions and were not strictly according to the law of the kingdom, still there was no interference in the working of the panchayats. As a general rule, the decision of the panchayat was binding upon the parties and no appeal was allowed from its decision.

(b) Mughal Period

The next part of the Muslim period i.e, the Mughal period begins with the victory of Babar in 1526 over the last Lodi Sultan of Delhi.

For the purpose of civil administration the whole empire was divided into the Imperial capital, provinces (subahs), districts (sarkars), parganahs and villages. The emperor created a separate department of justice (Mahukmae-adalat) to regulate and see that justice was administered properly. On the basis of the administrative divisions separate courts were established to decide civil, criminal and revenue cases[34]. A systematic gradation of courts with well defined powers of the presiding judges, existed all over the empire-discussed below.

(i) *The Imperial capital :* The important courts were established in the capital, Delhi. The Emperor's court, presided over by the Emperor, was the highest court of the empire. The court had jurisdiction to hear original civil and criminal cases. As a court of the first instance the emperor was assisted by a Darogha-e-Adalat, a Mufti, and a Mir Adil. In criminal cases, the Mohtasib-e-Mumalik or the Chief Mohtasib, like the Attorney-General of India today, also assisted the Emperor. The chief court of the empire was the second important court at Delhi. The court presided over by the Chief Justice had the power to try original, civil and criminal cases, to hear appeals from the provincial courts. In administering justice, the Chief Justice was assisted by one or two Qazis of great eminence. Four officers attached to the court were Darogha-e-Adalat, Mufti, Mohtasib, Mir Adil. The Mufti attached to the court was known as Mufti-e-Azam. The chief revenue court was the third important court established at Delhi. It was the highest court of appeal to decide revenue cases. The court was presided over by the Diwan-e-Ala.

Apart from the above stated three important courts, there were two lower courts at Delhi to decide local case[35]. The court of Qazi of Delhi, who enjoyed the status of Chief Qazi of a province, decided local civil and criminal cases. An appeal was allowed to the court of Chief Justice. The court of Qazi-e-Askar was specially constituted to decide cases of the military area in the capital. The court moved from place to place with the troops. In each court as stated above the four officers attached were-Darogha-e-Adalat, a Mufti, a Mohtasib, Mir Adil.

(ii) *Provinces :* In each province (subah) there were three courts, namely, the Governor's own court and the Bench, the Chief Appelate court, the Chief Revenue Court. The Governor's own court (Adalat-e-Nazim-e-Subah) had original jurisdiction in all cases arising in the provincial capital. It was presided over by the Governor (Nazim-e-Subah). The Provincial Chief Appellate Court was presided over by the Qazi-e-Subah. The court had original civil and criminal jurisdiction. Provincial Chief Revenue Court was presided over by Diwan-e-Subah. The court was granted original and appellate jurisdiction in revenue cases.

(iii) *Districts (Sarkars):* In each sarkar there were four courts, namely the Chief Civil and Criminal court of the district, Faujdari adalat, Kotwali and Amalguzari Kachehri.

The Chief Civil and Criminal court of the district was presided over by the Qazi-e-sarkar. The court had original and appellate jurisdiction in all civil and criminal cases and in religious matters. Qazi-e-sarkar was the Principal Judicial Officer in a district. He was officially known as Shariyat Panah. Six officers attached to his court were-Darogha-e-Adalat, Mir Adl, Mufti, Pandit or Shastri Mohtasib and Vakil-e-Shariyat. Appeals lay to Qazi-e-Subah[36]. Faujdari adalat dealt with criminal cases concerning riots and state security. It was presided over by the Faujdar. Appeals beg to the Governor's court.

Kotwali court decided cases similar to those under modern police Acts and had appellate jurisdiction. It was presided by Kotwal-e-sharkar. Appeals lay to the District Qazi.

The Amalguzari Kachehri decided all revenue cases. Amalguzary presided over this court. An appeal was allowed to the Provincial Diwan.

(iv) *Parganah :* In each parganah there were three courts namely, Adalat-e-parganah, Kotwali, and Kachehri.

Adalat-e-parganah was presided over by Qazi-e-parganah. The court had jurisdiction over all civil and criminal cases arising within its original jurisdiction. Four officers-Mufti, Mohtasib-e-parganah, Darogha-e-Adalat and Vakil-e-Shara.

Court of Kotwali was presided by Kotwal-e-parganah to decide such cases as are found in the Modern Police Act.

Amin was the presiding officer in Kachehri which decided revenue cases. Appeals lay to the District Amalguzar.

(v) *Villages :* The village was the smallest administrative unit. From ancient times the village council i.e., Panchayats were authorised to administer justice in all petty civil and criminal matters. The panchayat meetings were held in public places. It was presided by five panchs elected by the villagers who were expected to give a patient hearing to both the parties and deliver their judgment in panchayat meeting. Sarpanch or village headman was generally president of the panchayat. No appeal was allowed from the decision of a panchayat. Village panchayats were mostly governed by their customary law.

Judicial Procedure

A systematic judicial procedure was followed by the courts during the Muslim period. It was regulated by two Muslim Codes namely Fiqh-e-Firoz Shahi and Fatwa-i-Alamgiri[37] and discussed about these in the later chapter so far the related theme is concerned.

Crimes and Punishment

Islamic law or Shariat was followed by all the Sultans and Mughal emperors during the Muslim period. Three forms of punishments as recognised by the Muslim law were-'Hadd', 'Tazir', and 'Qisas'.

(i) 'Hadd' provided a fixed punishment as laid down in shara for crimes like theft, robbery, whoredom (Zina), apostasy (Ijtidad), defamation (Itteham-e-zina) and drunkenness (shurb). It was equally applicable to Muslims and Non-Muslims.

(ii) 'Tazir' was another form of punishment which meant prohibition and it was applicable to all the crimes which were not classified under 'hadd'. It included crimes like counterfeiting coins, gambling, causing injury, minor theft, etc. Under 'tazir', the courts exercised their discretion in awarding suitable punishment to the criminals. The courts were free to invent new methods of punishing the criminals e.g., cutting off the tongue, impalement. etc[38].

(iii) 'Qisas' or blood fine was imposed in cases relating to homicide. It was a sort of blood-money paid by the man who killed another man if the murderer was convicted but not sentenced to death for his offence.

The Muslim law considered 'treason' as a crime against God and religion and therefore against the state. Persons held responsible for treason by the court were punished with death. No consideration was shown for their rank, religion and caste. Only the ruler was empowered to consider a mercy petition like todays the President's mercy for a criminal accused.

It has been seen that the customary law was followed by the lowest court, panchayat during the Sultan as well as Mughal period. The decision of the panchayats were the final, no appeal was allowed from its decision. The tradition of the working of panchayats in the later periods remained same. Among the tribal groups, castes, religious group in India along with Assam the working of the panchayat is still alive. 'Jamat' of Muslim societies can do judgment within its jurisdiction when home conflict arises.

Legal System During East-India Company and Independence Era

The British started its establishment in India with the formation of East India Company which was formed by the merchants of London. The full name of the company was "The Governor and company of merchants of London".[39] The company was in corporated in England on 31st December, 1600 by a charter of Queen Elizabeth and was given exclusive trading rights in Asia and America.[40] But the company no longer remained a trading association and became a territorial sovereign by a subsequent Charter of 1668 when Bombay was transferred to the company. The Charter Act of 1726 conferred the overall control to the Governor-in-Council in each of the presidency towns where the company had established itself firmly and since then judicial system was organised on a uniform pattern in the company's territories. The development of legal history of India from the advent of East India company to British rule in India can be conveniently traced through the following phases:

(a) ***First phase :*** The East India company established their first settlement at Surat which was an important trading centre at that time. Subsequently, similar settlements were started at Bombay and Madras. The British settlers were entrusted with the responsiblities of governing these three settlements in India. For the administration they improved an elementary judicial system whereby they settled their mutual disputes. The notable feature of this system was that the administration of law and justice was entrusted to non-legal and non-professional Englishmen who belonged to the trading community having little knowledge of law and procedure.[41] As a matter of fact they were expected to follow the provisions of English law in discharging their judicial functions, but in practice they decided cases according to their common-sense notions of justice. The judiciary in the presidency towns was dependent and subordinated to the Executive which was the supreme administrative authority in British occupied territories in India. This position continued for about a hundred and fifty years.

(b) ***Second phase :*** The Supreme Court of Judicature established at Fort William (Calcutta) under the Regulating Act, 1773 enacted by the British parliament which is considered to be a land mark in the development of legal institutions in India.It was an English law court which consisted of professional English judges who were well-versed in law and legal practice. There was an English bar to assist the court in administration of justice. This court was modelled on the pattern of the court of Westminister of England. The Supreme Court was independent of the legislature as also the executive. It exercised some control over the executive and thus introduced in India the concept of judicial control of administrative actions. The net result was that the powers of the executive government were curtailed which eventually led to hostility and frequent clashes between the Supreme Court and the Supreme Council. It was only after the Settlement Act of 1781 that the differences between these two premier institutions of the company's govement in India were resolved by making the council independent of the jurisdiction of the Supreme Court[42].

(c) ***Third phase :*** The third phase begins when the Company took upon itself the administration of justice in Bengal by introducing Adalat system. In the initial stages the adalats were manned by the British executive civil servants of the company who had no legal training. They being primarily the executive officers of the company's government, considered judicial work as their secondary functions of a lesser importance. However, in course of time there was separation of the judicial functions from the executive, in civil matters while the administration of criminal justice still remained with the executive official called the Collector. Thus, the Collector-Magistrate played a significant role in the civil administration and also in the criminal justice system of the company's government in India.[43] The Adalat system was later extended to other newly acquired territories of the company in India.

(d) ***Fourth phase :*** In this phase the legal history of India is marked by the unification of legal system of courts prevailng in the presidency towns and the mofussil areas into a single one with the establishment of High Courts and the High Courts Act 1861. The judicial system of presidency towns was essentially based on the English law having a distinct British character while the mofussil territories outside the presidency towns had the Adalat system based on indigenous laws of Hindus and Muslims. The establishment of the High Court by abolishing the Supreme Court and Sadar Adalats of presidency town was an attempt to simplify the judicial system. Therefore as rightly suggested by Dr MP Jain, "these High Courts may rightly be considered as the precursor of the modern system of law and justice in India."[44]

Initially, High Courts were established in Calcutta, Madras (Chennai) and Bombay (Mumbai) which were later extended to other northern and western provinces as well.

(e) ***Fifth phase :*** The emergency of the Privy Council as the highest court of appeal from India constitutes another important phase of development in the legal system. It stimulated proper development of laws in India on a uniform pattern and also motivated the courts to apply high judicial standards in discharging their functions as dispensers of justice. The growth of laws became more conspicuous after 1833 with the setting up of the First Law Commission which started the process of codification of Indian laws to ensure uniformity and certainty in the administration of justice. The second and the third Law Commissions took in hand the task of major laws in India.

The Charter Acts and the Law Commissions in India

All India Legislature was established in India by the Charter Act of 1833 which forms a watershed in the legal history of India.With the creation of the new council under the Act the government of Bombay and Madras were deprived of their law making power.

The First Law Commision was appointed in 1834 under the chairmanship of Lord Macaulay. The law commission was to function under the direction and control of the Governor-General-in-Council which was authorised to determine from time to time the subject upon which the commission was to make enquiries and submit its reports. As directed by the government of India the law commission first started with the codification of criminal law. The reason for priority to draft penal code was that the existing criminal law was full of uncertainities and confusion throughout the country.[45]

In the presidencies, the English law of crimes was applied, while the provinces of Bengal and Madras followed the Mohammedan law of crimes. The province of Bombay followed the penal law under the Elphinstone code of 1827. It was also known as the 'Macaulay code'. However the draft could not be enacted into law till 1860. In view of the extensive modifications suggested by the First Law Commission in the administration of law and justice in India, it became necessary to enhance the law-making powers of the legislative council. This was achieved by the Charter Act of 1853. The Act defined the functions of executive and legislative councils more elaborately so as to enable these two organs of the government to function more efficiently and independently. The Act also provided for the appointment of a law commission for India in England to consider and examine the recommendations and proposals of the First Law Commission. The law commission was to submit its report to Her Majesty in England.[46]

The Second Law Commission consisting of seven members was appointed on November 9, 1853 under the chairmanship of Sir John Remilly. The commission held its sittings in London till the middle of 1856 and submitted four reports. Of these the second report, which was submitted in February 1855, was most important as it dealt with the grounds on which the codification of substantive law was to be carried out for India. The Second Law Commission submitted four draft codes on civil and procedure which were finally introduced as codified Civil Law under the Act no. VIII of 1859. The code was however, repealed twice in 1877 and again in 1882. Finally, the Civil Procedure Code of 1908 was enforced throughout the country which remain in force even today. The penal code drafted by Lord Macaulay in 1837 was revised by Sir Barnes Peacock who was one of the members of the Second Law Commission. It was finally enacted and passed in 1860. The Code of Criminal Procedure was enacted in 1861 which was based on the recommendation of the Second Law Commission. In 1859, the Limitation Act, was enacted. The Indian High Courts Act was passed in 1861 whereby the Supreme Courts, Sadar Diwani and Sadar Nizamat Adalats were abolished and in their place a High court was established in each of the presidencies.

At present the law Commission continues to function as a permanent body. Till now it has been reconstituted several times and submitted many reports in all. However, the more important of ones of twelfth and thirteen law commission are stated below[47]:

Legal System in the Post-Independence Era

With the Indian independence in 1947 the judicial system had to be modified to suit the changed conditions. The jurisdiction of the privy council over the Indian appeals came to an end with the establishment of the Supreme Court of India on January 26, 1950. The pattern of judicial administration even after the independence of India,

Table 1. Twelfth Law Commission (Chairman- Shri M.P. Thakkar)

Sl No.	*No of the Report* (1)	*Subject* (2)	*Date of presentation* (3)
1.	Hundred thirty-second	Need for amendment of the provision of charter (ix) of the Code of Criminal Procedure, 1973 in order to ameliorate the hardship and mitigate the distress of neglected women, children and parents.	19th April, 1989
2.	Hundred thirty-third	Removal of discrimination against women in matters relating to Guardianship and custody. of minor children and elaboration of the welfare principles.	29th Aug, 1989
3.	Hundred thirty-fourth	Removing deficiencies in certain provision of the workmen's compensation Act, 1923.	28th Sep, 1989
4.	Hundred thirty-fifth	Women in custody	14th Dec, 1989
5.	Hundred thirty-sixth	Conflicts in High Court decisions on central laws how to fore close and how to resolve.	21st Feb, 1990
6.	Hundred thirty-seventh	Need for creating office of ombudsman and for evolving legislative- administrative measure inter alia to relieve hardships caused by inordinate delays in settling provident fund claims of beneficiaries.	28th Sep, 1990.

(Contd.)

(Table Contd.)

7.	Hundred thirty-eight	Legislative protection for slum and pavement dwellers.	20th Dec, 1990.
8.	Hundred thirty-nine	Urgent need to amend under (xxi) Rule 92 (2), Code of Civil Procedure to remove an anomaly which nullifies the benevolent intention of the legislature and occasions in justice to judgment debtors sought to be benefitted.	4th April, 1991.
9.	Hundred fortieth	Need to amend Order V, Rule 19A of the Code of Civil Procedure, 1908 relating to service of summons by registered post with a view to foreclose likely injustice.	19th April, 1991.
10.	Hundred forty-first	Need for amending the law as regards power of courts to restore criminal revisional applications and criminal cases dismissed for default in apperance.	31st July, 1991.
11	Hundred forty-second	Concessional treatment for offenders who, on their own initiative choose to plead guilty without any bargaining.	22nd Aug, 1991.

Table 2. Thirteenth Law Commission (Chairman Justice K.N. Singh)[48]

Sl No.	*No of the Report* (1)	*Subject* (2)	*Date of presentation* (3)
1.	Hundred forty-fourth	Conflicting judicial decisions pertaining to the Code of Civil Procedure, 1908.	28th April, 1992.
2.	Hundred forty-fifth	Article 12 of the Constitution and public sector undertakings.	26th Nov, 1992.
3.	Hundred forty-sixth	Sale of women and children: proposed section 373-A, Indian Penal Code.	26th Feb, 1993.
4.	Hundred forty-seventh	Specific Relief Act, 1963.	6th Oct, 1993.
5.	Hundred forty-eighth	Repeal of certain Pre-Central Act.	26th Nov., 1993.
6.	Hundred forty –nineth	Removal of certain deficiencies in the Motor Vehicles Act, 1988 (No. of 1988).	11th Feb., 1994.
7.	Hundred fiftieth	Suggesting some amendments to the Code of Civil Procedure (Act No. V of 1908).	10th May, 1994.
8.	Hundred fifty-first	Admiralty jurisdiction.	
9.	Hundred fifty-second	Custodial crimes.	
10.	Hundred fifty-third	Inter-Country adoption.	

remained more or less the same. Thus, the modern legal system essentially the same as bequeathed to the independent country by the British rulers.

In modern times, India has an advanced legal system having a well defined hierarchy of courts with the Supreme Court at the apex and a number of subordinate courts below it. The whole of the judicial system of the country has been divided into two categories-(a) The civil judicature and (b) The criminal judicature. The following are the courts prevailing in the present legal system of India, stated with brief analysis:

(a) ***The Supreme Court of India :*** This is the highest court of the country. This court is constituted to function (i) as the protector of the fundamental rights and liberties of the individuals in exercise of its original as well as appellate jurisdiction; (ii) as the ultimate authority to interpret and enforce the provisions of the Constitution and the laws; (iii) as the final court of appeal in all matters, constitutional, civil, criminal, revenue, etc. against all decisions and orders of all courts and tribunals in the country, and (iv) as the sole tribunal to decide centre-state and inter-state disputes and to give advice in an advisory capacity on important questions of law or fact on reference by the Preseident.[49]

(b) ***High Courts:*** For every state, the High Court is the highest seat of justice and the highest authority for judicial administration. It has criminal and civil jurisdiction. The high court has original as well as appellate jurisdiction.

After the Constitution of India came into force the following new High Courts were established and the

Table 3. High Courts after Independance In India.

Name of State	*Name of High Court (1)*	*High Court seat at (2)*	*Date of establishment & the Act under which established. (3) (4)*
Andhra Pradesh	H.C. of Andhra Pradesh	Hyderabad	5-7 1954, the Andhra State Act, 1953.
Madhya Pradesh	Madhya Pradesh H.C.	Jabalpur	State's Reorganisation Act, 1956 Benches at Gwalior and Indore.
Gujarat	Gujarat H.C.	Ahmedabad	Bombay Reorganisation Act, 1960, 1-5-1960
Maharashtra	Bombay H.C.	Bombay	1-5-1960, Bombay Reorganisation Act, 1960. Extended for Goa, Daman & Diu 67 Act No. 18 of 1987.
Nagaland	Assam H.C.	Guwahati	State of Nagaland Act, 1962, N.E. Reorganisation Act, 1971.
Union territory of Delhi	Delhi H.C.	Delhi	24.10.1962
Himachal Pradesh	Himachal Pradesh H.C.		State of H.P. Act, 1970.
Assam, Nagaland, Meghlaya, Manipur, Tripura, Mizoram, Arunachal Pradesh	Gauhati High Court	Guwahati	N.E. Areas Reorganisation Act, 1971, Act 31 of 1986, Act 69 of 1986.
Sikkim	Sikkim H.C.	Gangtok	1975.

jurisdiction of certain High Courts was extended to include new territories.

By Act 57 of 1976 the Circuit Bench of the Patna High Court functioning at Ranchi since March 6, 1972 was made permanent by Act of Parliament. The Bench at Jaipur which was abolished was revived by the High Court of Rajasthan (establishment of a permanent Bench at Jaipur) order, 1976 in January 1977. The Calcutta High Court Act, 1953 extended the jurisdiction of the Calcutta High Court to the Andaman and Nicobar Island. The states Reorganisation Act, 1956 extended the jurisdiction of the Kerala High Court to Lakshadweep Islands. The Dadra and Nagar Haveli Act, 1961 extended the jurisdiction of the Bombay High Court over the Dadra and Nagar Haveli. The jurisdiction of Madras High Court was extended to cover Pondichery.[50]

Besides, there is Central Administrative Tribunal at central level comprising Judges of Supreme Courts. National Human Rights Commission is a major phenomenon today to administer the human rights and injustice. Like Central Administrative Tribunal and National Human Rights Commission there is State Administrative Tribunal and State Human Right's Commission to provide the Judical administration at state level.

(c) ***Administration of Justice in the districts and states:*** For the convenience of administration states have been divided into smaller areas that are now known as districts. Certain dominations of the districts are known as divisions. These divisions are put under the charge of Divisional Commissioner. In order to have a proper idea of the administration of justice in the states and districts, it will be worthwhile to divide the whole of the judicial system into the following three categories :

(a) Administration of criminal judicature

(b) Administration of civil judicature

(c) The revenue court.

(a) *Administration of criminal justice :* Below High Court there are other courts. The highest unit of the judicial administration in the district is the District Courts. In every district there are courts of first instance as well as appellate courts. These courts administer civil and criminal laws.

The Code of Criminal Procedure, 1973 provides that there shall be in every state the following classes of criminal courts,[51] namely-

(i) Courts of Session;

(ii) Judicial Magistrates of the first class and in any metroplitan area[52], Metropolitan Magistrate.

(iii) Judicial Magistrate of the second class; and

(iv) Executive Magistrate.

(i) *The Court of Session :* Each district of the state has a court of session which is presided over by a District & Session Judge. Additional Session Judges may also be appointed for assisting the Session Judge in his work. They are equal in rank and not subordinate to the Session Judge. The criminal cases of a grave nature are tried in the Sessions Court and the Session Judge can pass any sentence. However, the sentence of death passed by him requires confirmation of the High Court concerned for final execution. The Sessions Court hears appeals from the Courts of District Magistrates and those of Special Megistrates.

(ii) *Judicial Magistrates :* The Code of Criminal Procedure, 1973 provides for the appointment of a Chief Judicial Magistrate in every district.[53] He is assigned the powers of the Magistrate of the first class. Every Chief Judicial Magistrate is subordinated to the Sessions Judge. He can pass any sentence authorised by law except as sentence of death or of imprisonment for life or imprisonment for a term not exceeding seven years.[54] Besides the Chief Judicial Magistrate, there are also the courts of Magistrates which are further classified as Judicial Magistrates and the Executive Magistrates. There are two grades of Judicial Magistrates, namely the Judicial Magistrate of the first class and the Judicial Magistrate of the Second class. In Metropolitan areas, the court of a Chief Metropolitan Magistrate have the power of a CJM and the Metropolitan Magistrate have the powers of the First class Magistrate. The Chief Metropolitan Magistrate is subordinated to the Sessions Judge.[55]

(iii) *Executive Magistrates :* Sec 20(i) of the Code of Criminal Procedure, 1973 provides that in every district and in every Metropolitan area, the state government may appoint as many persons as it thinks fit to be Executive Magistrates and shall appoint one of them to be District Magistrate. The state government may appoint any Executive Magistrate to be an Additional District Magistrate who shall also have the same powers as those of District Magistrate in charge of a sub-division and the Magistrate so placed in charge of a sub-division shall be called a Sub-Divisional Magistrate. The state government may also appoint Special

Executive Magistrate for particular areas or for performing particular functions.

(b) ***Administration of civil justice :*** In general, the hierarchy of courts which exist in each state for the administration of civil justice consists of:

(i) *District Court :* There is a Court of District Judge in each district which is the principal civil court of original jurisdiction. It exercises appellate jurisdiction for the orders and decrees of the subordinate courts. The District Judge has the power to control and supervise the whole subordinate judicial courts in the district. He is assisted in his work by the Additional District Judges whenever necessary.[56]

(ii) *Lower courts :* Below the district court, there are number of courts of Judges having different designations in different states. In some states they are designated as Munsiffs while in others they are called as Civil Judge class I and class II as in case of Assam. Their pecuniary jurisdiction varies from state to state between Rs. 1000/- and Rs 5000/- as contained in the Civil Courts Acts of the respective state.[57]

(iii) *Other small causes courts :* Besides the lower subordinate courts, there are a few more courts of minor jurisdiction which are called the courts of small causes. They are meant to provide cheap and speedy justice in petty civil cases. The courts of small causes were first established in 1860 which were amended in 1865 and again in 1867. The same person may be appointed as a Judge of more than one such courts. Each court of small causes has a

Registrar who is a ministerial officer of the court. He may, however be empowered to try civil case. In addition to these, Family Court is now available to provide cheap and speedy justice of cases arising out of family dispute. Consumer Protection Council acts as a court for dispose of the cases embodying the consumer product and their transaction under the Consumer Protection Act.

In addition to the courts mentioned above, certain states also have courts of Mamlatdars and village Munsiffs as in Maharashtra or village courts in Madras (Chennai).

(iv) *The Village Panchayats :* After the Indian independence most of the states have established Village Panchayats which are commonly known as 'Gram-Panchayats' in compliance with the directive principle contained in Art. 40 of the Constitution of India. The Gram Panchayat conducts its proceedings in public and exercises petty civil as well as criminal jurisdiction. As regards civil cases, the Gram Panchayat decides petty cases involving money, goods, recovery of movabable property or compensation claims. Each Gram Panchayat consists of an elected head called the Sarpanch and a Up-sarpanch to assist the Sarpanch.[58] In the state of Assam the Secretary and the President with the help of members conduct the Panchayat. Now the 73rd amendment of the Constitution provides for its composition and Constitution which can make laws. The amendment provides constitutional protection to the local governments under the Panchayat which can govern local areas without direct interference from the state government.

(c) ***Revenue Courts :*** The system of courts adopted by different states for adjudication of revenue cases is more or less similar with minor deviations in the designations of the Revenue Officials. The different categories of Revenue courts functioning in the states are as follows:

(i) *The Board of Revenue :* The Board of Revenue is the highest revenue court in a state. It decides all judicial matters and cases relating the settlement in whole of the state.

(ii) *Commissioners and Additional Commissioners :* The whole of the state is divided into several divisions each having a commissioner who exercises powers and performs duties assigned to him by the code of Land Revenue of the state[59]. An Additional Commissioner assists the Commissioner in his work. The Commissioners and Additional Commissioner function under the Board of Revenue.

(iii) *Collectors and Additional Collectors :* Each division of the district like in the state of Assam, Additional Collectors or Commissioners are also appointed by the state govt to assist the Collector or Commissioner of the district.

(iv) *Assistant or Deputy Collectors :* Assistant collector of the first class may be placed in charge of a sub-division when they are called as Sub-Divisional Officer and a Deputy Collector is placed in the division like circle called Sub-Deputy Collector that is prevailed in Assam. They are subject to the control and supervision of the Deputy Commissioner or the Collector of the district.

(v) *Tehsilders and Naib Tehsildars :* These are revenue officers in the Tehsil which is a unit of collector of revenue. They deal with revenue matters according to the provisions of the land Revenue Act or Code.

Besides these Revenue officers there are a number of other petty revenue officials such as Superintendent of Land Records, Assistant Superintendant of Land Records, Kanugogois, as the state government may prescribe from time to time.

Although there is no uniformity as regards jurisdictional limits of different categories of subordinate courts in different states, nevertheless the organisation of these courts is more or less similar in most of the states. In case of Assam the history of the ancient and mediaeval legal system is somewhat different with the other states of the country. In context of Assam, so far the field of research work is concerned, the description of history of legal system is given below.

History of Legal System of Assam

Introduction

In the epics, puranic, early historical literature or in ancient lore Assam is mentioned as Pragjyotisha and Kamrupa.[60] Assam is mentioned as Pragjyotisha in the *Ramayana* and *Mahabharata.* Pragjyotisha included not only the whole of Assam and parts of north and east Bengal (at present Bangaladesh) but also the hill tracts upto the boarder of China. It is known for the first time as Kamarupa in the Allahabad pillar inscription of Samudra Gupta (fourth century A.D.) and in the early *Puranas.* The territory is called "Asham" in the *Ain-i-Akbari* and Asam in the *Padshahnamah* and the same name was applied by Francis Hamilton in his *Account of Assam* compiled during 1807-1808.[61] S.P. Sen writes in his *Sources of the History of India-*

> "In a few royal epigraphs the country is called Saumara or Saumara-Kamarup. In later writings the state is known as Assam or Acam."[62]

The boundaries of Pragjyotisha, Kamarupa did not remain static or constant throughout, but underwent changes in different ages for reasons political or otherwise. At present Assam lies between the latitude $28^0 18'$-24^0N and Longitudes $89^0 46'$-97^0 E in the north east corner of the Republic of India covering an area of 78, 438 sq.km.[63].

Legal System of Assam in Ancient time

Administrative divisions in ancient Assam : Several administrative units i.e., group of villages signified the ancient Kamarupa/ Bhukti, mandala, vishaya, pura and agrahara were such administrative unit. The two main divisions of the kingdom-the portion to the north of the Brahmaputra called Uttarakuladesha and that to the south known as Dakshinakuladesa.[64] The term bhukti signified the biggest administrative divisions like Pundravardhana of the Gupta period representing Dinajpur, Borga and Rajshahi or Tirakbhukti comprising Muzaffarpur and Darbhanga divisions of that time. The Kamauli grant mentions Pragjyotisha as a bhukti while Kamarupa is called a mandala, a lower administrative unit[65]. The administrative terms connoted different interpretations in different times. It is equally likely that a few new ones were evolved in some period while at another time the two might have been merged into one. Sometimes a term connoting a smaller unit was used for a big kingdom. According to the lexicons the terms vishaya signifying a district is equated with desa, upavartana, janapada and rashtra which were equally applicable in case of other states of the country as R.S. Tripathi describes in his *History of Ancient India*-

> "The empire (rastra) comprised desas or janapadas (regions or provinces) sub-divided into vishayas (dividions), nagaras (cities) or puras (towns), and gramas (villages)."[66]

The next administrative unit in descending order was mandala corresponding to a modern district. The Kamauligrant mentions Pragjyotisha bhukti and Kamarupa mandala. Kamarupa is mentioned as a vishaya in a grant of the Ganga king Anantavarman. The head of the vishaya was called Vishayapati or Vishayanaka. Below the district was grama or village and pura or city. There are references to a number of villages such as Abhisuravataka, Hensiva, Trayodasa, Haposa, Bhavisa, Kanjia, Guhesvara, Digdola, Chadi etc. Some of the names are sanskritised ones while others are tribal names. There are also references to agraharas like Mayurasalamalagrahara and Srigatikagrahara which were made up of many village settlements.

Officers and administration in the department of justice : The chief officials of judicial department were Dandika, Dandapasika and Chouradharanika. Literally speaking, Dandika was the officer in charge of a court, or Sitting Magistrate, responsible for judging and punishing criminals. The actual infliction of punishment after the delivery of the judgement was carried out by the Dandapasika. The Chauroddharanika was the highest officer concerned with the apprehension of thieves, robbers and brigands; his functions being the same as those of the Cauroddhartr or Cauragraha of the Hindu law books. Among the police officers, are included certain semimilitary officers, Cata and Bhata. Cata is equivalent to the modern head of a paragana responsible for the internal management of a district for the collection of revenue and the apprehension of criminals.[67] The Chief Judge is called Pradvivaka and other

Judges called Dharmadkikarins as called in the context of ancient Indian rule. Inscriptions mention officers with titles such as Nyayakaranika, Vyavaharika, Kayastha ordinarily at the head-quarters of a district (visayadhikarana). Each vishaya had an adhikarana with his officer Visayadhipati as the head.[68] The adhikarana was responsible not only for justice but also for revenue and other aspects of the administration. In the Indian context at the same time a Mantriparisad consisted of four Brahmanas, eight Kshatriyas, twenty-one Vaisyas, three Sudras and one of the suta caste helped the king in the administration besides other officers subordinate to them. The subordinate rulers were the Yuvaraja (Crown-Prince), the aristocracy and such high officers as Purohita (Priest), Camupati (Commander-in-Chief), Dvarpala (Chamberlain), Pradesta (Chief Justice), Dharmadhyaksa (Superintendent of Justice), Dandapala (Presiding Judge of the criminal courts), Nagaradhayaksa (city-Prefect), Karagaradhikari, (Superintendent of prisons), Durgapala (warden of forts)[69] etc.

In ancient Assam along with other states of the country justice was administered according to the Vedas, Angas, Dharmasastras and Puranas. The sources of law were the code of sacred laws (Dharmasastras), case-law (Vyavahara), customs and traditions (Caritam) and the king's orders (Sasana). The laws were expounded by the Brahmanas. Another official closely associated with the Nyayakaranika was the Vyavaharin or Vyavaharika. The Vyavaharin was an official who conducted judicial proceeding like a lawyer of present system. He was a lawyer either engaged by the Brahmana doneess to plead their case against the revenue officer assessing the land, or he was the king's lawyer responsible for the correct drafting of the grant [70].

The judicial system was in no way different in Assam from that of other dynasties in India. Closely connected with the problem of law and order, the officials in charge of law and justice had dual functions, prevention of crime and punishment of offenders. There was no division or bifurcation between the executive and judicial powers[71]. The Dharmadhikarin was the judicial officer along with the Nyayakarinikas. The defensive system seems to have been properly planned with plans for civil defence through fortification backed by a good fighting force under the Mahasenadhipati. The Baladhyaksha seems to have looked after the organizational wing and the supply line was maintained under Bhandagarika. On the whole the legal administrative as visualised on the basis of the available evidence seems to be fair enough to look after the interest and welfare of the people of Kamarupa.

Legal Administration in Medieval Assam

Kingship, Patra Mantris, Local Governors, the Paik or Khel system etc. in the Ahom dynasty : In the days of Ahom rule the king was the source of all power, the fountain head of the justice, but he had to abide by the recommendations of the council of ministers. The king was called Swargadeo, an Assamese equivalent to the Tai-Ahom word Chaopha (the king of heaven). All honours and prerogatives emanated from him and all superior appointments were made by him. The main duty of the king was the protection of his people. Another important function of the king was to conduct the foreign policy. Theoretically the king was bound to consult the council on all important matters and was not permitted to issue any general order, embark on war, or engage in negotiations with other states until he had done so. Neither was he considered to have been legally enthroned unless they had concurred in proclaiming him as king. But the personal influence and character of the king varied the rules.[72] Some kings, such as Pratap Singha, Gadadhar Singha and Rudra Singha appear to have followed own wishes without much regard, while others like Sudaipha, Lara Raja and Kamalesvar Singha were mere puppets in the hands of one or other of the great ministers of state. Next to the king was the council of the five known as the Patra-Mantris, consisting of Buragohain, Borgohain, Borpatragohain, Barbarua and the Barphukan. The three 'Gohain', who were hereditary were entitled to the appellation 'Dangariya'. It was their duty to select a king from amongst the legal claimants. To each of the 'Dangariya', the king assigned territories in which they exercised most of the rights of independent sovereignty. In times of war they supplied soldiers to the king's army and in normal times contributed labourers for carrying on such works as construction of roads, bridges and temples. Within their respective territories they could inflict the penalty of death. All important matters connected with defence, survey or settlement were carried on under the direct supervision of the Gohains. The Barbarua was the Chief Executive Officer and the head of the judiciary, who however could not act independently of the Gohains. The Barphukan was the Viceroy, who had his headquarters first at Kaliabar[73]. He enjoyed a great amount of executive power and could inflict death sentence not accompanied by blood-shed.

The princes and the near relatives of the reigning king were appointed as governors in certain areas and they were given the title 'Raja'. The frontiers of the Kingdom were placed under wardens like Sudiyakhowa Gohain, Marangi Khowa Gohain, etc.

Chaw-lung-Siu-Kapha the first king of Ahom dynasty introduced a system of exacting personal service from the members of the tribal communities, who were to serve the ruling tribe as fuel-suppliers, water- drawers, honey-suppliers etc. The ruling tribe of the valley divided into two classes- the rulers and the ruled, the latter tending to identify itself with the rest of the subject population, the non-Ahoms. With the extension of the Ahom power, the load of administrative work also increased, which necessitated the appointment of different new officers. In order to meet the internal exigencies, they elaborated the existing system of exacting personal service from the subjects. The result was the Paik or Khel system, systematically implemented by Momai-Tamuli Barbarua under the patronage of king Pratap Singha.

Legal administration : In the earlier period, the judges decided the cases according to the customs of the country and their own standards of right and wrong. These practices were withdrawn when the Hindu law were expounded by the Brahmins. According to this law the king was the supreme court of law, who assisted by a Chief Justice called Nyay-Sodha Phukan, dispensed with the cases received from the lower courts, which were controlled by the Patra-Mantris. The senior executive officers like the Phukans, Rajkhowas and Baruas had judicial power over the paiks[74] under their control. Appeals from the lower courts in upper Assam could be made to the court of the Barbarua and in lower Assam to that of the Barphukan. A second appeal could also be made to the king from the courts of the Barbarua and the Barphukan. The other courts of the Patra-Mantris, the frontier wardens and the local governors[75] were subordinate tu the king's court. These courts could decide all cases within their jurisdiction but the right of inflicting capital punishment was reserved to the three Gohains and the Barphukan only. The king alone could execute death-sentence accompanied by blood-shed; others were to do it by drowning, striking with hammer, etc.

No record was kept in criminal cases, but in civil cases, a summary of the proceeding was drawn up and a copy of it was given to the winning party. Trials for crimes were characterised by extreme and horrible sterness. Severity and retaliation were the guiding principle of the penal code. Offenders were put to death in various manners-by cutting throats, by impaling, by grinding between two cylinders, by sowing asunder between two planks, by starving to death, etc. The common punishments were extraction of eyes and knee caps, slicing of noses and ears, blowing, slapping, beating with sticks and so on. A traitor was punished by execution which in many cases extended to the members of his family. Another severest form of execution consisted in cutting off slices from the body, before final decapitation and hoeing from head to foot. Crimes were then not defined by law, and punishments were inflicted less with a view to dispensing justice than to subduing enemies.[76] Only at the lower of the khel social justice was defended effectively. The village namghars or prayers halls served as the village-court, where criminal and minor civil cases of the village were dispensed with by the Raij-mels or village councils. Aiming at the general welfare of the village the decision of these village courts were binding upon the offender. Similarly, the Gabharu-mel dispensed the cases in case of female matrimonial conflicts or like that. In those days the group identities of the parts of the population were preserved. As such in appointing the junior officers like Boras, Saikias and Hazarikas, who were directly related to the paiks, the government had to pay proper attention to their being acceptable to the subjects. The smaller units of the social organization maintained their respective identities. The paiks could demand the removal of a junior officer up to the rank of a Hazarika and hence any allegation made against such an officer was first discussed and usually disposed of in the village courts in the namghars. Therefore, such an officer was a member of the commonalty and hence bound to maintain social justice in accordance with the general will of the community. This autonomy of the village community was never threatened or questioned by the state.[77] In this way the traditional life and administration were continued till 1826, when western part of the Brahmaputra valley came under the British rule.[78] In December 1826 David Scott[79] reported to the supreme government that on account of a very considerable accumulation of civil cases, he had considered it indispensable to establish native courts for the administration of civil justice. As such the three courts namely Munsifs in Bengal to exercise the power upon it, another to exercise the powers vested in the Sadar Amins for the purpose of hearing original suits and deciding appeals from the tribunal first mentioned and a third to decide criminal cases of minor importance and to hear appeals from the Rajas (kings), Chaudhuris[80] and other Malguzars who agreed to the custom of the country exercise powers in their respective parganas[81] were came into existence, which paved the way later on for establishment of the adalat system.

The Judicial System (Reported by A.J. Moffatt. Mills, Judge of the Sadar court on deputation to Assam) During the early days of British administration: In these days the courts were guided by a brief code of rules. The Principal Assistants and their subordinates of the court recorded every judgement and order, whether relating to fiscal, civil or criminal matters in their own handwriting. The character of the civil litigation was very simple and the suits were mostly of small value. The stamp laws were in force only in the then Gowalpara district. J.Mills stated that litigiousness was a prominent feature in the character of the Assamese.[82] The Assam Civil Code was defective in various aspects, for instance clause 8, section I, which prescribed that suits for money instituted in the court of the assistant and clause 5, section II which gave to the assistant the power to make a summary inquiry into the merits of the cases by confronting the parties, extended only to assistants and the assistants had no time to take up these cases themselves and was extremely harased.[83] The system of having four written pleading and filing in every case had been prevailed and not well suited to the simple habits of the people of Assam. There were no provisions for the confronting and mutual examinations, simple debt, damage etc. The pleaders in the courts of Assam were a most ignorant set and it was not practicable to introduce the rules regarding the settling of issues by the pleaders on the hearing of a case. In the administration of criminal justice the salutory provisions of clause 6, section II of the Assam Criminal Code authorised the taking of evidence viva-voce and the recording of the substance either in English or in Bengalee as the commisioner directed in misdemeanours, thefts to the amount of fifty rupees and offences for which Magistrates were empowered to pass sentence of imprisonment not exceeding six months, Mills reported it as greatly neglected. The Deputy Commissioner was empowered to enhance punishment and penalty. Persons charged with the offences of murder or other heinous crimes were tried in the presence of a jury.[84]

As per observation made by Baboo Anandaram Dhekial Phookan the judicial system of the province Assam had utterly failed to afford any satisfaction to the people. All classes were unanimous in declaring that the mode in which justice was administered by the British government was ill adapted to the simple habits of the people. The public courts of justice were exclusively for the benefit of the rich and powerful, that it was imprudent and foolish for men in humble life to resort to them for relief, that cunning and deceit, falsehood and perjury hemmed in the courts on all sides and that in the civil and criminal courts, truth was often transformed into falsehood and falsehood into truth.[85] Men of all ranks appeared to be impressed with this opinion and the necessary consequence was entertained. Under the judicial system of early British administration, a party how trivial soever might be the nature of his complaint, could never obtain relief without submitting to a vexatious and harassing course of procedure, extending from at least six months to an unlimited length of time, and even when he obtains an award in his favour, the execution of the same was attended with so many obstacles that he was in many instances actually compelled to relinquish all hopes of recovering his dues.

Whenever questions of Hindu law arised in the courts of the province, they had no proper authority to whom they can apply for expositions. The consequence was that every court was obliged to refer to and guided in their decisions by the pundits in their immediate vicinity. But the pundits were influenced either by improper motive or by ignorance of the law, delivered opinions not only conflicting with each other, but often erroneous.[86] Questions of Mohammedan law were of very rare occurance, and they had been facilitated by the District Kazees assisted by two or three Mohammedans acquainted with the local law and usage of Assam. As a result some legal terminnology of Persian origin such as Adalat, Paroana, Hazoor, Kaidi, etc. became the language of court. Under the provision of Act XXIX of 1937, the vernacular language of a district was directed to be used in the courts. However, notwithstanding the provisions of this wholesome law, a foreign language viz., the Bengallee had been introduced into the courts of Assam. It was only to the officers and other persons connected with the courts that Bengallee was generally intelligible. For more than ten years after the annexation of the province the Assamese was the language of the courts. The Assamese being the vernacular language as well of the people as of the majority of the judges and ministerial officers of the courts no inconvenicences arised from its use.[87]

Legal System of Assam in Modern Period

With the passage of time the position of the legal system in Assam had changed. In 1860, the general Codes of Civil and Criminal Procedure were extended to the Brahmaputra valley, and in 1862 the Indian Penal Code came into force. These enactments superseded the Special Assam Code, which had been drafted in 1837 and revised ten years laters, but there was still great uncertainty as to the operation of the other laws in force in Bengal. These laws as a rule contained no local extent clause. All legislative enactments had been provided since about 1870 with a clause showing precisely how and where they are to operate. The difficulty in respect of the earlier enactments which did not contain these particulars was met in 1874 by the passing of two Acts the Scheduled Districts Acts, XIV of 1874 and the Laws of Local Extent Act XV of 1874. The latter enactment was designed to specify the laws which were in force in India generally, except in certain backward tracts, which were described as scheduled districts.[88] The Schedule District Act gave power to government to declare by notification in the Gazette what laws were in force in such districts and to extend to them any enactments inforce elsewhere which it might seem desirable to bring into operation. The whole of Assam, including Sylhet was classed as a scheduled district and all doubts as to what laws are and what laws are not in force have been removed by a series of notifications under the Scheduled District Act. The effect of these notifications had been to place the plains of Assam in much the same legal position as other parts of India. The elaborate legal rules laid down in the procedure code were not suited to the inhabitants of the hilly tracts. It was therefore provided by the Frontier Tracts Regulation II of 1880 in all the hill districts. Notwithstanding, that the customary laws were more effective in hill areas than the plain areas, which is still observable. By orders issued under this regulation the tracts in question had been excluded from the operation of the enactments relating to criminal procedure, stamps, court-fees, registration and transfer of property; and a simpler system of administrating justice in civil and criminal matters had been prescribed by rules framed under the Scheduled District Act.[89] The Inner Line Regulation was the first law promulgated in Assam to prevent the quarrels and disturbances arised from the unrestricted intercourse existed between British subjects in Assam and the tribes living across the frontier. Then some changes were made in the legal system of Assam in later decades of British administration. Supervision of the administration of justice for the valleys of Assam was left to the High Court of the Fort William in Bengal. The District and Session Judge at Guwahati continued to hold sessions at various districts when required. The Deputy Commissioners of the districts had civil powers of subordinate judges and under Criminal Procedure Code of trying all offence not punishable with death and awarding a sentence of seven year's imprisonment. The Assistant and Extra-Assistant Commissioners had ordinary power of a Magistrate of first, second and third class and in Assam proper the civil powers of a Munsiff for the disposal of civil suits. In Cachar the Session Judge was the Judge of Sylhet who held sessions at Silchar whenever necessary, but the Deputy Commissioner had the special criminal powers under sections 30 or 34 of the Criminal Procedure Code.[90] The Deputy Commissioner or the Judge of Sylhet was the District Civil Judge and the Assistant and Extra Assistant Commissioners exercised powers of Munsiffs in addition to their normal duties as Magistrates and executive officers. The constant elaboration of the system of administration in the context of law and order pave the way for setting up the different courts and procedure in Assam. The following may be referred to as the existing court system in the legal administration in Assam:

(a) ***High Court :*** Prior to the establishment of the Gauhati High Court, the Calcutta High Court administered the legal order at the apex. On a motion of the Assam Legislature the Governor General of India established a High Court with headquarters at Gauhati for the state of Assam. Then the state of Assam was taken away from the jurisdiction of the Calcutta High Court and Calcutta High Court had the limited jurisdiction of West Bengal. So, the Gauhati High Court, Assam came into existence before enactment of the Indian Constitution i.e., in 1948. Like other states Gauhati High Court of Assam consists of a Chief Justice and such other Judges as the President of India may from time to time deem it necessary to appoint. It derives its power and authority from the Constitution of India contrary to the custom and tradition. It has the highest authority for judicial administration which embraces criminal, civil along with appellate and original jurisdiction.

(b) ***Administration of Justice in the Districts of Assam :*** Besides the High Court, there are subordinate courts in Assam like other states of the country for the administration of civil and criminal justice along with the revenue administration.

For the convenience of the administration the state of Assam has also been divided into 23 districts. Besides the districts, it has been divided into two divisions - Upper and Lower. The judicial system may be categorised in Assam into three divisions like in other states of the country (as mentoned earlier).

(a) Administration of criminal justice

(b) Administration of civil justice and

(c) The revenue administration.

(a) ***Administration of criminal justice :*** Below the Gauhati High Court there are other courts in Assam. Like other states, the highest unit of the judicial administration in the district is the district court. These courts administer civil and criminal laws. The following classes of criminal courts now existed in Assam as per the Code of Criminal Procedure, 1973.

(i) *The court of session :* Each district of Assam has a court of session which is presided over by a District & Sessions Judge. Additional Session Judge assists the Sessions Judge in his work. The criminal cases of a grave nature are tried in these courts. The sessions court hears appeals from the courts of District Magistrates and those of Special Magistrates. The Session Judge can pass any sentence.

(ii) *Judicial Magistrates :* The power and functions of the Chief Judicial Magistrate, Magistrate of 1st class and 2nd class are the same in Assam as prevailed in other states of the country. There is no court of Metropolitan Magistrate in Assam like in the metropolitan area of Mumbai, Chennai or Bengal.

(iii) *Executive Magistrate :* As mentioned earlier in the context of Indian judicial system, there are District Magistrate and Additional District Magistrate who have been categorised as Executive Magistrate as per sec.20(i) of the

Code of Criminal Procedure, 1973. The Govt. of Assam also appoints Sub-Divisional Magistrate and Special Executive Magistrate whenever necessary for particular areas or for performing a particular function.

(b) ***Administration of civil justice :*** The hierarchy of courts which have been existed in each district of Assam consists of:

(i) *District court :* In the state of Assam the power and various functions of these courts are the same as in the case of other states of the country as mentioned earlier.

(ii) *Lower courts :* Below the district court, there are number of courts of Judges designated as Munsiffs or Civil Judge of Class I and II in different states. But in Assam instead of Munsiff the Civil judges Class I and II are existed with limited pecuniary jurisdisction.

(iii) *Other small cause courts :* Like other states of India there are courts of minor jurisdiction in Assam which are known as courts of small causes as mentioned earlier in case of modern legal system of the country.

(iv) *The village panchayats :* As in case of other states, in Assam too, the village panchayats which are known as 'Gaon panchayat' have been prevailing. As mentioned earlier, here the president, the secretary along with the other members elected by the public (citizens) conduct the panchayat.

(c) ***Revenue Courts :*** The Board of Revenue, Commissioners, Additional Commissioner, Collector and

Additional Collector, Sub-Deputy Collector performed the revenue matter in Assam as available in other states. Under Sixth Schedule, Regional Councils and District Councils are empowered to make Laws.

Legal Administration in respect of Tribal Areas of North Eastern Region of India including Assam Under Sixth Schedule of the Constitution : After Independence the problem of legal administration in tribal areas of the North-Eastern Region including Assam attracted serious attention of the Constituent Assembly. A Sub-Committee of the Constituent Assembly called the North-Frontier (Assam) Tribal and Excluded Areas Sub-Committee with Late Lokpriya Gopinath Bordoloi as its Chairman reported that uniform, general administration which prevailed in the plains should not be introduced in these areas, due to the special circumstances of this region. The special circumstances arose from the distinct way of life, social customs, their attachment to and dependence on land and forests, peculiar mode of cultivation and the manner in which disputes were resolved. Then the Sub-Committee recommended on the principle that the local customary laws should be interfered with as little as possible and that the tribal councils and courts should be maintained, the hill people should have full powers of administering their own social laws, codifying or modifying them. The Sub-Committee submitted it to the Constituent Assembly and incorporated in the Sixth Schedule of the Constitution. Article 244 (2) declared that the provisions of the Sixth Schedule shall apply to the administration of the tribal areas in the state of Assam. The old terminology like 'backward tracts', 'excluded areas' and 'partially excluded areas' was dropped and instead these areas were called 'Autonomous Districts'. Each Autonomous District could establish a District Council which was given certain powers of legislation. Paragraph 4 under the Schedule the District Council may constitute village councils or courts for trial of civil and criminal disputes between parties both of whom are tribals. The power of a council or a court to try criminal cases is limited to offences which are not punishable with death, transportation or imprisonment for five years or more. Above the level of the village council or court, the District council, or any court constituted by the District Council, shall exercise the powers of a court of appeal from the decisions of the village council or court. No other court except the High Court and the Supreme Court shall have any jurisdiction over the village council or court. Paragraph 5 provides that Governor may confer powers, under the Criminal Procedure Code, on the District Council or and officer appointed by Governor, to try this class of cases. In actual fact Governor has not yet conferred such powers on any council, court or officer under this paragraph.

Recent development of legal system : Amongst the new areas of development of legal system and service mention may be made of National as well as State Human Rights Commissions, Lok Adalats and Legal Aid Programmes, the Consumer Protection Movement, Family court etc.

The Human Rights Commissions on national and state level have been set up on the basis of Universal Declaration of Human Rights as per the proclamation made by UNO in 1948. These are being empowered equally with the Indian courts. At the state level in Himachal Pradesh, West-Bengal, Madhya Pradesh, Tamil Nadu, Assam, Punjab and in Kashmir the commissions have been set up so far. Judges of Supreme Court and High Court and veteran legal personnel have headed these commissions for securing the rights of the citizens provided by the Constitution of India. Lok Adalats, which are peculiar process of deciding disputes by negotiations via benevolent middle agency, is a recent successful movement started first in Gujarat and now spread all over the country. The awards passed by the Lok Adalats are deemed to be the decrees of the Civil Court or the order of any other court and are binding on all the parties to the dispute. No appeal lies against an award. All categories of cases can be settled through Lok Adalats except criminal cases which are not compoundable. 42, 477 Lok Adalat bave been held in the country wherein 90, 74971 cases have been settled amicably through negotiations.*

Under Article 39-A the state has to promote justice on the basis of equal opportunity and to provide free legal aid by suitable legislation or schemes so that opportunities for securing justice are not denied to any citizen by reason of economic or other disabilities. For this purpose legal Aid and Advices have been provided by setting up the Legal Aid Programmes i.e., State Legal Services Authorities and Commitees. As per reported on 9th Nov. '99 (Legal service Day) 24, 10, 450 persons have been provided Legal Aid and Advice in Law courts by various State Legal Services Authorities and Committees.

The public controls on the freedom of trade assume greater importance and various legislations aimed at the Consumer Welfare have taken shape. Quality control is one measure which aims at consumer protection and the producer welfare too. In spite of the various Acts enacted by the Govt. the interest of the consumers were not satisfactorily protected. Consequently the Consumer Protection Act 1986 was passed to provide better protection to consumers. As a result Consumer Protection Council at the central and state level and Consumer Disputes Redressal Agencies at the central, state and district level have been set up to promote and protect the rights of the consumer.

Another addition in the recent development of legal system is the establishment of Family Court. In the big cities like in Guwahati of Assam it has been established to promote and protect the family rights, legal matter embodying women and speedy and easy disposal of the disputes arising out of them.

Conclusion : It appears that judgement made by the king and the learned Brahmin or Puruhita was considered as laws which was based on religious scripture and spiritual thinking in the early Hindu legal period. In the early period king's power was under religion and the religion was more powerful than the sovereign. There was much caste prejudice in matters of legal dealings and against woman in the country including Assam. In the medieval period of India law was reformulated and modified according to the tradition, convenience and religious fanaticism. The Sultan or the Emperor administer justice with the help of systematic court system and procedure. But, the law and justice were guided by religious traditions and scripture. However, in lower level, most settlements were based on customs and traditions.

In the medieval period of Assam as regards to legal system, the king was the fountain head of justice who administered the justice with the help of council of ministers. A systematic procedure of law has been observed in this period. Notwithstanding this the crimes were then not defined by law and punishments were inflicted although less according to one's whim but in view of dispensing justice for to subduing enemies. Severity and retaliation were the guiding principle of the penal code. The legal administration was not based on any Hindu religious scripture or constitution. In lower level, customs and traditions were followed to administer the justice. The paik system of Ahom rule paved the way for introducing the co-operative system in the societies in later periods.

In the modern period of India as well as in Assam law is based on justice on the concepts of democracy, liberty and equality. Modern laws have been made according to the constitutional rights which makes no distinction between man and woman. Under Hindu Succession Act, girls have the right to inherit the property. At present, widow can marry under Hindu Family Law which was not permitted by legal custom in ancient Hindu period of the country as well as in Assam. But the distinction in respect of civil code of India for Hindus and Muslims has still remained the same, which should be constitutionally amended for uniform civil code for the people of the country. India is a Sovereign Socialist Secular Democratic Republic and no state religion. The uniform civil code would help in establishing the rule of law. Examples of Roop Kanwar, Shah Bano and many others like Urmila Saho of Assam indicate that woman are in many cases trapped as they are often wedded to their oppressors and their subordination is thus clothed in religious rhetoric or fundamentalism. If a common or uniform civil code is enacted and enforced, it would help and accelerate national integration.

As such, the country and its indispensable part Assam have been administerd by different administrators of different dynasties and in different ways since the ancient period. The information about the system relating to administration have been recovered in varying ways in different periods of time. The formal and informal literature available in the country are worth-mentioning in this regards and the searching of these literature will pave the way to have knowledge in connection with the legal system embodying the customs and traditions prevailing throughout the age in the country as well as in Assam.

References

1. V.D. Mahajan, Ancient India, 4th ed. Delhi, S. Chand., 1968, p. 5.

2. Manorama yearbook 1995, Kochi, Malayala Manaorma, pp. 455. See also India: A Reference Annual, edited by Research, Reference and Training Division, Ministry of Information & Broadcasting Govt of India, p. 1.

3. Ronald Segal, The Crisis of India, Ch. II., pp. 34-37. See also Society in India by David G. Mandelbum, Bombay, Popular Prakashan, pp. 5-6.

4. V.D. Kulshreshtha, Landmarks in Indian Legal and Consistitutional History, 7th ed., Lucknow, Eastern book Co., 1995, p. 2.

5. The rite of commemorating the ancestors at which balls of rice called pinda were offered. Sradha defined the family and those who were entitled to participate in the ceremony were 'Co-pindas' (Sapindas), members of the family group, *Ibid.*

6. Most families of Bengal and Assam follow the rules of Dayabhaga while the rest of India generally follows Mitaksara, *Ibid.*

7. Rama Jois, Seeds of Modern Public Law in Ancient Indian Jurisprudence, Lucknow, Eastern book, 1990. pp. 1-2.

8. V.D. Kulashreshtha, Landmarks in Indian Legal and Constitutional History, Lucknow, Eastern book, 1995, p. 4.

9. Ram Sharan Sharma, Aspects of Political Ideas and Institutions in Ancient India, Delhi, Motilal Banarisidas, 1996, p. 103.

10. *Ibid*, p. 112.

11. V.D. Kulashrestha, Landmarks in Indian Legal and Constitutional History., Lucknow, Eastern book, 1995, p. 6.

12. P.V. Kane, History of Dharmashastra, Vol. II, p. 65.

13. Radhakumud Mukherji, Local Government in Ancient India, pp. 29-34, See also Landmarks in Indian Legal and Constitutional History, Lucknow, Eastern book, 199, p. 7.

14. P.V. Kane, History of Dharmashastra, Vol. III, Chap. XV, Poona, Bhandarkar, Oriental Research Institute, p. 379.

15. *Ibid*, pp. 330-360.

16. V.D. Kulashreshtha, Landmarks in Indian Legal and Constitutional History, Lucknow, Eastern book, 1995, pp. 9-10. See also I.D. Bernett Antiquities of India, 1964, p. 155.

17. Jagadishlal Shastri, ed., Manusmriti, Delhi, Motilal Banarsidas, 1996, Chap. VIII, p. 329.

18. P.V. Kane, History of Dharmashastra, Vol. III, Poona, Oriental Research Institute, pp. 388-390.

19. Jagadishlal Shastri, ed, Manusmriti, Delhi, Motilal Banarsidas 1996, Chap, VIII, p. 129.

20. Rajanikanta Dev Sharma, ed, Kautilya's Arthasastra, Vol. IV, Asom Prakashan Parishad, 1977, p. 10.

21. Jagadishlal Shastri, ed, Manusmriti, Chap-3., Delhi, Motilal Banarsidas, 1996, p. 102.

22. Panas - a copper coin.

23. *Ibid.*

24. Rajanikanta Dev Sharma ed, Kautilya's Arthasastra, Chap-IV Asom Prakashan Parishad, 1977, pp. 8-11.

25. The system of employing Pandits to expound the Law in Civil Cases between Hindus was introduced by Illtutmish.

26. S.K. Puri, Indian Legal and Constitutional History, pp. 18-19. See also. A Rahim, Muhammadan Jurisprudence, Allahbad, pp. 36-37.

27. *Ibid.*, p. 19.

28. M.B. Ahmed, The Administration of Justice in Medieval India, Lucknow, Eastern book, 1995, pp. 104-125.

29. Mufti was a lawyer of eminence attached to the court to expound law and was appointed by the Chief Justice in the

name of the Sultan. Law as expounded by Mufti was accepted by the Judge as authoritative.

30. A Brahmin lawyer generally known as Pandit, was appointed to explain personal law of Hindus in Civil cases. His status was the same as that of Mufti.

31. He was in charge of prosecutions on original side and in appeal he answered for the prosecution.

32. An Administrative officer of the court. See - V.D. Kulashrestha, Landmarks in Indian Legal and Constitutional History, Lucknow, Eastern book, 1995, pp. 17-19.

33. Person selected as Qazi usually possessed a good knowledge of law. See - M.Elphinstone, History of India, Bombay, Orient Longman, 1987, p. 421.

34. M.B. Ahmed, The Administration of Justice in Medieval India, Lucknow, Eastern book, 1995, pp. 14-166.

35. V.D. Kulashrestha, Landmarks in Indian Legal and Constitutional History. pp. 22-24.

36. *Ibid.*

37. *Ibid.*, p. 24.

38. M.B. Ahmed, The Administration of Justice in Mediaeval India, Lucknow, Eastern book, 1995, p. 225.

39. S.K. Puri, Indian Legal and Constitutional History, Allahabad, Allahabad Law Agency, 1995, p. 32.

40. A.B. Keith, Constitutional History of India, Lucknow Eastern book, 1936, p. 2.

41. N.V. Paranjape, Indian Legal and Constitutional History, Allahabad, Central Law agency, 1994, pp. 2-4.

42. *Ibid.*

43. *Ibid.*

44. M.P. Jain, Outlines of Indian Legal History, New Delhi, 2nd ed., pp. 1-4.

45. V.D. Kulashreshtha, Landmarks in Indian Legal and Constitutional History, Lucknow, Eastern book, 1995, pp. 65-73.

46. *Ibid.*

47. *Ibid.* pp. 268-269.

48. See Paranjape .... and Kulashreshtha.

49. Kulashreshtha, pp. 211, See also Universal Encyclopaedia, Vol. 15, pp. 85-92.

50. V.D. Kulashreshtha, Landmarks in Indian Legal and Constitutional History, Lucknow, Eastern book, 1995, pp. 175-180.

51. See - Sec. 6 of the Code of Criminal Procedure, 1973.

52. Each of the Presidency towns of Bombay, Calcutta and Madras and the City of Ahmedabad shall be deemed and metropolitam area according to sec. 8(1) of Cr. P.C.

53. See - Sec. 12, Code of Criminal Procedure 1973.

54. See - Sec. 29, Code of Criminal Procedure 1973.

55. See - Sec. 19, Code of Criminal Procedure 1973.

56. N.V. Paranjape, Indian Legal and Constitutional History, Allahabad, Central Law, 1994, pp. 142-145. Also collected by personal interview with Sr. Advocates and Magistrates of Assam.

57. *Ibid.*

58. M.P. Jain., Outlines of Indian Legal History, Delhi, 1986, pp. 143-150.

59. N.V. Paranjape, Indian Legal and Constitutional History, Allahabad, Central Law, 1994, pp. 14-150.

60. S.P. Sen. ed., Sources of the History of India, Vol. III, Calcutta, Institute of Historical Studies, 1988, pp. 10-15. See also H.K. Barpujari ed., The Comparative History of Assam, Vol. I, Guwahati, Pubn. Board., pp. 1-2.

61. H.K. Barpujari, ed., The Comparative History of Assam. Vol. I, Guwahati, Pubn. Board, pp. 1-2.

62. S.P. Sen, ed., Sources of the History of India, Vol. III, Calcutta, Institute of Historical Studies, 1988, pp. 10-15.

63. Brian Hunter, ed., The Statesman's Year Book, 134th ed. 1997-98, pp. 656-657.

64. H.K. Barpuzari, The Comprehensive History of Assam, Vol. I, pp. 180-181.

65. B.K. Barua, A Cultural History of Assam, Gauhati, Bina Library, 1986, pp. 58-60.

66. R.S. Tripathi, History of Ancient India, Delhi, Motilal Banarsidas, 1960, p. 78.

67. B.K. Barua, A Cultural History of Assam, Gauhati, Bina Library, 1986, pp. 61-63.

68. P.C. Choudhury, The History of Civilisation of the People of Assam to Twelfth century A.D., Delhi, Spectrum Pubn, 1987, pp. 282-283.

69. R.S. Tripathi, History of Ancient India, Delhi, Motilal Banarsidas, 1960, pp. 70-71. See also V.D. Mahajan, Ancient India, Delhi, S.Chand, 1067, pp. 126-127.

70. B.K. Barua, A Cultural History of Assam, Gauhati, Bina Library, 1986, pp. 60-61.

71. H.K. Barpujari, ed. The Comprehensive History of Assam, Vol. I, Guwahati, Pubn. Board, 1990, pp. 193-194.

72. E. Gait, A History of Assam, Guwahati, Lawyers book stall, 1994, pp. 222-223.

73. S.L. Baruah, A Comprehensive History of Assam, Delhi, Munshiram Manoharlal, 1985, pp. 381-386.

74. Under the khel or paik system, every adult male between the age 16 to 50 was registered as paik for state service. Four paiks (Later three) formed a unit called got. The paiks of some specified areas whose number did not exceed 3,000 were placed under the control of a class of officers called Rajkhowas who could administer justice.

75. Such as Sadiya khowa Gohain, at Saidya, Morangi Khowa Gohain, governor of the Naga marches west of the Dhansiri, The Solal Gohain who administered a great part of Nowgong and a portion of Charduar etc. See, E.Gait, A History of Assam, 2nd ed. Guwahati, Lawyer's book stall, 1994, p. 226.

76. S.L. Baruah, A Comprehensive History of Assam, Delhi, Munshiram Manoharlal, 1985, pp. 395-408.

77. *Ibid.*, pp. 405-410.

78. S.K. Chatterji, The Place of Assam in the History and Civilisation of India, Gauhati, University of Gauhati., 1970, pp. 74-75.

79. David Scott was a Covenant Civil servant on the Bengal Establishment. As Commissioner in Cooch Bihar from 1816 Scott was required to discharge duties which were primarily political in character. He had to conduct the East India Company's relations with Bhutan, Assam and other principalities and chiefs on the northern and eastern frontiers of Rangpur, See-H.K. Barpuzari, ed. Comprehensive History of Assam, Vol. IV, pp. 4-5.

80. The Chouduris occupied a position similar to the Zamindars of Bengal before diecennial settlement, i.e., they were not recognized as owners of the soil and were liable to be removed at the pleasure of the govt.

81. In Kamrup the pargana system was mixed up with the Khel system. There were 26 parganas; Settlements were made with the Chaudhuris on the basis of records relating to a survey made in the mid-eighteenth century. See-H.K. Barpuzari, Comprehensive History of Assam, Vol. IV, pp. 303.

82. A.J. Mills. Report on the province of Assam, 2nd ed., Guwahati, Pubn board, 1984, pp. 113.

83. *Ibid.*, p. 114.

84. *Ibid.*,

85. *Ibid.*, pp. 93-117.

86. *Ibid.*, p. 131.

87. *Ibid.*

88. E. Gait, A History of Assam, 6th ed. Guwahati, Lawyers book stall, 1994, p. 315.

89. *Ibid.* pp. 316. See also H.K. Barpuzari, The Comprehensive History of Assam. Vol. IV. pp. 220-222.

90. H.K. Barpuzari, The Comprehensive History of Assam. Vol. IV, pp. 280-283.

* As per news published in the 'Asamiya Pratidin', 9th Nov., 1999.

3

History of Legal Literature

Meaning of Law and its Kinds

Definition : Law has been defined by Blackstone, a legal jurist as follows—Law in its most general and comprehensive sense signifies a rule of action, and is applied indiscriminately to all kinds of objects whether animate or inanimate, rational or irrational[2]. Laws according to Austin, a prominent legal jurist, are divisible into two kinds, i.e., (a) laws properly so-called and (b) laws improperly so-called. Laws properly so-called are the general commands, i.e., addressed to the community. Austin sub-divided laws properly so called as general commands into two categories i.e., (i) Laws of God; and (ii) Laws set by men to men i.e., positive laws. Positive laws also fell into two categories i.e., (a) laws set by political superior and he defined them as commands of the sovereign and (b) Laws set by men to men neither as political superior nor in pursuance of rights, conferred upon them by such superiors, i.e., positive morality. Austin classified 'Laws improperly so called' in two categories: (a) Laws by analogy, i.e., Laws set and enforced by mere opinion e.g., laws of fashion and international law and (b) Laws by metaphor, which express the uniformities of nature.

Though there are many criticisms of Austin's definition of law, it is in a more systematic form. He defined it as follows: "A law in the most general and comprehensive acception in which the term in its literal meaning, is employed may be said to be a rule laid down for the guidance of an intelligent being by having power over them".[3]

Law is defined by A.S. Hornby in his dictionary as Rule made by authority for the proper regulation of a community or society or for correct conduct in life.[4] H.M. Sinha defines law in his Legal dictionary: (i) "The most general term for all rules to which people in any society conform, whether by custom or by enforcible governmental regulation, (ii) properly the body of all rules enforced in any community through courts or administrative agencies or through any official acts within the authority granted to his office, (iii) the rule and bond of men's actioner, a rule for the well governing of civil society, to give every man that which both belong to him; a rule of action to which man are obliged to make their moral conduct conformable."[5]

Salmond classified the law in the following kinds neither based on logical decision nor there is anything to prevent one kind falling under the other heading.[6]:

(i) Imperative law;

(ii) Physical or scientific law;

(iii) Natural law;

(iv) Conventional law;

(v) Customary law;

(vi) Practical or Technical Law;

(vii) International law;

(viii) Civil law or law of the state.

(i) *Imperative law :* It is the command imposed by superior authority upon men. This command must be obeyed by those for whom it is meant. Being a command it is issued from a determinate authority. If the imperative law is not obeyed the punishment is to follow.

(ii) *Physical or Scientific law :* The expression of the uniformities of nature are these types of laws. They show harmony and regularity in the observation of the activities and operation of the universe, e.g., law of gravitation, law of tides and chemical combination.

(iii) *Natural law :* It is the principle of natural right and wrong- the principles of natural justice. This law of nature has taught all animals and is not peculiar to the human race, but belongs to all living creatures, birds, beasts and fishes. It is a general idea and common law of all humanity. It is not a body of actual law which can be enforced in actual court but mother of all laws.

(iv) *Conventional law :* These are the body of rules which have been agreed upon by person themselves for regulating their conduct towards each other. When the parties agree to a certain pattern of conduct, it becomes law for them, e.g., laws of a club, cricket, etc.

(v) *Customary law :* Custom are the rules of human action which are established and evidenced by long usages founded on pre-existing rules sanctioned by the will of the community. Custom is that source of law which is not set down in any written statute or ordinance but is based on immemorial usages. When these customs are recognised by judicial authority and clothed with legal sanctions, i.e., codification takes place they become customary law of which detail discussion is made in the fourth chapter.

(vi) *Practical or Technical law :* With the help of these laws, the desired goal may be obtained. On account of them it is ascertained what ought to do or refrain from doing in order to fulfill the aim. The examples of such laws are—laws of health, laws of musical and poetical composition, rules of architecture etc. According to Salmond rules of game may be divided into two kinds, firstly the rules which are conventional. i.e., those rules which are agreed upon by the parties themselves (similar to conventional law as mentioned earlier) and secondly practical or technical laws formulated for playing game successfully.

(vii) *International law :* International law expressess those rules of conduct in accordance with which nations are expected to act in a particular manner in relation to each other. These rules may be in persuance of usages of the civilized world or due to their expressed consent. CTBT is an example in this regard.

(viii) *Civil law :* Civil law is the law of the state also known as municipal laws or civitis or law of the land as applied in the state's courts of justice. According to Hobbes, it is the law which men are bound to observe. Civil law included Constitutional Law as the latter provides the constitution of a country and describes the working of three organs of the state namely

Executive, Legislature and Judiciary besides the rights and obligations of the citizens, etc. Civil law also includes Administrative law and Municipal law. Civil law as a matter of fact includes Criminal law in its ambit although in its narrow sense it excludes Criminal law. Civil law broadly speaking involves all man-made law of the country. Civil law may be divided into substantive law and formal law. Substantive law deals with the substance and the topic of the law, e.g., contract etc., while formal law deals with the procedural aspect of law e.g., evidence and procedures adopted in the court.

The Meaning and Kinds of Literature

The term literature denotes a body of writing by people using the same language whose value lies in beauty of language or in emotional effect. The term itself derived from the latin word littera ('Letter of the alphabet', litterae, 'letters'); but in ancient times literature tended to be considered separately in terms of kinds of writing, or genres as they came to be called in the 18th century when the term literature took on its modern meaning.[1] Thus, literature may be confined to the writings of a particular language of a particular kind or may be confined to publications or printed matters in a particular field of subject. Literature is a way for human expression. It represents a record of achievement of human race. In general literature means a body of knowledge. Any composition of letters, words or sentences cannot form literature.

In nature it is multilingual, complex and diverse. Literature is becoming more and more interdisciplinary and growing at a fast pace. Informational needs of various kinds of users are served by respective literature.

Information or knowledge generated from different sources is communicated through different media like published or formal and unpublished or informal document. A published document is one which is accessible to the public and which can be acquired through normal trade channels. Unpublished documents or informal literature are produced in limited quantities for specific uses and are not meant for wider circulation which includes personal diaries, notebooks etc. Again in the modern age along with print-on-paper media, non-paper media like microphones and electronic medium are gradually gaining inportance. Notwithstanding these divisions, according to the sources of generation, information can be grouped into three broad categories- Primary, Secondary and Tertiary. So, the corresponding documentary channels are accordingly categorised as Primary, Secondary and Tertiary literature.

(a) *Primary literature :* These type of literature record the direct, first hand information of any kind and original research and develpopment or describe new application. These are primary documents representing unfiltered ideas recorded by the persons concerned. These sources are sometimes unorganised sources. Periodical papers, Research monography, Research reports, Survey reports, Patents, Standards, Acts, Agreements, Laboratory experiments and Unpublished sources like Memoranda, State papers, Oral history, Coins, Inscription, Epigraphs, Diaries, etc. are the instances of this type of literature.

(b) *Secondary literature :* These type of literature contain information compiled from primary literature. The original information having been usually analysed, modified, selected or reorganised so as to serve a definite purpose or groups of users. These contain organised repackaged knowledge meaningful for making judgements. Statistical reviews, Historical studies, Indexes, Bibliographies, Indexing periodicals, Abstracting periodicals, Reference books, Manuals, Digests, Commentary, etc are the instances of this type of literature.

(c) *Tertiary literature :* Distilled informations are available in this type of literature, which are collected from primary and secondary literature. The primary function of tertiary literature is to aid the searcher of information in the use of primary and secondary literature. Bibliography of bibliographies, Guide to reference books, Text-books, Directories etc are the examples.

Formal sources of information like Research organisation, Societies, Industries, Government departments, Universities, Consultants, Informal sources like Television programmes, Radio programmes; Theses, Dissertations, Feasibility Reports, Manuscripts etc produce a considerable amount of information.

Evolution of Law

(a) *Primiiive law :* The growth of law appears to be much more complex and it is not easy to generalise that in all societies law developed in the same line. The course of conduct of the primitive man was entirely based on customs and religion. The supernatural sanctions compelled him not to depart from the prescribed behaviour. Hence the primitive man did not dare to break the recognised customs of the community. Early law, therefore appears to have its origin in religious sanctions.

Before the era of courts the primitive law had a very limited scope. There were very few rules regarding marriage, succession of property and few rules regulating crimes such as witchcraft etc. As the institution of courts developed it took into cognizance the question of compensation. The members of the family of the injured party could accept the compensation and if the wrongdoer did not pay the compensation, then physical violence even may be inflicted on him. In primitive law the community itself took an action against any one guilty of certain wrong, e.g., witchcraft. In tribal societies law has been still based on customs.

Early codes in the legal literature were closely associated with religion. But all codes were not influenced by religion, some were secular in character. In the earliest society the notion of law could hardly be divorced from religion and it is difficult to reject the idea that legal duties are derived from religious duties. Pound, the legal jurist is of the opinion that the Hindu system of law has close relation with religion. A man was bound by law because he was bound by religion. Early codes were largely the result of a consolidation of scattered legislation. The view that all law was based on the work of one legislator and it was inconceivable that such a system was created by one Act.[7] Hence, Hindu philosophy was taken as Hindu religion. Law owes a part to Hindu philosophy in earlier times.

(b) *Law in the middle age :* In this period the rigidity and technicality in law through the medium of codes were gradually developed. Codes are nothing but the mainfestation of the legislative activity. Some writers claim that legislation, which may create new laws and change existing laws is of late growth, while others believe that it appears very early. The era of codes was preceded by the era of themists or judgements and the era of customs. Greeks believed that when a king decided a dispute, he was guided by the divine will. 'Themis', their goddes of justice was actively instrumental in the judicial awards.

When custom and its force became visible, adjudiction and the decisions of the suits was based on it. It was observed by Allen in his book *Law in the Making* (pp. 29) that before any clearly articulated system of law making and law dispensing power had developed, the conduct of men in society was governed by the customay rules. With the invention of writing it was felt that these customs must be reduced into writing and thus written laws in the form of codes begin to appear except the prevailing customary laws of the tribal people of the country including Assam.

Legal fiction, equity and legislation were three instrumentalities which brought law into harmony with the society.

Legal fiction meant any assumption which concealed or affected to conceal the fact that a rule of law had undergone alteration its letter remaining unchanged, its operation being modified. Thus it is useful weapon to a judiciary which wishes to maintain the view that its task is but to declare the law.

Equity also played an important role in the development of law. Technicality, conservation of law etc can be removed by adopting rules of equity. Legal rules are mere generalisation and hence they are incomplete as absolute uniformity cannot be achieved in the operation of any law. Unless a margin is left for extraordinary cases, the essential purpose for which law was created is obstructed. This margin is completed by the rules of equity. It is a force working through and not in opposition to the law. Equity tries to correct legal rules as if the legislator would by himself have done it.

(c) *Classical law :* The society had marched ahead. Developments from all sides had taken place. The community was economically well advanced but the development of laws was not so rapid. The new social changes and new economic developments demanded new laws and it was felt by the society that the old rules in spite of modifications and interpretations needed new shape as the laws of undeveloped age were of no practical utility in the advanced civilization. The old law was to be replaced by new law which could fulfill the ambition of new society. Thus a need for classification, analysis and synthesis was felt.

(d) *Post-Classical law :* As the society becoming more complex, the development of law also became very rapid and complex. The social welfare programmes of the community influenced the pace of law making process. The effect on law in this period have placed due to the new theories of planning collectivism and social security. Laws relating to nationalization of many industries are to be seen in the codes. Thus, in the post-classical period the law has changed its function and its old characteristic of concentration on individualism has yielded way to the new dimensions of law. There was a tendency in this period to mature systems, as economic and social conditions became more complex to deal with new situations by statutes designed for a particular mischief only. It was the task of the lawyer to point out how much the old order changed and what reforms were necessary to make the body of the law again consistent with itself. Hence in this period there was a challenge to lawyers to study the basis of statutory law[8], as in the classical period attention was concentrated on the basis of case law[9], otherwise law might cease to be a systems.[10]

Notwithstanding the fact that the new developed law has been executed to general people of economically, socially developed area, the under-developed tribal areas of plains as well as hills of the countries including India and Assam remained same. Their course of conduct or laws still based on customary practices. They have their own laws which are still original in nature. Notwithstanding that, as the customs of some particular group of particular areas have been entered into the court of law and recognised by judicial authority i.e., codifications take place, the original customs and traditions have obtained legal sanctions. But the content of the customs still involved with religion, philosophy and some traditonal beliefs of the concerned societies leaving some conducts which are inconsistent with the prevailing ages.

Legal Literature, its Meaning and Kinds

The meaning, kinds and information relating to law may be effected through literary or documentary works. Besides formal literary works in context with legal affair, informal or unpublished documents or literature like Correspondence Files on legal matter and the Special Category of Documents-Case studies on legal matter, Reports on legal matter etc produce a voluminous literature. So, the recorded knowledge or recorded meaningful information relating to law is legal literature and the ramifications of these legal literature are same as in case of types categorised under literature in general. These legal literature confined to particular kind of field of information or subject like Folk literature of Assam, which reflects the particular kind of information to supplement the culture of Assamese people, their customs and traditions. Since the folk-literature donot convey any legal message, this has not been discussed in detailed in this report.

In the field of tribal societies the information, knowledge, transacted through practices, conducts in various aspects and occasions reflects their culture besides through their usual literary works and other cultural activities. But recorded information or documents are not sufficiently available through which information relating to their customs and traditions can be obtained. That is why amphesis has been given on the study of their behavioural actions and practices which is discussed in the later chapter.

Development of Legal Literature in Ancient India including Assam

(a) *The Rigveda :* Veda meaning literally knowledge, is the name given to certain ancient works which formed the foundation of the early beliefs religiously adhered to or law of the Hindus. These are the *Rigveda,* the *Samaveda,* the *Yojurveda* and the *Atharvaveda* and these were supposed to have been compiled in tenth centrury B.C. All of these the *Rigveda-so* called because its Samhita or collection of mantras or hymns consists of verses intended for loud recitation.[11]

Regarding sources of law, Manu says:

"Bedotkhilo dharmamulang smritisile so tadwidam,

Acharachaiba sadhunamatmanstustirebo so."[12]

i.e., the whole Veda is the first source of sacred law, next the traditions and conducts of those who know the Veda, also the customs of holymen and finally self satisfaction. 'The whole Veda' here means that not only the direct texts themselves are authoritative but also rules which are deducible from them. Vedas donot contain positive precepts (vidhi) on matters of dharma in a connected form. They only contain incidental references to various topics that fall under the domain of dharmashastra as conceived in latter times.

One instance is-

(i) *Marriage*-In early vedic age the marriage rite resembled in essence the Brahma form. The Asura form of marriage was also known. The Gandharva form is hinted at in these words.

"Bhadra badhurmabati yatsapesa sayang sa mitrang banute jane sit."[13]

i.e., when a bride is good looking and well adorned, she seeks by herself her friend among men.

The Rigveda is a collection of 1017 hymns, supplemented by 11 others called Valakhilyas and is systematically arranged into 10mandalas or books.[14] The hymns represents compositions of different periods[15], and are of varying degrees of literary merit, being productions of priest-poets-mostly men and women of various families or as orthodox traditon regards it revelations to the Rishis. It is only invocations to the gods, conceived as personifications of the powers of nature to give spiritual and material favours on the worshipers. In various state of affairs the Aryans those were divided into several tribes[16] followed the law believing it as command of the creator. The regular word for law or custom in the Rigveda is Dharma. Theft, burglary, highway robbery and cheating are among the crimes recorded.[17]

(b) *The Manusmriti in the age of Dharmahsastras : The Manusmriti* is the most authoritative work on Hindu law which is supposed to be compiled between 2nd century B.C. and 2nd century A.D.[18] Manu is not the name of one person. A number of Manus are mentioned in Puranas which differ in the names and number of Manus. e.g., the Vayu and Padma refer to14 Manus; the Visnupurana, Brahmanda enumerate 12.[19] Manu may be regarded as a legendary sage with whom law is associated. The extant *Manusmriti* consists of twelve chapters and 2684 shlokas (verses). *The Manusmriti* informs the legal matters in various aspects and it appears to have undergone several recasts. Manu provides that a Brahmana can marry a Sudra wife[20]. But in later chapter it is strictly forbidden. Manu mentions statements about the suitable forms of marriage for different castes. Comprising twelve chapters, the *Manusmriti* deals with the usual topics which can be divided into four classes, viz., Acara, Prayascitta, Vyavahara and Rajadharma. Under Vyavahara discussions have been made on the usual eighteen titles of law, the judge, legal procedure, inheritance and succession, evidence, etc. Under Rajadharma the important matters are the necessity and modes of punishment, policy on taxation etc. In various chapters of the smriti the following legal topics have been mentioned: Mutual relation of husband and wife, five yajnas, duties of householders (ch.iii); Means of livelihood, rules of conduct, condemnation of enjoyment of others' wives (ch.vi); the use of instruments of punishment (ch.vii); Administration of justice, eighteen titles of law, viz., Rnadana (non- repayment of debt), Niksepa (deposit), Asvami-Vikraya (sale by one who is not the owner), Sambhuyanutthana (partnership business), Dattasyanapakarma (non-delivery of what is promised), Vetanadana (non-payment of wages), Samvrd-Vyatikrama (breach of contract), Svamipala-vivada (dispute between the owner and keeper of cattle), Simavivada (boundary dispute), Dandaparusya (too severe punishment), Vakparusya (abuse), Steya (theft), Sahasa (violence), Stri-Samgrahara (abduction of women), Stripumdharma (duties of wife and husband), Vibhaga (partition), Dyutasamahvaya (gambling and animal-betting) (ch.viii); Duties of women and men, inheritance and succession, stridhana, gains of learning (ch.ix); Duties of

Brahmanas and mixed castes, duties in emergency (ch.x); Snataka (Characteristics and duties, Sin and expiation) (Ch.xi); Results of good and bad deeds (ch.xii).

Relating to laws of Manu in the book *The sacred books of the East*[21] the following have been referred.

1. A king, desirous of investigating law cases, must enter his court of justice, preserving a dignified demeanour, together with Brahmanas with experienced councillors.
2. There either seated or standing raising his right arm, without ostentation in his dress and ornaments, let him examine the business of suitors.
3. Daily (deciding) one after another (all cases) which fall under the eighteen titles (of the law) according to principles drawn from local usages and from the Institutes of the sacred law.
4. But if the king does not personally investigate the suits, then let him appoint a learned Brahmana to try them.
5. Either the court must not be entered or the truth must be spoken, a man who either says nothing or speaks falsely becomes sinful.
6. Property stolen by theives must be restored by the king to (men of) all castes (varna); a king who uses such (property) for himself incurs the guilt of a thief.
7. (A king) who knows the sacred law, must inquire into the laws of castes (gati), of districts of guilds, and of families, and (thus) settle the peculiar law of each ....

The important commentaries on *Manusmriti* dealing with legal matters are: the *Bhasya of Medhatithi* (C. 900 A.D.) and of *Govindaraja* (C. 1100 A.D.); the *Manvartha-muktavali* of Kulluka (earlier than 1100 A.D.). Besides these *Narayana* (earlier than 1500 A.D.),[22] *Raghavananda, Nandana* and *Ramacandra* may be mentioned.

(c) *Yajnavalkya smriti :* Next to Manu in date and authority is Yajnavalkya. This smriti is more systematic than that of Manu. Yajnavalkya divides his smriti into three chapters: viz., Acharadhyaya, Vyavaharadhyaya and Prayachitadhyaya, and he deals all topic to their proper positions and avoids repetitions. He treats only 1009 instead of 2684 verses of Manu[23]. There are numerous verses in *Yajnavalkya* that show remarkable agreement with the text of Manu. But there are several points in which *Yajnavalkya* differs from Manu and shows in general more advanced state of thought and feeling than the *Manusmriti*. The privilege of Brahmin is cut down to a minimum in *Yajnavalkya*. The smriti of Yajnavalkya treats the woman as a full legal persona, and it follows her to inherit property. Yajnavalkya has no repressive law against a Shudra disputing with the Brahmans or against a Shudra teaching owning property. Yajnavalkya limits the prerogative of the king. He limits it even in a conquered country. He says that the conquest gives exactly the same right to, and imposes the same duty on the king with regard to new subjects as the king has got in his own country. The conquerer could not even introduce new laws there i.e., their belief in tradition. The new subjects have to be ruled in the same way as the subjects of his own country.

In *Yajnavalkya smriti* the largest space in Civil law (Vyavahara) is given to contract. The partnership to sea-traders and artisans and the law of corporation find place in Yajnavalkya. He defines partnership as-

"Samabayen bonijang labhayo karma Kurbatam,
Labhalabhau jathadrabyang yatha ba
Sangbidangkritam."

i.e., where a group of traders do business for the purposes of profit, the distribution of profit and loss shall be in the absence of a contract to the contrary, in the proportion of the sums subscribed.[24]

The definition given by Yajnavalkya is the same as provided by the Indian Partnership Act, 1932, in section 4.[25] The definition of partnership contained in Partnership Act is carbon copy of the definition of partnership given by Yajnavalkya, 2000 years back.

Chief commentaries on Yajnavalkya are :

(i) *Balakrida* written by Vishvarupa;

(ii) *Mitakshara* written by Vijnaneshwar;

(iii) *Apararka* written by Aparaditya;

(iv) *Deepakalika* written by Sulapani; and

(v) *Virmitrodaya* written by Mitramisra.

(d) *Narada smriti : Narada-smriti* was compiled in about A.D. 200, latter than *Yajnavalkya smriti.* In the beginning of his smriti Narada states that his smriti is an abridgement of the larger work of Manu said to have originally been in one lakh verses. A feature of *Narada smriti* is that it deals solely with Positive law (Vyavahara), and does not contain chapters on Achara or Prayachitta. Narada is the first to give a Legal Code unhampered by the man of religious and moral teaching. He regarded king's edict as the final authority in judicial matters. He gives a very high place to custom by stating, the custom is powerful and overrule the sacred law. *Narada smriti* contains three introductory chapters on the principles of judicial procedure and on judicial assembly (sabha). He speaks of the plaint as of the essence of a law-suit and stresses the rule that it must disclose a proper cause of action. Narada allows a woman to remarry in cases where the husband is not known, is dead, is impotent, becomes sanyasi, or becomes outcaste (or convert) like modern Hindu family law. Narada prescribes remarriage for widows and for woman whose husband are impotent. There are about 50 verses that are common to Manu and Narada.

(e) *Brihaspati-smriti : Brihaspati smriti* is among the most precious relics in the early legal literature of India[26]. Brihaspati supplemented Manu on many places. Manu expresses apparantly two conflicting views on niyoga (levirate). First Manu allows niyoga and later condemns it as 'Pashudharma' (animal custom) or as the violation of eternal law. Brihaspati is obviously against the practice of niyoga, the appointment of wives and widows to raise offspring to their husbands. Therefore Brihaspati gives the jurisdiction of the rejection of niyoga:

Uktwa niyogamanuna nishida syamebatu,

Yugahrasadaskiyong kotu sarbai bidhanata.

i.e., first Manu allows niyoga but later condemns it owing to the inferior virtue of the men of Kaliyuga.Yajnavalkya and Kautilya allow gambling under Government supervision. Brihaspati gives elaborate rules regarding partnership, and mutual agency. He holds an enlightened view on the subject of women's rights and declares the right of the widow and daughter to inherits as heirs. He argues for widow to succeed a sonless man, - "In vedas, smritis and customs, the wife is regarded as half the body of the husband; So, so long as half the body of the husband survived, no one else would take the inheritance."[27]

Brihaspati was the first jurist to make a clear distinction between civil and criminal justice. He divides the "eighteen tiles of law" into two groups-Arthamol, springing from wealth and Hingsamol, springing from injury to beings. The rules of procedure laid down by Brihaspati are a great advance. He seems to provide for the first time for the examination, cross-examination and re-examination of the witnesses.[28] Brihaspati mentions four kinds of courts : fixed (Pratisthita), moving (Apratisthita), meeting under the king's seal (Mudrita) and directed by the king himself (Shasita) . The Pratisthita meets in town or village; the second, Apratisthita is itinerant; the third Mudrita is presided over by adhyaksha (probably by Chief Justice known as Pradavivak) and the fourth, Shasita is attended by the king. Brihaspati gave a rule of fundamental importance when he recomended 'Yukti' (equity) in the decision of a case. He says that the decision must not be made solely having recourse to the latter of the written codes, since if no dicisions were made according to the reason of the law, there might be a failure of justice. The date of Brihaspati is later than Manu and Yajnavalkya, P.V. Kane thinks that Brihaspati is not later than Narada and places him between 200-400 A.D.[29]

(f) *Parashara smriti : Parashara smriti* deals only with the subject of Achara and Prayaschitta and omits discussion on Vyavahara. The smriti is divided into twelve chapters and contains 592 verses. Parashara found the positive law (Vyavahara) considerably modified by usage that he felt it unsafe to refer his readers to refer those laws, therefore Parashara says that some positive laws are to be determined by the decisions of a parishad or an assembly of the learned. The present *Parashara-smriti* has been assigned to a period between the first and fifth century A.D.[30]

The introductory verses of the smriti narrate that Rishis went to Vyasa and requested him to tell them the dharmas and conduct beneficial to mankind in Kali age and that the great Vyasa took them to his father Parashar who then propounded the dharmas of four castes.

Parashara appears to have been a practical man. He exhorts his readers to save their bodies first in invasions, journeys, diseases, famines and calamities and then care for dharma. He recommends the non-observance of rules of purity in times of difficulty and adherance to the strict rules of dharma when one is at ease.[31]

(g) *Katyayana smriti :* Katyayana occupies a very prominent place among smriti-writers on law and procedure. Next to Narada and Brihaspati he is cited on Vyavahara (positive law) more frequently than any other Smritikara in such commentaries and digests as the *Mitakshara,* the *Smritichandrika,* the *Viramitradaya* and the *Vyavahara-mayukha.* Katyayana is later than Manu, Yajnavalkya, Narada and Brihaspati. His smriti is placed to be compiled between 300 to 600 A.D.

Katyayana looked upon Brihaspati as a model and as an author whose dicta were entitled to respect. On form and nature of reply (written statement as present day procedure) Katyana provides four form of answers, viz., Confession (Satya), Denial (Mithya), Special exception (Pratyabskandan) and Res-judicata (Purbanyai).

Katyayana smriti marks an advanced stage of development in adjective law. He provides the rule of constructive Res-judicata thus: when a litigant abandoning a strong ground resorts to a weak one (to prove his case), he would not be again entitled to rely on that (strong ground) after the members of the court have decided as to who should succeed. This rule of Katyayana is similar to the rule of constructive Res-judicata contained in Explanation IV to section 11 of the C.P.C.[32]

Katyayana defines at great length 27 verses to Stridhana. He prescribed that over women's wealth of the type called Saudayika she had absolute power of disposal even as regards immovable property. Nor even the husband nor her son had any power over her wealth. Sir D.F. Mulla says, the whole law relating to the rights of women over their stridhana has been evolved from the four texts, of which the first three are the texts of Katyayana, and the last is the text of Narada. Manu, Yajnavalkya, Vyas, Brihaspati and Narada made widow an heir of her sonless husband. She was considered as full legal persona and the heritage was not limited to her life. But Katyayana restricted the widow's right in her husband's heritage. He provides:

Aputra sayanang bharta palayanti gugrau sthita,

Bhunjita marnat khyanta dayada ordhamapnyu.[33]

i.e., a sonless widow keeping unsullied the bed of her husband and staying at her father-in-law's house shall enjoy the inheritance abstemiously until her death, the heirs of her husband shall take after her death.

Katyayana provides the rule of bailment and liability of the bailee as provided under sections 151 and 152 of the modern Contract Act. He says that a person by whose fault anything (i.e., deposit) is destroyed should be made to pay the thing together with interest, except in the case of fate (act of God) or king. Where a thing (without the negligence of bailee) is destroyed even without the act of God or king together with the goods of bailee, the loss is declared to be that of the bailor.[34]

(h) *The Dharma-sutras in the age of sutras :* The sutras were manuals of instruction in a brief but definite language. The sutra literature contained the *Vedangas, Niraukta* of Yaska, *Ashtadhyayi* of Panini, *Srauta-sutras,* the *Griha-sutras* and the *Dharma-sutras.* As regards the six *Vedangas* they included *Kalpa, Siksha, Vyakarana, Nirukta, Chhandas* and *Jyotisha.* The *Ashtadhyayi* of Panini as a book on

Sanskrit grammar. The *Srauta-sutra* deal with a large number of ceremonies which were performed by priests. *Griha-sutra* deal with domestic sacrifices and rites to be performed by the householders. The *Dharma sutras* refer to customary law and practices.

The *Dharma-sutras* are assigned to the period between 7th century B.C. and 2nd century B.C. and their authorship is ascribed to Gautama, Baudhayana, Apastamba and Vasistha.[35] In many points regarding law all the writers differ from one another. While Gautama and Baudhayana refer to eight kinds of marriage, Apastamba refer to only six and omits altogether the Paisacha and Prajapatya marriages. Baudhayana says that the eldest son should be given a greater share than others, but this view is not accepted by Apastamba. Apastamba does not allow the ceremony of upanayana to a charioteer but Baudhayana allows the same. Gautama allows usury to a Brahman if it is done through an agent, but Apastamba condemns it and says that nobody should eat at the house of a Brahman who is an usurer. According to Baudhayana usury is like Brahmahatya and a Brahman who practices it becomes a Shudra. According to the *Dharmasutras* the sovereign was not the source of law but merely the upholder of law, which is supposed to be the custom. Gautama speaks that the administration of justice shall be regulated by the *Veda,* the *Dharmashastras,* the *Vedangas,* the *Puranas* and the *Upvedas*. According to Vasistha, the king's duty is to pay attention to the special laws of regions, castes and clans-i.e., to local, family, caste customs etc in addition to the laws of the country. According to Gautama widows were not given the right of inherit. A daughter could inherit only if there was no son, pupil or teacher of the deceased. Women were not allowed to offer sacrifices. They were considered as property.

Three kinds of important crimes assault, adaultery and theft were prevailed in this age. The punishments awarded to persons belonging to the various castes varied. If a Vaishya abused a Brahmana, he was fined 150 coins. If Brahmana abused a Kshatriya he was fined 50 coins. If he abused a Vaishya, he was fined 25 coins. If he abused a Shudra, he was not fined at all.[36]

(i) *The Ramayana and the Mahabharata in the epic age: The Ramayana* is the oldest i.e., in the present form it was composed in the period from second century B.C. to the second century A.D.[37] It consists of seven books and 2, 400 couplets - which was written by Valmiki Rishi. The theme of the *Ramayana* is the conflict between Rama and Ravana who can be taken to be the representatives of the Aryan and non-Aryan civilizations.

The Mahabharata consists of 18 books and about one lakh of couplets. It was written by Vyas and supposed to have been completed in the periods from the fourth century B.C. to the fourth century A.D. The epic describes a conflict among the Aryans themselves. From these two epics a lot of informations about the then existing customary practices as well as social, political or religion legal situation can be obtained, which had traditionally been prevailed. In the time of the epics in addition to the four traditional castes many other castes came into existence. That was partly due to the inter-marriages between the different castes. The institution of marriage lost its old sanctity. Polygamy and polyandry were both practised. Dasaratha, the king of Ayodha (in the *Ramayana*) had three wives. Ravana, the king of Ceylon or Srilanka also had many wives. Draupadi married the five Pandavas. A man was not allowed to marry a wife from a higher caste although he could marry a woman from the lower caste. Women were not allowed much freedom in the matter of their marriages. However, the practices of Swayamvara for the royal families existed. This is clear from the Swayambara of Sita and Draupadi. Maidens were exhibited for sale and given to the highest bidders. The practice of the custom can be witnessed from the fact that Kaikeyi and Madri were secured by giving large presents. Rakshas marriage was another name for abduction and the abductor was allowed to keep the girl if he could defeat her relatives.

In this age the Kshatriyas kept long hair but the Brahmanas shaved their heads and their chins. The tradition of loving of athletics has been observed. Krishna, Balram and Bhim were great athletes. The deliberation of Krishna to Arjuna at the battle of Kurukshetra contained a lot of social, political as well as religious or legal values which is found in the shape of *Bhagawad Gita.*

The recognition of the private ownership of land by the state was practised which was contented by claiming only one- sixth of the produce as land revenue. The king was entitled to demand forced labour from the people once in a fortnight or 10 days. It was the custom that the Brahmanas learned in the *Vedas* were exempted from taxes but those Brahmanas who were not learned in the *Vedas* had to pay taxes. The taxes, on the whole, were not oppressive. The king was always to see that the income was more than the expenditure and there was always a large money in the reserve fund which has traced from the historical point of view of then kings of Bharata tribe.

In this age the tradition of addiction to gambling and drinking were practised (Dice of Sakuni).

Justice was administered by the king with the help of a minister and the council. Witnesses were examined by the parties. There was also the system of ordeals (in the case of Sita, after recovery from Ravana). He who died in the battle field went straight to heaven. A warrior was not to fight a woman or a person resembling a woman which was traditionally accepted, for instance the killing of Bhishma before Sikhandi in Kurukshetra. A person who was wounded or who fell in the battlefield, was not to be attacked. The use of war-chariots was common. Fire-weapons or missiles were freely used. Krishna used the Sudarshana Chakra to destroy the Kauravas.

(j) *The Arthashastra of Kautilya :* The work of Kautilya or Chanakya as is popularly known was compiled about fourth century B.C. Chanakya was the Minister of Chandra Gupta Maurya and advised him on financial matters of the state. Detailed rules relating to civil rights, duties, wrongs, criminal law, procedure which made these later to customary practices, are dealt with in great detail and in their manifold aspects in this work.

In the ancient texts (Veda, Smritis) the law and religion were intermixed and there was no clear cut distinction drawn between them simply due to the reason that rules were meant for spiritual and moral uplift of the human beings. *Arthashastra* of Kautilya is a treatment of entirely different branch of law as he deals with the rights, duties and responsibility of the king in the administration of the state including judicial administration. The king is a central figure in the entire work. According to Kautilya the calamity of a king is more serious than that of a minister (Amatya). Kautilya makes it clear that it was their tradition to receive the revenue by the king from the people as his fee for the service of protection. The custom that practised in the kingdom that the king was avoided to injuring women and property of other and shuned falshood. According to Kautilya four tests had been practised to find out the Amatyas. Those tests were fear, virtue, wealth and law. Kautilya emphasised the necessity of civil service in these words:

> "Sovereignty can be carried on only with assistance. A single wheel does not move, hence the king should employ the ministers and hear their advice."[38]

Kautilya's Authashastra describe the law of the land (country's) many of which had been followed traditionally in later time. This various aspects of law those have customary in nature or qualities or had been supposed to discussed in the Arthashastra are arranged under the following headings:

(i) *Civil law :* Chapters II to IV of book III deal with the topic of 'marriage'. According to Kautilya, 'marriage is at the root of all disputes including property disputes. He recognises eight types of marriages namely-brahma, prajapatya, arsha, daiva, gandharva, asura, rakshasa and paisacha. Each earlier form of marriage was traditionally treated as superior to each later form. The first four forms of marriages were valid on approval by the father. He favoured monogamy but accorded sanction to a man who could marry any numbers of women for whom he could pay the sulka (money in consideration of marriage) and stridhana. The custom that the possessing the right of re-marriage till her husband was alive did not prevailed. But if the husband was abroad or dead or had become ascetic then the woman could marry the brother of her husband or with the permission of judges any person of her liking.

(a) *Divorce :* In the four kinds of marriage divorce can be obtained. In the later four forms of marriages it could be obtained on the ground of mutual enmity between the spouses. But neither of the spouses could obtain a divorce against the will of the other. A wife could abandon the husband who (a) was of bad character or (b) had long gone abroad or (c) had become a traitor, or (d) was likely to endanger the life of his wife or (e) had fallen from his castes or (f) had lost virility. He accorded equal status to men and women in contrast to later developments in Hindu law through customary.

(b) *Partition :* Partition was to take place when all the heirs had attained majority. Self acquired property or gains of learning were not liable to be partitioned. The partition was made in accordance with the local custom.

(c) *Contract :* A contract was valid if made in the open with free consent by competent parties and if it was not against public policy and morals. Fraud and misrepresentation vitiated the contract. The invalid contracts could be rescinded by the party and the wrongdoer suffered the damages as well as penalty.

(ii) *Criminal law :* The last four chapters of book III and book IV deal with the concept of crimes and prevention of offences. Crimes in the nature of robbery, defamation, assault and gambling, etc are dealt with in great in *Arthashastra*. Sudden and direct seizure of property was termed as robbery and fraudulent and indirect seizure as theft. Contemptuous talk or intimidation constituted the offence of defamation. Truth was no defence for abusive words. Gambling was an offence but not punishable. The king regulated it through his own officers who collected percentage from the gamblers. Kautilya mentions offences against animals, trees, offences in the nature of murder, abortion, rape, adultery, sedition and offences against the king of which procedures and punishment had been followed traditionally.

Under miscellaneous, slavery was not recognised and the sale of an Aryan by any caste was punishable though in certain calamities his life could be mortgaged for money. This was based on local custom.

The rules concerning the infliction of (for secret conduct) punishment has been described by Kautilya as R.P. Kangle writes[39] :

> ... A secret agent, after inciting a brother of the treasonable high officer, not honoured by him, should show him to the king. The king should induce him to fight against the treasonable officer by granting the use of the treasonable man's property. When he has acted with a weapon or poison, he should cause him to be executed on that very ground, declaring, 'He is a murderer of his brother".

It may be mentioned that the whole book is divided into 15 adhikaranas or sections and 180 prakaranas or sub-divisions. It has about 6, 000 slokas. The book was discovered in 1909 and has been ably translated by Shamasastri and R.P. Kangle. Kautilya has described the legal system in the light of autocratic form of governcent. The free will of the autocrat was restricted to a certain extent by the customary reverence for Brahmanas. The Brahmanas were exempted from capital punishment. Kautilya suggests the king to turn aside eight specific kinds of spiritual punishment, viz. fire, flood, pestileness, famine, rats, snakes, tigers and demons. Kautilya had his own views on punishment. According to him, he who inflicts severe punishment becomes oppressive to all creatures. He who inflicts mild punishment is over-powered. He who inflicts just punishment is respected.

Arthashastra is a highly beneficial legal document for those of information seekers in this regards along with for learning the procedure to implement in this modern legal system so far the tactful laws concerned in those days.

(k) *Other Legal documents in the Gupta age (Third century B.C.):* In addition to *Arthashastra* the Gupta age accrued many literature where legal matters were included. Along with the Smritis of Narada, Brihaspati, the *Smritis of Vyas, Harita, Pitamaha* and *Pulastya* were written during the age of Gupta. The *Kamandaka, Nitisara* was written in the time of Chandra Gupta II by Sikhara Prime Minister of Chandra Gupta II.[40] In the *Mudrarakshas,* Visakhadatta describes the method of execution adopted in the Gupta period. Kalidasa in his *Malvikagnimitram* (the first work of the poet) describes about the political history comprising the legal aspect.

The Harsacharita of Banabhatta ascribed to the early part of the 7th century A.D., contains political and historical aspect. The work is of great value for the study of legal administration of the 7th century Kamararupa. The *Hara-Gauri-Samvada, Kalhan's Rajtarangini* also give light on this sphere.

(l) *The Puranas, Tantras etc in ancient India including Assam :* Among the other literary works in ancient India mention may be made to the Puranas, which are 18 in number[41]. These are found uptodate in Gupta age only. They are of inestimable value from the point of view of law. It may be relied as a source of law. The *Vishnu Purana* and *Bhavishya Purana* are the important from the point of view of law among others. Every Purana deals with five topics, viz., Sarga, Prati-Sarga, Vamsha, Manavantra and Vansha-Charita. It is the fifth topic mostly dealt with history with law. *The Puranas* start with the rulers who trace their origin from the Sun and the Moon. They describe the various kings who ruled in the Madhyadesh with their administrative system embodying legal matter. They fill in the gap from the end of the epic age to the rise of Buddha (9th century B.C. to 6th century B.C.).

The ancient Assam i.e., Pragjyotisa and Kamarupa along with its rulers have been mentioned in most of the Puranas. The *Garuda Purana* mentions Kamarupa and Kamakhya as great centre of pilgrimage. The *Naradiya Purana* refers to Hidimba. The *Markandeya Purana* mentions Pragjyotisa along with Udayachala, Lauhitya and Kamarupa as countries in the east. The *Skanda Purana* refers to the prevalence of the Sakti faith in Kamarupa. Of all the Puranas, the most important work is the *Kalika Purana*, which was composed in Assam itself in or about the tenth century A.D.[42]

(i) *The Kalika Purana (10th -11th century A.D.):* The greatest elaboration of the political as well as legal system of Assam is found in the Upapurana entitled *Kalika Purana*. It indicates that certain ideal standards of administration based on the Hindu law books were laid down for the king.[43] These ideals emphasised that an ideal ruler was one who worked for the welfare of his subjects and treated them as his own children. The *Kalika Purana* advises the king to take all measures for his own safety. It also enjoins upon him the duty of protecting his family and his people. The *Kalika Purana* lays emphasis on King's good qualities, training, education and observance of the injunctions of the Shastras. The Rajniti section of the *Kalika Purana* emphasises on the king's duty and responsibility to different varnas comprising the subjects. Certain kings of Kamarupa like Sthitavarman and Harjaravarman performed their coronation ceremonies. The *Kalika Purana* describes the ceremony based on the injunction of the Shastras performed by the Purohita. It also mentions regarding administration that a king should appoint learned and wise Brahmanas as Ministers. The information about legal system like spy, punishment, etc. are also described apparantly in this work.

(ii) *Tantrik-Buddhist literature with the Yogini Tantra:* The Tantrik-Buddhist literature of Eastern India, Tibet and Nepal contain materials relating to the religious and political history of ancient Assam, where the legal aspect followed traditionally by the people are also depicted. All of them mostly mentioned in *Kamarupa-Kamakhya*. The *Kamarupa-Yatra* based on *Yogini Tantra*, the *Kalika Purana* and the *Kularnava*, a Sanskrit work composed in Assam deals with the mode of worship of Kamakhya which has been followed customarily and it records the origin of the names of Pragjyotisha and Kamarupa. The *Tikkha-Kalpa* deals with the worship of Tara. The *Kamakhya Tantra* gives an account of Naraka-Bhagadatta. The *Dipikachanda* of Purusottama Gajapati, another religious work contains legendary accounts of the rulers of ancient Assam. The tantrik work entitled *Hara-Gaurisamvada* was composed after the first decade of the nineteenth century.[44] It aims to give an account not only of Indian history from the days of Yodhishthira, but also of the early history of territories like Kamarupa as well as of the medieval Kamarupa rulers of the Indra-vamsa. The administration with legal affairs of the dynasties of Pushyavarman, Salastambha and Brahmapala are mentioned in this work.

The *Yogini Tantra* is of special interest for the material it contains on political and cultural history of Assam. It is a 16th century A.D. work. It describes about funeral oblation.[45] Pinda, sacrifices, other rites and rituals relating to legal affairs. *Kamarupa-Kamakhya* has been described along with its political, religious social conditions and identification. The

Yoginitantra also mentions who has or lacks the right upon sacrificial activities.[46]

The other tantrik works that have legal value along with other aspects (cultural, political, socio-religious) are: *Pag Som Zon Zan, Grub' tob* and *Bka Abab Bdun Idan, Kahgyur* and *Tangyur, Dakarnava Kaulajnananirnaya, Akulavira tantra* and *Kamakhya Guhyasiddhi,* attributed to Minanatha; *Vyaktabhavanugata tattvasiddhi,* attributed to Sahajayoginicinta; *Goraksa samhita; Goraksa vijaya; Sadhanamala* etc. In the work *Sources of the History of India*[47] an account of the religio-legal aspect has been laid about the *Kalikapurana* and *Yoginitantra.* Dr N.N. Acharyya of Gauhati University writes in the aforsaid book:

> ...literary works came into existence in the eastern portion of India specially in the kingdom of Kamakhya ... The *Satapatha Brahmana* records the progress of the Aryans... The *Griha* and *Dharma sutras* are useful sources for studying the socio-economic and political life (which embraces the legal aspect) of the people of India in general and north-eastern part of it in particular. The works of Panini and Patanjali bear similar importance...[48]

(iii) *Inscription, Epigraphic grants etc. (Unpublished literature):* Inscriptions, epigraphs etc in the grants are the sources of information relating to geographical, political as well as historical aspects of the land. These are important literature emphasised for legal matter in the shape of historical account of earlier days.

Different inscriptions in Doobi grant of Bhaskarvarman, a Khonamukhi grant of Indrapala, Guwahati grant of Indrapala, Kamauli grant of Vaidyadeva, Hayungthal grant of Harjaravarmana, Nagaon grant of Balavarman, Tezpur grant of Vanmala etc. are the valuable sources for getting information in connection with legal system which were followed customarrily in the days of respective rulers in ancient Assam.

The Doobi grant mentions whatever the origin of kingship, the divine nature of the rulers of Assam was believed. Some of the ancient rulers of Assam was compared with gods. The grant describes, Pusyavarman was like a second Visnu.[49]

The Nagaon grant records that the donee's land was immuned from entry of the Chourodharanika (examinator of thieves) along with others. Tenants who had no occupancy right had to pay extra revenue as compared to the rightful occupiers and the king had to face no troubles to get them realised. Along with this grant Gauhati grant, Bargaon grant etc. mention the officers like Dandika and Dandapasika who were associated with the department of justice and the infliction of punishment.[50] Nidhanpur grant of Bhaskarvarman mentions that the Nyayakaranika (officer relating to justice) Jonardana Swami not only dealt with justice but also acted as an adjudicator, who had to inspect and decide if the boundaries of lands were properly demarkated or not and to settle all cases of dispute arising out of the land.[51] Epigraphs mention various types of lands, such as Kshetra (arable land), Khila (waste land), Vastu (building sites) etc., which were made classified for the purpose of proper assessment of taxes. Epigraphs mention about Chourodharanika and Chata-bhata (Police Officers). Inscriptions of Kamauli grant describes Govinda Gonandana as the Dharmadhikara (a Judge). Again the inscirptions of Nidhanpur and Nawgong grant mention officers with titles such as Nayakaranika, Kayastha and others ordinarily at the head-quarters of a district (visaya-dhikarana). That the king had to give proper attention in the courts is found in epigraphic literature of Nidhanpur grant.[52] Besides these the following copper-plate inscriptions are important for historical information embodying legal matter:

(1) Parbatiya plates of Vanamalavarmadev of nineth century.

(2) Uttarabarbil plates of Balavarman of tenth century.

(3) Ulubari plates of Balavarman of tenth century.

(4) Bargaon plates of Ratnapala of eleventh century.

(5) Saikuchi plates of Ratnapala of eleventh century.

(6) Gachtal inscription of Gopala of eleventh century.

(7) Puspabhadra grant of Dharmapala of twelfth century.

(8) Subhankarapataka plates of Dharmapala of twelfth century.

In the medieval period the legal system for the whole country practised under the respective rulers including North Eastern Region of India. In this period basically the Ahoms in Assam differs in the legal system with the other parts of the country. The information in connection with social, political or legal matters have been laid in some historical documents or in other medias like numismatics or epigraphs, inscriptions, coins etc. Which are referred to as unpublished legal literature. So, the following are the points which have been laid for sources of information relating to historical account in the long Ahom age, besides, it gives light on the laws and practices which had been customarily practised age after age.

Legal Literature in the Medieval Period

(a) *Buranjis in the Ahom age:* Medieval period of Assam history have began with the coming of the Ahoms to this land in the early part of the 13th century and covers the entire period of their rule

> till the formal inauguration of the British regime in 1826. The Ahoms had become the supreme power in Assam during this period and as a consequence the entire literary activities shifted from Western Assam to Estern Assam where the capital of the Ahoms was situated.[53] Sukapha, the first Ahom king in Assam, when reached the Brahmaputra valley advised his nobles to keep record of all events, which was the glorious beginning of the history-writting in Assam.[54]

Buranjis, the historical works which are numerous and voluminous, literally means 'a store that teaches the ignorant'.[55] The Ahom conqueror and settlers when started to record the events that happened within the land and outside it, conserved the language, customs, institutes, officials and judicial procedures, social and religious usages and the details of state machinary.[56]

The complete and comprehensive Ahom Buranji from the earliest times to Purandar Singha (1832-38 or end of Ahom rule) in Tai-Ahom script is divided into two parts: *Deo-Buranji*, history of heavenly bodies, creation up to descent of Khunlung and Khumlai; *Din-Buranji*, history of earth, from the extension of the rule of the Tais and migration of Sukapha from Maulung to Mungdanshunkham (country full of gardens of gold) on Assam i.e., rise and fall of the Ahom power in Assam. The *Assam Buranji* is an important chronicle of Assam from earliest Ahom kings to Gadadhar Singha (1681-96). It throws light on administrative measures of the period where the legal system of that time is also contained. The *Satsari Assam Buranji* is a collection of seven old Assamese Buranjis which deals with political history: (i) Political history refers to the victory of Pratap Singha (1603-41) over the Mughals at the battle of Bharali (1615), to Mir Jumla's invasion and the role of Bejdoloi and loss of Assamese soldiers, (ii) history from Swarganarayan to Suhummong

(Dihingia Raja), (iii) Suhummong to Pramatta Singha (1497-1751); (iv) Suhummong (1497-1539) to Gaurinath Singha (1780-1795), gives supplementary information (v) from Jayadhwaj (1648-1663) to Chakradhwaj (1663-1670), (vi) 1795-1838 (which is not relevant) (vii) Court etiquette and diplomatic relation. This seventh part of the Buranji gives the aparant description of the legal system.

Deodhai Assam Buranji is a collection of some old chronicles in Assamese describing the earlier period of Ahom history, its relation with neighbouring tribes, the Koches, Jayantias, Kacharis, Mikirs, Chutiyas, Naras and with the Mughals and social customs and legal administration of the Ahoms etc. The *Tungkhungia Buranji* also gives the account of administrative machinary in legal aspect of Tungkhungia dynasty of Ahom kings (1681-1826)[57]. Day-to-day annuals of the courts, proceedings of important judicial trials, etc. were written with accurate description of other events. This has been the process since the reign of Suhummong or Dihingia Raja, that Buranjis in Assamese were first written.[58] Besides the Buranjis mentioned above there are many other chronicles dealing with the reigns of Ahom kings of different periods of Assam history, like Rajniti and other historical miscellany by S.K. Bhuyan which gives an account of Ahom legal administration and other miscellaneous events. *Assam Buranji Puthi* is a history of Ahom rulers from earliest time to the British occupation of Assam.

(b) *Other historical works containing legal information :* Persian chronicles, account of contemporary foreign travellers and British Officers etc : So far as the earlier Muslim invasions to Assam are concerned the Persian chronicles like *Tabaquat-i-Nasiri* (1260) by Minhaj-ul-Siraj[59], *Tarikh-i-Firoz-Shahi* by Ziau-din-Barani, *Bahrristan-i-Ghaibi* by Mirza Nathan Allaud-din-Ispahani, the *Akbarnamah* and the *Ain-i-Akbari* by Shaikh Abul

Fazal, the *Alamgirnamah*, the *Maasir-i-Alamgiri*, the *Masir-ul-Umara*, the *Muntakhab-ul-Labab*, the *Zafaranamah-i-Alamgiri* and *Fathiya-i-Ibriyah* of Shiha-buddin Talish (16th century) etc[60]. are all valuable sources of information for social, political, economic condition of medieval Assam where the legal system practised through caste, local custom are also depicted apparantly.

The accounts left by the contemporary foreign travellers who visited Assam are informative and interesting. Ralph Fitch, a Portuguese traveller, who visited the kingdom of Koch Behar during Naranarayan's reign (1540-84 A.D.) left an account that throws light on its administrative set-up with the system of legal affair and social, economic conditions. A Jesuit traveller Stephen Cacella visited Koch Behar and Kamrupa upto Pandu and left his observation in the form of letter. His letter throws new light on legal history of Mughal Kamrupa of that time. Captain Welsh in his expedition to Assam in 1792-94 was accompanied by Dr. John Peter Wade[61] as Asstt. Surgeon to the detachment. His account on the working of the Ahom administration is also important for legal aspect in the medieval Assam.

(c) *Information on Numismatical sources :* Coins indicate the names of rulers, titles, firm dates and gives idea of the extent of the dominion of a ruler from which legal matter of that time can also be withdrawn. The legends on the coins indicate the various aspects of the cultural and riligious condition and thus a critical study of these enable to assess the legal system prevailing in the country.

A silver coin of Jayadhwaj dated saka 1570 or A.D. 1648, now in the State Museum, Guwahati, weighing 173.2 grams has this legend: Sri Sri Swarganarayana devasya Saka 1570/ Sri Sri Haricharana Parayanasya[62]. Three silver coins of

Gadadhar (1681-95), found at Sibsagar and now in the State Museum Guwahati, weighing 172, 171.5 and 171.1 grams have the Tai legend Chaosu Patpha pin Khun lak ni raisa'n/ Ka'e bay pha len dan be u chu[63]. The coins of Lakshmi Narayana bear the legend, Sri Srimat Lakshmi Narayanasya Saka 1509/Sri Sri Sivacharana Kamala Madhukanasya. The full rupee coins weighed between 1479 and 1555 gram, the majority being approx-153 gram.[64]

As coins are symbols of sovereignty these help in resolving the inter-relation between the Koch, Kamrup and Mughal. The epithets in the coins indicate the deities worshipped. The Ahom coinage was peculiar because its octagonal shape which is said to have represented eight sides of the country according to the *Yogini-tantra*.

Legal Literature in the Modern Period of Assam

Assam passed into the hands of the East India Company in 1826 by the treaty of Yandabo.[65] There is a large mass of historical materials dealt with legal matter in the despatches of Assam's first commissioner David Scott. His report on Assam is a genuine historical contribution in legal aspect. A.J. Moffatt Mills, Judge of Sudder court letter to Cecil Beatton, Secy to the Govt. of Bengal, letter from Lieut-Colonel Francis Jenkins to A.J.Moffatt Mills, various letters and statistical lists incorporated in the *Report on the Province of Assam* by A.J. Moffatt Mills highlight the general sketch of the system of administration as prevailed in erstwhile Assam of the early British days. The letters and reports also belong to the suggestions to improve the civil, fiscal, judicial administration of Assam. In the letter from Cecil Beatton to Mills[66] regarding the character of civil litigation and value of suits are apparantly found in these words-

> "The character of the civil litigation is generally very simple, and the suits are mostly of small value. One of the chief subjects of litigation is the

enforcement of conjugal rights or the recovery of money expended in the ceremony of betrothal, in consequence of nonfulfilment of engagements. Cases of this description and claims on simple bond-debts and balances of accounts, constitute three fourths of the suits in the Province, and should be all decided on viva voce examination. The Assam Code clauses 5 and 6, section II provides for the summary disposal of these cases by the Principal Assistant."[67]

Information about Assam Civil Code, Stamp laws, Criminal Justice etc are also available in this letter.

From the points of observation made on the administration of the province of Assam by Anandaram Dhekial Phookan, the informations regarding the revenue system, the judicial system, law of procedure, law of evidence, oaths, administration of Hindu law, Judges, language of the courts, registry of deeds, registration of marriges etc in the early modern Assam can be obtained. Apart from these, Mill's Report mentions the various aspects of legal administration held in different districts-'Gowalpara', 'Gowahatty', 'Luchimpore', 'Nowgong', 'Seebsagar' and Darrang (as pronounced in those days) in Assam. For instance the Nagaon district he describes that:[68]

Table 4 : Civil Suits in 'Nowgong' district

Sl.No.	*Nature of suits*	*No. of suits instituted in 1852*
1.	Suits on account of advances made for produce	326
2.	Money lent	215
3.	Wages or hire	33
4.	Breach of promise of marriage and recovery of money expended in the ceremony	49

(Contd.)

(Table 4 Contd.)

Sl.No.	Nature of suits	No. of suits instituted in1852
5.	For enforcement of conjugal rights	22
6.	For rent	49
7.	For share of movable and immovable property	12
8.	For value of property taken away	90
9.	For land	24

As regards the recommendation of Second Law Commission provided by the Charter Act of 1853 the *Indian Penal Code* was passed in 1860, the *Code of Criminal Procedure* was passed in 1861.[69] In the sphere of civil law, the *Civil Procedure Code* was passed in 1859 and the Limitation Act was also passed in the same year. These laws and Acts were made and executed for the whole of India including Assam. In 1860 the general Codes of Civil and Criminal Procedure were extended to the Brahamaputra valley and in 1862 the Indian Penal Code came into force in Assam. These enactments superseded the Special Assam Code, [70] which had been drafted in 1837 and revised ten years later. Prior to these codes the four districts, Goalpara, Kamrup, Darrang including Bishnath and Nowgong were administered under the Act II of 1835, which placed all functionaries employed in them under the control and superintendence of the Sadar court in civil and criminal cases and of the Bengal Board of Revenue in revenue matters. Act VI of 1835 was passed to provide for the judicial control of the Khasi and Jaintia hills-embracing their strong customary laws. Since about 1870 all legislative enactments have been provided with a clause showing precisely how and where they are to operate. The difficulty in respect of the earlier enactments which did not contain these particulars was met in 1874 by the passing of two Acts- The Scheduled District

Act, XIV of 1874 and the Laws of Local Extent Act XV of 1874. The later enactment was designed to specify the laws which were inforce in India generally except in certain backward tracts, which were described as 'scheduled districts'. This Act gave power to govt to declare by notification in the Gazette what laws were inforce in such districts and to extend to them any enactments inforce elsewhere which it might seem desirable to bring into operation. The whole of Assam, including Sylhet was classed as a 'scheduled district.' All doubts as to what laws are and what laws are not, inforce had been removed by a series of notifications under this Act.

A.J.Mills mentions in his *Report on the Province of Assam* regarding some other Acts and Regulations which were prevailed in the early British administration in Assam, e.g., Regulation VII of 1799, Regulation II of 1819, Regulation X of 1822, Regulation III of 1828, The Act IV of 1840, The Act of 1845 etc.[71] The elaborate legal rules laid down in the procedure codes and in several other enactme nts of the same class were not suited to the inhabitants of the hilly tracts. It was therefore provided by the Frontier Tracts Regulation II of 1880, that the operation of unsuitable laws might be barred in all the hill districts, in the North Cachar subdivision, the Mikir hill tract in Nawgong and the Dibrugarh frontier tract in Lakhimpur. The tracts in question had been excluded from the operation of the en actmen ts relating to criminal procedure, stamps, court-fees, registration and transfer of property, by orders issued under this Regulation. The Civil Procedure Code never was inforce in the hill district [72] only because of strong traditional base of customary laws.

The Inner Line Regulation of 1873 was the first law promulgated in Assam under the authority conferred by the Statute 33, which provides the executive power of summary legislation for backward areas to parts of Assam and Cachar which were beyond revenue settlement, but not to areas under occupation of Europeans. George Campbell the successor of A.E. Campbell, Deputy Commissioner, Sibsagar, sought to apply the Statute 33 to all the districts not excluding the Europeans because it was afraid that any one of the numerous European settlers living in the frontier might any moment be the cause of a frontier war. Besides these, the planters and the frontier tribes were so intermixed that it was necessary that there should be law and tribunals to cover them. Thus the Inner line came into force which was considered essential to define the line beyond which the jurisdiction under the statute should not be extended.[73]

By Acts VIII and XII of 1874 the legal powers which were previously vested in the Lieutenant Governor or the Board of Revenue, Bengal were transferred to the Governor-General in Council who was at the same time authorised to delegate all or any of them to the Chief Commissioner. The powers delegated, combined with those conferred by the General Clauses Act which vests in the Chief Commissioner the powers of a local government in respect of the Imperial Council passed since the year 1874. These powers were placed the Chief Commissioner in the position of a local govt in respect of all legislative enactments such as Bengal Regulation of the Governor of Fort William, Acts of the Governor- General in Council, Acts of the Lieutenant Governor of Bengal in council, some powers of extension of the Scheduled District Act etc. These all subsequently included laws made by the Assam Legislative Council which was created in 1920.[74]

To provide the funds for the construction of roads, a regular public works department which was established in the year 1868 and the local boards established in 1880 for the management of affairs of local interest, were given half the proceeds of a local rate of one-sixteenth the annual value of all landed property, the levy of which was authorised by Regulation III of 1879.[75]

The Assam Land and Revenue Regulation, 1886 has been brought into force in all the plains district of the province and contains all the necessary provisions of the revenue law of Bengal, which it repeals so far as Assam is concerned.[76]

Although maintenance of law and order and collection of revenue had been the main concern of the British Indian government, attention had to be paid before long to welfare activities. The first attempt to introduce municipal govt outside presidency town was made by Act X of 1842. The subsequent Act XXVI of 1850 provided for the whole of British India the appointment of commissioners to manage municipal affairs and authorised to levy taxes. To remedy the defects of the Act XXVI of 1850, the District Improvement Act III of 1864 was introduced. The elective principle of municipality was followed by the Act 1868 which was inforce in the town of Sylhet and Goalpara. At the close of the century, there were nine municipalities in the province of Assam of which constituted under Act of 1884 and the remainder under Act of 1876.[77]

Assam became a separate province under a Chief Commissioner in 1912. The change occured further in 1921 when, in accordance with the provisions of the Government of India Act 1919. Assam was constituted a governor's province.

In the changing circumstances British Government felt the need of fresh reform in Indian administration and they came out with Government of India Act, 1935. The Government of India Act, 1935 envisaged a federal system of government. It was a very elaborate and lengthy Act comprising 321 sections and 10 schedules. The basic features of the Act were: (1) All-India-federation, (2) Dyarchy in the centre, (3) Provincial autonomy, (4) Safeguard provided in the constitution to the government of India.[78]

The Indian Independence Act was the legislative culmination of the announcement made by his Majesty's government on June 3, 1947. A draft of the Indian Independence bill was prepared and circulated to the leaders of the Congress and the Muslim league for their consideration. The bill was then introduced in the British parliament on July 5, 1947 which finally became an Act on July 18 to be operative on August 15, 1947. The Act provided for the partition of India and establishment of two independent dominions—India and Pakistan from August 15, 1947. The word 'independent' signifies the absence of any external restraint.[79]

The Constitution of India is a most wide and lengthy legal literature, which came into force on January 26th 1950, has been abided by all the citizens of India including Assam. It was framed by the Constituent Assembly of India under the chairmanship of Bhim Rao Ambedkar. The new constitution was adopted and signed by Rajendra Prasad on November 26, 1949.[80] The constitution is comprised of 400 articles and 12 schedules. 400 articles are laid down in 22 parts in the entire Constitution. The subjects in different parts along with the schedules are embodied as given below.[81]

Table 5 : Feature of the Constitution of India

Part	*Basic feature of the Constitution of India*
Part I	The union and its territory
Part II	Citizenship
Part III	Fundamental rights
Parts IV	Directive principles of state policy.
Part IVA	Fundamental duties
Part V	The union

(Contd.)

(Table 5 Contd.)

Part	*Basic feature of the Constitution of India*
Part VI	The states
Part VII	The states in part B of the first schedule.
Part VIII	The union territories.
Part IX	The territories in part D of the first schedule and other territories not specified in that schedule.
Part X	The scheduled and tribal areas.
Part XI	Relations between the union and the states.
Part XII	Finance, Property, Contracts and suits.
Part XIII	Trade, Commerce and Intercourse within the territory of India.
Part XIV	Services under the union and the states.
Part XIV A	Tribunals.
Part XV	Elections.
Part XVI	Special provisions relating to certain classes.
Part XVII	Official language.
Part XVIII	Emergency provisions.
Part XIX	Miscellaneous.
Part XX	Amendment of the constitution.
Part XXI	Temporary, Transitional and special provisions.
Part XXII	Short title, Commencement and Repeals.

Schedules		
First :	I	The states.
	II	The union territories.

Second:	Part A	Provisions as to the President
	Part B	[Repealed]
	Part C	Provisions as to the Speaker and the Deputy Speaker of the House of the people and the Chairman and the Deputy Chairman of the council of states and the Speaker and Deputy Speaker of the Legislative Assembly and the chairman and the Deputy Chairman of the Legislative Council of a state.
	Part D	Provisions as to the Judges of the Supreme Court and of the High Courts.
	Part E	Provisions as to the Comptroller and Auditor General of India.
Third :		Forms of oaths or Affirmations.
Fourth :		Allocation of seats in the Council of states.
Fifth :		Provisions as to the administration and control of scheduled areas and scheduled tribes.
	Part A	General
	Part B	Administration and control of scheduled areas and scheduled tribes.
	Part C	Scheduled areas.
	Part D	Amendment of the schedule.
Sixth :		Provisions as to the administration of tribal areas in the states of Assam, Meghalaya and Tripura and in the Union Territory of Mizoram.

Seventh :	List I	Union list
	List II	State list
	List III	Concurrent list.
Eight :		Languages.
Ninth :		Validation of certain Acts and Regulations.
Tenth :		Provisions as to disqualification on ground of defection.

Notwithstanding the existence of these Codes, Acts and Rules, gradually came to the province of Assam, the legal administration has been basically performed under the Code of Civil Procedure and Criminal Procedure. From the legal literature point of view some other legal documents such as Current Legislative materials, Commentaries, Manuals, Digests, Private Law Reports etc are the important and are briefly described below :

(a) *Current legislative materials :* To be aware of the current orders, amendments, etc. legal professionals refer to state Gazette like Karnataka Gazette, Assam Gazette etc.

(b) *Commentaries :* These are found on each subjects on particular branch of law where legal points are discussed in detail.

(c) *Manuals :* These are found on different branches of law, e.g., Civil Manual, Criminal Manual, Excise Manual, etc. which are like handbook on particular law. In addition to these there are manuals like Civil Court Manual, AIR Manual, etc. In these manuals all branches of law are discussed. They deal with Central Acts and Ordinances and the arrangement is alphabetical of legal Acts. They also provide subject index in order to help in quick identification of the required information.[82] Civil Court Manual is being published by Madras Law Journal pubn, Madras (now Chennai), AIR Manual is being published by AIR pubn., Nagpur.

(d) *Digest :* Digest provide abstracts of the cases, some of the popular digests are :-

(i) Supreme Court Digest.

(ii) Fifty Years Digest.

(iii) Quinquenial Digest etc.

These Digest are brought out by *All India Reporter*, Nagpur. These are multivolume publications. In these Digests all the Supreme Court cases are abstracted. It covers legal judgements covering a particular period viz, *Supreme Court Digest, 1956-1986.* In *Fifty Years Digest* cases are abstracted covering the period of fifty years. These will be published for every fifty years. In all these Digests arrangements are alphabetical and it is provided with subject index, e.g., *Fifty Years Digest 1901-1950.*

(e) *Private Law Reports :* These are issued in the form of journals which gives the information about latest judgements in the Supreme Court, High Court etc. Besides these some of the important journals relating to law are :

(i) All India Reporter.

(ii) Criminal Law Journal

(iii) Indian Judicial Report

(iv) Guwahati Law Report (Assam)

(v) Accident Claims Journals.

(vi) Rent Control Journal.

(vii) Rent Control Reporter.

(viii) Karnataka Law Journal

(ix) Labour Law Journal

(x) Indian Law Reporter (Karnataka, Chennai, Calcutta, Patna, Lahore, Allahabad, Bombai)

(xi) Calcutta Weekly Notes.

(xii) Crimes etc.

All the cases contained in these journals are used as references in varities of litigations held in different courts of the States of India.

(i) *All India Reporter : It's best use :* Majority of the advocates refer to AIR which is monthly publication published by AIR, Nagpur. It covers all the branches of law like civil, criminal, labour, rent control, tribunal etc. It covers the judgements of Supreme Court and High Courts of all the states of india. The arrangements of the decisions in this journal are simple and very easy to locate the required decision on particular branch of law. The first issue of AIR starts from January every year. The arrangenment of decision starts from journal section with photographs of legal professionals of current interest and next Supreme Court decision and then alphabetically by states i.e., Allahabad first covers all the states of India like Andhara Pradesh, Arunachal Pradesh, Assam, Bombay (Mumbai), Delhi etc. Separate paginations are started for each-state and continued the same in the next issues. It provides subject index, nominal table and comparative table. Thus AIR helps the legal professionals to have access to Indian legal materials and it is an important legal literature to the researcher who have been dealt with legal study.

(f) Few Acts with their dates of publication have given below (In respect of Assam)[83]

(1) Assam Act XXXIV of 1950. The Assam Land Requisition and Acquision (2nd Amendment) Act, 1950. Date of publication in Assam Gazette- 13-12-50. Actual date of publication -01-12-50

(2) Assam Act VII of 1954. The Assam Appropriation (No.II) Act, 1954 Date of publication in Assam Gazette- 31-03-54 Actual date of publication - 30-03-54

(3) Assam Act I of 1958. The Assam Municipal (Amendment) Act. Date of publication in Assam Gazette - 15-01-58. Actual date of publication -07-01-58

(4) The Assam Legislative Assembly Members Salaries and Allowances (Amendment), Act, 1965.

(5) The Assam Fixation of Ceiling on Land on Land Holdings (Amendment) Act, 1972. Date of publication in Assam Gazette - 13-10-72. Actual date of publication -10-10-72.

(6) The Assam Contingency Fund (Amendment) Act, 1985. Date of publication in Assam Gazette -10-12-84. Actual date of publication -08-12-84.

(7) Assam Fire Service Act, 1985. Date of publication in Assam Gazette - 01-10-85. Actual date of publication -26-09-85.

(8) The Assam sericulture (silk-worn seed cocoon and silk yarn control) Act, 1987.

(9) The Assam Taxation (on specified land) Act, 1990. Date of publication in India Gazette- 25-05-90. Actual date of publiction- 23-05-90.

(10) The Jogighopa (Assam) unit of Ashok Papermils Limited (Acquisition and Transfer of Undertaking) Act, 1990. Date of publication in India Gazette-25-09-90. Actual date of publication -12-09-90.

(11) Assam Finance (Sate Tax) (Amendment) Act, 1990. Date of publication in Assam Gazette -29-10-90. Actual date of publication -27-10-90.

(12) The Assam Panchayati Raj (Amendment) Act, 1990.Date of publication in Assam Gazette -23-11-90. Actual date of publication -21-11-90.

(13) The Assam Co-operative Societies (Amendment) Act, 1990. Date of publication in Assam Gazete-23-11-90. Actual date of publication- 21-11-90.

(14) The Assam Preferential Stores purchase (Amendment) Act, 1990. Date of publication in Assam Gazette -23-11-90. Actual date of publication -21-11-90.

(15) Some other Acts, Rules, Manuals, Reports and Codes dealt with legal aspect in the existing decade:-

(i) Assam General Sales Tax Act, 1993

(ii) North- East Region Stamp & Court fees Act.

(iii) North-East Region Urban Areas Rent Control Act.

(iv) Bodoland Autonomous Council Act.

(v) Assam Panchayat Act.

(vi) Guwahati Metropolitan Development Authority Act.

(vii) Assam Jail Manual.

(viii) Assam Forest Manual

(ix) Assam Police Manual

(x) Contingency Manual

(xi) North-Eastern Region Education Code.

(xii) Assam and Meghalaya Pension Code.

(xiii) Assam and Meghalaya Service Code.

(xiv) State of North-East India.

(xv) Rules and Orders of North East India

(xvi) Assam, Meghalaya and Manipur Delegation of Financial Powers Rules.

(xvii) Gauhati High Court Rules.

(xviii) Assam and Meghalaya Travelling Rules

(xix) Assam Service Discipline and Appeal Rules, 1964.

(xx) Assam Financial Rules.

(xxi) F.R and S.R (Fundamental Rules and Subsidiary Rules) Assam & Meghalaya.

(xxii) Law Relating to Protection of Backward Classes in Assam.

(xxiii) North-Eastern Fisheries Rules, etc.

(h) Few Books and Reports prepared and published so far by the Law Research Institute, Gauhati High Court, Guwahati (Assam) are:

(i) The Customary Laws and Practices of the Pati-Rabha of Assam.

(ii) The Customary Laws and Practices of the Dimasa of Assam.

(iii) Land System of Assam.

(iv) Administration of Justice Among the Tribes and Races of North-Eastern Region.

(v) Model Police Manual (Assam)

(vi) Criminal Justice System in Assam

(vii) Legislations in Changing Society, 1996.

Conclusion : It appears that most of the legal matters have been introduced at the time of *Manusmriti*. Caste discrimination did not prevail as a Brahmana could marry a Sudra wife. But in later days it was strictly forbidden. Status of woman appears to be existed as the law dealt with condemnation of enjoyment of others' wives, mutual relation of husband and wife have been prevailed. The law of Niksepa (deposit), Sambhuya nutthana (partnership business), Samvrd Vyatikarama (breach of contract) etc. analogous to our modern law of the country.

The law of remarriage, divorce, etc. are the derivation of Smriti age and Narada Smriti which was compiled 1800 years back is worthmentioning. At this age of smriti, Brihaspati argued for the right of the widow and daughter to inherits as heirs. The distinction between civil and criminal justice was made by him which have been prevailing for subsequent periods. The rules of court procedure made by Brihaspati like examination, cross- examination and re-examination of witnesses are still have been prevailing as modern law of procedure in the court of the country. Positive laws of Parasara were determined by the decisions of

Parishada or an assembly of the learned about fifth century A.D. like the law making procedure in the Parliament of today in the country. Katyayana made the rules of form and nature of reply in the court like written statement as present day procedure about 1700 years back from today. The modern rule of constructive Res-judicata contained in Explanation IV to section II of the Civil Procedure Code is similar to that of the rule made by Katyayana.

Most of the present laws are found as religious custom of ancient time, e.g., Katyayana prescribed that over women's wealth (stridhana) of the type called Saudaysea she had absolute power of disposal even as regard immovable property. In the age of Sutras the caste discrimination prevailed e.g., the punishment awarded to persons belonging to the various castes varied. The present revenue system was practised in the epic age. It appears that caste discrimination have been existed as the Brahmanas were exempted from taxes who learned in the Vedas. The separate existence of present law can be witnessed since the period of Arthashastra of Kautilya. Arthashastra of Kautilya is a treatment of entirely different branch of law as he deals with the rights, duties and responsibilities of the king in the administration of the state including judicial administration. The present civil law of the country is not lesser different from that of the laws laid down in the Arthashastra as it appears from the laws in respect of marriage, re-marriage, divorce, partition, contract etc. Kautilya accorded equal status to men and women in contrast to later developments in Hindu law through customary. The information laid down in the Arthashastra is most beneficial for present law maker, personnel involved with law and procedure and information seeker in this regard.

It appears that the inscription and epigraphic sources available in Assam inform about the system of systematic land settlement, proper assessment of taxes etc., as modern land settlement procedure. The information recorded in the Buranjis, Persian Chronicles, Documents of foreign travellers depicts the picture of anti corrupted administration along with socio-cultural and legal aspects in the medieval period which are immitable for the present country citizen or leaders.

While disputes were resolved according to the principles laid down in the Smritis and the Dharmasutras in the rest of India, in the tribal and hill areas of Assam these were settled on the basis of perennial customs which are still being prevailed.

So far as the common man of the villages of Assam is concerned, it must have been admitted that a sizeable number of them are not apprised of their rights and duties and also about the sanctions behind the laws even on the eve of Golden jubilee year of the Indian independence. If something which is done in violation of a law was not known the same will not protect an individual from the clutches of laws. Bigamy is an offence under the Indian Penal Code (Sec.494-495). It is also prohibited by the Hindu Marriage Act, 1955. A majority of the common people commit the offences of such type, who are ignorant. The mass media like radio, television, newspapers, lectures, meetings etc have been playing a vital role to eradicate such problems towards well administration of social justice. A little effort has been made toward this end in Assam. viz., the first publication in Assamese language relating to legal aspect was *Ain Aru Samaj* by Dr. Minati Sharma. *Bibahitar Surakshyat Ainor Byabastha* by Abha Bora, published in Payabhora, May 1991, Vol. 22, no. 4, ed. by D.K. Bhardevaj; *Adalator Kahini* by Late Suren Saikia and Bodhen Borah, Published by Eastern printers, Ghy, 1991, *Ainor Saran Aru Prahasan* by Harin Mahanta, Ghy, Janaki Prakashan, 1994; *Ain Chayanika* by Panindra Kr. Burman, Biswanath Prakashan etc. Among the articles published in local news papers *Ain Aru Apuni* by Haren Das, in the newspaper 'Agradoot', published bi-weekly ed. by Kanak Sen Deka, and 'Nijar Adhikar' a radio broadcasting by Akashbani Dibrugarh, the television serials arranged by Guwahati Doordarshan occassionally in this regard may be worthmentioned. These are all the contributions through which the general people of the regions become aware of the laws prevailing in the country and it depicts the informal type of sources which have been controlling the information produced in legal aspects.

After having the comprehensive knowledge about the historical development of the legal literature in general and customary application in the country as well as in Assam since ancient period of the same, it is required to highlight the matter in persuit of behavioural pattern of the people of Assam which is described in the next chapter and is the gist of the investigating work.

References

1. Encyclopaedia Britannica, 15th ed. Vol. 23, Chicago Ency. Brit. Inc. pp. 86-87.
2. B.S. Sinha., Jurisprudence, Allahabad, Central Law, 1987, p. 54-55.
3. *Ibid.* p. 55.
4. A.S. Hornby., ed. Oxford Advanced Learner's Dictionary of Current English, 10th ed., Delhi, Oxford Univ. Press, 1986, p. 476.
5. H.M.Sinha, Legal Dictionary, Delhi, Pioneer books, 1997, pp. 114-286.
6. *Op. cit.* B.S. Sinha, p. 37.
7. Pound, An Introduction to the Philosophy of Law, n.p. , n.d. p. 243.
8. The written law which is derived from the interpretation of statutes (legislative enactments).

9. The law which is created by and appears in the decisions of the courts.

10. B.S. Sinha, Jurisprudence, Allahabad, Central Law, 1987, pp. 29-35.

11. R.T.H. Griffith, The Hymns of the Rigveda, ed. by J.L. Shastri, Delhi, Motilal Banarsidas, p. V.

12. J.L.Shastri, ed. Manusmriti, Delhi, Motilal Banarsidas, 1996, p. 30.

13. *Op. cit.* R.T.H. Griffith, p. 548. See also Rigveda, book VII, hymns 58.

14. R.S. Tripathi, History of Ancient India, Delhi, Motilal Banarsidas, 1960, p. 27. See also the Hymans of the Rigveda.

15. The Rigveda itself speaks of older and later Rishis and their composition. Great case was taken to preserve its textual purity by a number of devices like padapatha, Krama-patha, Anukamanis etc.

16. Anus, Druhyus, Yadus, Turvasas and purus (who dwelt on either side the Saraswati). Bharatas (later merged into the Kurus), Tritsus, Srinjayas, Krivis etc.

17. Book I. hymn II: Mitra and Varuna, through law, lovers and cherishers of law, have yeobtained year mighty power. Book I, hymn XIII: Those who by law uphold the law, Lords of the shining light of law, Mitra I call, and Varuna. Book II, hymn LV Where the two Cows, the Mother and the Daughter, meet and give suck yeelding their lordly necter, I praise them at the seat of law eternal. Great is the God's supreme and sole dominion. etc.

18. Sacred Book of the East, Vol. XXV, Buhler's Introduction, Delhi, Motilal Banarsidas, n.d., p. 15.

19. J.L. Shastri, ed. Manusmriti, Delhi, Motilal Banarsidas, 1996, pp. IX.

20. *Ibid.* p. 81.

21. F. Max Muller, ed., The Sacred Books of the East, Vol. 25, trans. by various oriental scholars., Delhi, Motilal Banarsidas, 1998, Chap. VIII, pp. 254-277.

22. *Op. cit.* J.L. Shastri, p. VIII.

23. i.e., Yajnavalkya compresses two verses of Manu into one, e.g., Manu II-243, 247, 248 are equal to Yajnavalkya I-49.

24. R.R. Maurya, Hindu Law, Allahabad, Central Law, 1985, pp. 14-15. See also V.D. Mahajan, Ancient India, S Chand & Co., pp. 132-133.

25. Sec. 4 defines, Partnership is the relation between persons who have agreed to share the profits of business carried on by all or any of them acting for all.

26. *Op. cit.* Sacred book of the east, Vol. 33, p. 271.

27. Brihaspati Smriti (Gackward's series) Vol. XXVI, Delhi, Banarsidas, n.d., pp. 92-93.

28. R.C. Majumdar ed., Age of Imperial unity, Bombay, Vidya Bhawan, n.d. p. 354.

29. P.V. Kane, History of Dharmashastra, Vol. 1. Poona, Oriental Research Institute, n.d., p. 210.

30. *Ibid.* p. 195.

31. *Ibid.* p. 191.

32. Any matter which might and ought to have been made ground of defence or attack in such former suit shall be deemed to have been a matter directly and substantially in issue in such suit. Exp. IV to sec. 11 of C.P.C.

33. D.F. Mulla, Principles of Hindu Law, Delhi, Oriental Research, 1982, Para-141, p. 192.

34. R.R. Maurya, Hindu Law, Allahabad, Central Law, 1985, p. 20.

35. S.K. Chatterji, ed., The Cultural Heritage of India, Vol. V, Calcutta, The Ramakrishna mission, 1991, pp. 72-87.

36. *Op. cit.* V.D. Mahajan, pp. 115-118.

37. H.K. Barpuzari, ed. The Comprehensive History of Assam Vol. I, Guwahati, Pubn board, 1990, pp. 80-81.

38. V.D. Mahajan, Ancient India, Delhi, S. Chand, 1968, p. 257.

39. R.P. Kangle, The Kautilya Arthashastra, Part-II, Ch-I, Delhi, Motilal Banarsidas, 1997, pp. 268-270.

40. V.D. Mahajan, A History of India, Vol. I, New Delhi, S. Chand, 1990, pp. 153-176.

41. The name of the eighteen Puranas are the - (i) Brahma Purana (ii) Padma Purana (iii) Aishnava Purana (iv) Saiva or Vayavya Purana (v) Bhagavata Purana (vi) Naradiya purana (vii) Markandeya Purana (viii) Agneya Purana (ix) Bhavisyat Purana (x) Brahmavaivarta Purana (xi) Laing Purana (xii) Varaha Purana (xiii) Skanda Purana (xiv) Vamana Purana (xv) Kaurmu Purana (xvi) Matsya Purana (xvii) Garuda Purana (xviii) Brahmanda Purana.

42. P.C. Choudhury. The History of Civilisation of the People of Assam to the Twelfth Century A.D, 3rd ed., Guwahati, spectrum pubn, 1987, pp. 10-13. See H.K.Barpujari, The Comprehensive History of Assam, Vol. I, Guwahati, Pubn board, 1990, p. 87.

43. Nitya karma rajniti Sartrer bidhane, Koho Dev daya Kari amar sadane.. Sastrokta bisoy sab sunibe srabane, Asastriya upadesh na sunibe kane. Arupe je Raj kare karjya anusthan, Nahi heri jitendriyo taharo saman. See A. Bondopadhyay, tran., Brihat Kalika Puran, ed. by Kaliprasanna, Calcutta, Benimadhav Children's lib., Ch. 95, n.d., p. 233.

44. H.K. Borpuzari, ed. The Comprehensive History of Assam, Vol. I, Guwahati, Pubn board, 1990, p. 45.

45. "Agnidagdhassho je kesinnagnidagdhastathapore, Bidyachourohata je so tesang pindang dodamyahang". See- Yoginitantra, tans. by S.B. Doloi, Guwahati, Dutta Baruah, 1994, p. 359.

46. "Kamarupa mahapithang gujyadgujyatam parang, Sada so sangsthita statra parbatya saha sankara". Diddhakhyetresu tirthasu nashi kurjyat parushya sa, Gocsheditohanyatra hi boi tilong gancha bisesat, Na grihiyato sudrasya joto Jagyabahirmutha, Jashya gyashya jat patrang tatra pape na lipyate Tasmat sarbbaprajatnen parajyogyang bibarjayet". See *Op. cit.* Yoginitantra, pp. 292-293.

47. S.P. Sen ed., Sources of the History of India, Vol. III, Calcutta, Institute of Historical Studies, 1988, pp. 10-15.

48. *Ibid*, pp. 20-22.

49. *Op. cit.* H.K. Barpuzari, Vol. II p. 184.

50. *Op. cit.* P.C. Choudhury, p. 284.

51. *Ibid*, p. 282.

52. S.L. Baruah, Comprehensive History of Assam, pp. 135-151. See also Sources of the History of India ed. by S.P. Sen, Vol. III, Cal, Institute of Historical Studies, 1988, pp. 60-62.

53. International Encyclopaedia of Indian Literature, Vol. III, edited by Ganga Ram Garg, Delhi, Mittal Pubn, 1987, pp. I-IV.

54. *Op. cit.* S.L. Baruah, p. 222., Gait mentions that as Sukapha crossed the river Khamnamjang and came to the Nongnyang lake he commanded one of his noble to rule the conquered country and record all the events which was a beginning of recorded chronicle.

55. Bu means ignorant persons, ran-teach and ji-store hence it means a store that teacher the ignorant. *Op. cit.* Borpuzari, Vol. II, pp. I and Op. cit: Studies, pp. 25-26.

56. S.K. Bhuyan, Studies in the History of Assam, 2nd ed. Guwahati, Omsons, 1985, p. 229.

57. *Op. cit.* H.K. Borpuzari, Vol. II, pp. 9-11.

58. *Op. cit.*; S.L. Baruah, p. 44.

59. B.K. Baruah, A Cultural History of Assam, Vol. I, 3rd ed., Guwahati, Bina library, 1986, p. 72.

60. *Op. cit.* H.K. Borpuzari, Vol. II, pp. 10-12.

61. S.K. Bhuyan, Studies in the History of Assam, 2nd ed., Gauhati, Omsons pubn, 1985, pp. 124-142.

62. H.K. Barpuzari, Vol. II, The Comprehensive History of Assam, Ghy, Pubn board, 1992, pp. 19. See also C.J. Brown, Goins of India, 1922, p. 69.

63. R.Das Gupta, Coins of Medieval Assam, JARS, 1971, pp. XIX, 58.

64. *Op. cit.* H.K. Barpuzari, Vol. II p. 19.

65. In February 1826 the British army under General Sir Archibald Combell reached Yandabo, by the treaty of Yandabo which was concluded on 24th February, the Burmese had accepted whatever the British proposed. See-Beli Mar Gol by Leela Gogoi, Appendix.

66. The letter was written on 27th July 1853.

67. A.J. Moffatt Mills, Report on the Province of Assam, Gauhati, Pubn board, 1853, p. 33.

68. *Op. cit.* Mills Report, p. 464.

69. N.V. Pranjape, Indian Legal and Constitutional History, Allahabad, Central Law, 1994, p. 123-124.

70. *Op. cit.* Gait, p. 284.

71. *Op. cit.* Mills Report, pp. 32, 411, 657.

72. *Op. cit.* Gait, pp. 315-316.

73. H.K. Barpuzari, Comprehensive History of Assam, Vol. IV, Ghy, Board of pubn, 1992, pp. 220-221. See also-Gait, p. 317.

74. Gait, p. 318.

75. *Ibid*, pp. 327-328.

76. *Ibid.*

77. *Op. cit.* H.K. Barpuzari, Vol. IV, pp. 285-287.

78. *Op. cit.* Paranjave, p. 351.

79. *Ibid*, p. 405.

80. 21st Century Universal Encyclopedia, Vol. 15, 1996, pp. 81-82.

81. The Constitution of India, Allahabad, Law agency 1988, pp. I-IX. See also. D.D. Basu, Commentary on the Constitution of India, Calcutta, S.C. Sarkar & Son., 1972.

82. S. Maheswari, Information sources in law : their role for the legal profession, In: Herald of Library Science, Vol. 31, no-1-2, 1992, pp. 22-26.

83. As per office record (1995), Assam Legislative Assembly, Dispur, Assam.

4

Survey of Customs in the Context of Legal Literature

Custom: Its Interpretation

Custom is a habitual practice of a number of persons. It is an usage which is observed by people and adopted by the courts on the fulfilment of certain conditions in personal matters in different religions. A custom signifies that fact where a number of persons are in the usage of observing certain things in their dealings with each other and further expect that they would be followed by others. Custom is that source of law which is not set down in any written statute or ordinance but is based on immemorial usages. As T. Hussain in his *Customary law and Indian Constitutions* mentions that the innate desire in man to obey the will of the community.[1] Practice and rules of these customs made by the people or the customary practices and rules are the uncodified, unwritten or sometimes written codes of conduct in a particular socio cultural unit like various type of mantras, rules of marriage, etc. These acquire public sanction in due course because of their uninterrupted continuity. Customary practices are not universal in character as mentioned by Jeuti Barooah.[2] Although they are observed in some societies, savage or civilized, illiterate or literate the same is not seen in all societies in this world. B.S. Sinha in his book *Jurisprudence* has divided the customs as (a) legal and (b) conventional customs. A legal custom is that whose legal authority is absolute. It is codified and operative as a binding rule of law. A conventional custom on the other hand is one whose authority is conditional. It operates only indirectly through the medium of agreements and as such it is accepted and adopted in individual cases. Legal customs are again divided into (a) local customs and (b) general customs. Local custom is that which is prevalent in a particular group of a locality. It affects the inhabitants of particular area. The general custom is that which is prevalent throughout the kingdom.[3] R.R. Maurya in his book *Hindu Law* describes that the smritikars mention three kinds of customs (a) local custom (b) caste custom and (c) family custom,[4] which are more adequate as the third sources of Hindu Law[5]. A local custom is one binding on all persons in the local area within which it prevails. The local area may consist of a state, division, district or even a part of it. The local custom in the state of Gujrat and Maharashtra that a man may be adopted at any age, though he may be married and have children has been prevailed. In Assam along with other states of India if the lower part of leg of anybody touches unknowingly other's any part of the body, he or she seeks mercy by paying regards with 'Sewa'. It is a local custom of India.

The largest area of custom in Hindu law is covered by the caste custom. A caste custom is binding to all members of the caste wherever they may be. A caste in Bihar namely 'Kamath' beliefs that he or she would be free from all sins committed in this world or even in the past world if confesses and swears with pure mind before any temple of great Rishi, Lord Siva or any Deity. It is a caste custom of 'Kamath' caste of Bihar. The marriage among most of the population of Hindus is solemnized in accordance with the customary rites and ceremonies of the caste or community. Saptapadi is an essential part of shastric ceremony of marriage and the marriage is completed as soon as the seventh step is taken. But amongst the various communities of Uttar Pradesh, Bihar, Madhya Pradesh and Bengal the Saptapadi ceremony is not considered as essential ceremony of marriage. But the ceremony called 'Sindurdana', that is the smearing vermilion on the forehead of the bride by the bridegroom is an essential part of marriage and the marriage is complete and binding with the Sindurdana. Amongst the Ahom community of Assam Swearing of the groom with sword in hand and exchange of rings is binding part of the ceremony of 'Saklong marriage'. Among the Chettiar caste and Nadar Community of Tamil Nadu the tying of sacred thali round the neck of the bride complete the marriage.

Use of 'Khaj', a particular type of rice beer usually prevalent among Ahom community have been existed in a Muslim family at Nazira of Sibsagar District of Assam. It is an instance of family customs in this particular family.

Paul Vinagradoff in his *Historical Jurisprudence* (p. 363) mentions that customs may be laws even before their adoption by the courts. There are two grounds for holding that customs may be laws even before their adoption by court, firstly because of the retrospective nature of Judicial adoption of custom. Secondly, it is often asserted that judges are bound to decide in accordance with custom. Customs were there before the establishment of the courts and the judges recognised them. Customs were moulded and modified by the judges, and they have been creating laws in times past and even at the present age they are only made judiciary law and the customary law. If custom has been proved and recognised by the court, it becomes law and its judicial notice may be taken as establishing a principle of law.

Customs have strong base as source of Hindu law. Maurya in his *Hindu Law* mentions that the Lordships of the Privy council in Collector of Madura V. Mootoo

Ramalinga, gave the fullest effect of the custom, when observed :

> "Under the Hindu system of law, clear proof of usage will outweigh the written text of the law."[6]

To have the force of law a valid custom must have the following requirements: (i) A custom to be valid must be an ancient custom and not be of recent origin. Antiquity of a custom depends upon the circumstances of each case. Custom must have been handed down from generation to generation. Plucknett in his *Concise History of Common Law* (part-iii, chap-3), describes that a custom can be called long if it was introduced within ten or twenty years, very long if it dates from thirty years and ancient if it dates from forty years. However on evidence of prevalence a custom even for twenty or thirty years the courts have held that a presumption may arise that the custom is ancient unless rebutted. (ii) Custom must be certain and uniform. The court must be satisfied that custom existed as a matter of fact. (iii) The essential condition for the validity of custom is that it should not be unreasonable. It cannot be said that the custom should always be founded on reason and customs are not to be enlarged beyond the usage by parity of reasoning. For example, there has a custom to marry one's elder brother's widow. An instance is observed in 1999 in a family headed by Kanhailal of a Behari community at Golaghat Town of Golaghat district of Assam. This custom cannot be enlarged by the parity of reason to marry one's younger brother's widow, since it is the usage that makes the law and not the reason of the thing, for no reason (even the highest whatsoever) could make a custom. Another example may be referred to here that suppose in a village all persons have a customary right to catch fish from a common pond. One day a person sets a net on the pond and catches all fish. This would be unreasonable and the courts may not approve of this right. (iv) It must not be immoral or against public policy.

Customs which are immoral or opposed to public policy will not be recognised and are void. A custom by which a woman can marry again during the life time of first husband without the first marriage being dissolved is void being immoral one. (v) Continuity is essential to the validity of a custom. In case of local custom and caste custom the 'continuity' is not very material; the want of continuity would evidence that it never had a legal existence; but it is difficult to imagine that such a custom once thoroughly established, could come to a sudden end. In case of family custom which is founded on the consent of a small number of persons, the discontinuance of the custom will destroy it. (vi) Custom must not be opposed to statutory law. It is not to be contrary to an Act of parliament.

Though a custom is generally in derogation of the general law, it cannot override a statute which does not save it from its operation either expressly or by necessary implication, e.g., many ancient usages as sati, infanticide, slavery, forced labour, dedication of women as devadasi to temples, marriage of children under a certain age, practice of polygamy or polyandry have been prohibited by statutes and no court will allow any party to plead for a custom against them. (vii) The custom must have been enjoyed peaceably. *Encyclopaedia Britannica* describes that secret custom does not possess any validity. The law is public, similarly a custom, which rests on the revocable license, has not any legal reality because in that case its operation depends on the will of an individual or a group of individuals and not on public recognition.[7] (viii) The courts have accepted that a custom in order to be valid must be obeyed from consciousness of its obligatory character. A mere convention between family members or an arrangement by mutual consent for peace and convenience cannot be recognised as custom. (ix) It is recognised that there is hidden authority behind a custom. (x) The custom must be clear and unambiguous. (ix) It is the assent of the community that gives a custom its validity.

(xii) Custom is founded neither on common-sense nor on reason. (xiii) Customary law is a fluid state and changes with times. (xiv) A custom to be valid must not be contrary to justice, equity and good conscience.[8]

Customs may be codified in various ways:

(a) by judgements and decrees of courts recognising them,

(b) by the evidence of persons who give their opinions,

(c) by instances in which the customs were followed or enforced,

(d) by entries in public documents made by public officers,

(e) by producing works of eminent authors dealing with customs.

The evidence of these several kinds must be such as to make the court feel assured that the custom has the characteristics of a valid custom described above.

The elaborate legal rules are not suited and not applied in tribal areas as they are not in modern society e.g., the Civil Procedue Code was never in force in the hill districts during British-time and even today. The administration of justice of tribal peoples of hills and some particular castes of particular plain areas of Assam have been governed by customary laws and principles which are strictly observed by them. The members of the general community are required to follow these only to some extent. Though the study upon different types of castes and the people of general community have been made, basically the tribes are considered more so far the majority of customary law follower is concerned.

Difference Between the Tribal Areas of Assam and the Rest of India in respect of Administration of Justice

Administration of justice among the tribes and races of Assam is significantly different from that in the rest of the country. It differed in the past and differs even at the present time.

In Pre-British Days: In the past, before the advent of the British, while in the rest of India (barring of course the tribal areas) disputes were resolved generally according to the principles laid down in the Smritis and the Dharmasutras, in the tribal areas of Assam these were settled on the basis of perenial customs. These customs varied from ruthless retribution to peaceful amicable settlement.

The authorities which dispensed justice were also different. After the vedic period, either the king or the judges appointed by the king dispensed justice among the people of India, though Panchayats in some areas continued to dispose of certain types of cases. In the tribal areas of the Sub-Himalayan Regions of the North-East, the village councils disposed of all cases including those relating to commision of heinous offences like murder, arson, rape, robbery, etc. Among only a few tribes of then Assam, the Mizos and the Kukis the chief was the absolute judicial authority, notwithstanding that he used to take the advice of his council of elders.

When the British occupied these areas, they didnot alter the basic structure of the authorities which dispensed justice nor in the general customs related to it. But they prohibited trial of certain heinous offences continued by the traditional authorities. Reference may be made in case of drowning of lovers among the Mishings which is observed in the fiction *Miri-Jiyori* written by Rajani Kanta Bordoloi, etc. These offences made by customs were to be tried either by the political officer or his assistants. Even in respect of other offences (i.e, non heinous) the British administration attempted to regulate their trial by laying down certain procedural rules. These rules were known as the Administration of justice rule. Though different sets of rules were promulgated in different areas, the provisions were almost identical. While in the rest of India the criminal and civil laws enacted by the British government of India were followed, in the tribal areas these were barred by specific regulations.

After Indepencence: After the independence, tribal areas of the then state of Assam except the North-East-Frontier Tracts came under the purview of the sixth schedule of the constitution according to which certain categories of offences and civil disputes could be tried by the village councils or courts established by the Autonomous District Councils. The district councils framed new rules for administration of justice within their respective jurisdictions. The Code of Civil Procedure and the Code of Criminal Procedure do not apply to the trial of any civil suit or criminal case in these districts.[9]

Castes and Tribes in Assam: Tribe, the term commonly used to denote a group of primitive clans under recognised chiefs. *21st Century Universal Encyclopaedia* refers that the word denotes in Roman history each of the political divisions of the Romans, originally three in numbers, probably representing clans and ultimately numbering 35. The term is used also in respect of the social organisation of contemporary peoples in Africa, Oceania and America, where it is used by anthropologists and others in the technical sense of a single, indigenous, teritorially defined, political unit. These tribal societies can be further defined by their scale, economy and common culture.[10]

A.S. Hornby, the editor of the *Oxford Advanced Learners Dictionary* defines tribe as the racial group united by language, religion, customs, etc and living as a community under one or more chiefs. Encyclopedic edition of *Webster Comprehensive Dictionary* describes it as among primitive peoples a group of aggregation of persons, usually consanguineous and endogamous, under one chief, characterized by its own culture and having a name, a dialect, a government and usually a territory of its own.

Article 46 of the Indian Constitution directs that the state shall promote with special care the educational and economic interests of the weaker sections of the people and in particular of the scheduled castes and scheduled tribes and shall protect them from social injustice and all forms of exploitation. That schedule was initially promulgated by Presidential order and can now be modified only by an Act of Parliament. So the administrative definition of who is a tribesman was set by Presidential or Parliamentary decision without much social analysis.[11]

Webster's Comprehensive Dictionary defines 'caste' as one of the hereditary classes into which Hindu society is divided in India.[12] Mandelbaum refers in his *Society in India*, that the term 'caste' have been used by both Indian and non-Indian writers originally from the Portuguese for the prevalent social order in India as well as the component groups within that order.

Ram Ahuja in his book *Indian Social System* refers that there is no single and accepted criterion by which to distinguish a tribe from a caste. Regarding India the concept of 'tribe' can be understood clearly not on the basis of its existing definitions but by finding out the attributes and analyzing the specific conditions in India which are distinctive of groups conventionally regarded as tribes.[13] Likewise in Assam too, there is hardly any tribe which exists as a separate society. Almost all tribes have been absorbed in varying degrees into the wider society. It has been said that what we find today in India are tribes in transition.

Total population of Assam as per 1991 census is 22,414,322 including 11,657,989 males and 10,756,333 females. Total population of India in 1991 was 8,46,302,688 and the total population of Assam constitutes only 2.65 per cent of the total population of India. The decadal growth of population in Assam is shown below[14]:

Table 6. Population of Assam 1901-1991

Year	*Population*	*Decade Variation*	*Percentage decade variation*
1901	3,289,680		
1911	3,848,617	+ 558,937	+ 16.99
1921	4,636,980	+ 788,363	+ 20.48
1931	5,560,371	+ 923,391	+ 19.91
1941	6,694,790	+ 1,134,419	+ 20.40
1951	8,028,856	+ 1,334,066	+ 19.93
1961	10,837,329	+ 2,808,473	+ 34.98
1971	14,625,152	+ 3,787,823	+ 34.95
1981	18,041,248	+ 4,373,074	+ 29.90
1991	22,414,322	+ 7,789,170	+ 24.23

List of Scheduled Tribes and Scheduled Castes and their distribution in Assam[15]:

A. Twenty One districts in Assam cover the plain tribes as follows:

(i) Bodo-Kachari

(ii) Miri (Mishing)

(iii) Sonowal-Kachari

(iv) Rabha

(v) Laloong (Tiwa)

(vi) Deori

(vii) Barmans of Kachar

(viii) Mech

(ix) Hozai

The following Hill tribes of Assam scattered in North Cachar Hill and Karbi Anglong District of Assam:

(i) Chakma

(ii) Dimasa Kachari

(iii) Garoo

(iv) Hajong

(v) Hmar

(vi) Khashi, Jayantia, Synteng, Hnar, Warbhoi, Lingngam.

(vii) Any Kuki tribes including –

(a) Biat, Biet

(b) Changsan

(c) Ghongloi

(d) Doungel

(e) Gamalbeu, Gangte, Guite, Haneg, Haokip, Haupit, Haolao, Hengna, Hongauhgh,

Hrangktogwal, Rongkhoi, Lengthang, Lhangum, Lhoujem, Lhouvun, Lupheng, Mangjet, Misao, Riang, Sairhem, Selnam, Singsong, Uibul, Sukto, Thado, Thamgngeue, (Uibul), Vaiphei.

(viii) Lakher

(ix) Man (Tai-speaking)

(x) Any Mizo (Lusai tribes)

(xi) Mikir (Karbi)

(xii) Any Naga tribe

(xiii) Pawi

(xiv) Syntheng

B. Name of Scheduled castes of Assam [16]:

(i) Bansphor

(ii) Bhuimali or Mali

(iii) Bri Hial Bania or Bania

(iv) Dhupi or Dhubi

(v) Hira

(vi) Jalkeot

(vii) Jhalo, Malo or Thalo-Malo

(viii) Kaibortta or Jolia

(ix) Mahara

(x) Mehtar, Thamoi

(xi) Namasudra

Table 7. Districtwise Distribution of Scheduled Castes and Scheduled Tribes and their Percentage to Total Population

Name of State/ District	*Scheduled Caste*	*Percentage of S.C. to total population*	*Scheduled Tribes*	*Percentage of S.T. to total population*
1	*2*	*3*	*4*	*5*
Assam	1,659,412	7.40	2874,441	12.82
Dhubri	64,161	4.82	32,260	2.42
Kokrajhar	30,114	3.76	329,461	41.15
Bongaigaon	86,744	10.74	141,542	17.52
Goalpara	36,746	5.50	115,099	17.23
Barpeta	90,687	6.54	110,452	7.97
Nalbari	89,194	8.78	179,641	17.67
Kamrup	150,743	7.54	214,340	10.72
Darrang	64,350	4.95	224,957	17.32
Sonitpur	81,000	5.69	152,498	10.71
Lakhimpur	60,180	8.01	177,156	23,57
Dhemaji	30,482	6.37	210,312	43.92

(Contd.)

(*Table 7 Contd.*)

Name of State/ District	*Scheduled Caste*	*Percentage of S.C. to total population*	*Scheduled Tribes*	*Percentage of S.T. to total population*
1	*2*	*3*	*4*	*5*
Marigaon	88,136	12.78	98,483	15.40
Nagaon	189,693	10.02	69,848	3.69
Golaghat	46,262	5.59	84,916	10.25
Jorhat	66,311	7.61	105,307	12.09
Sibsagar	32,303	3.56	34,496	3.80
Dibrugarh	41,927	4.02	82,920	7.95
Tinsukia	25,137	2.61	51,493	5.35
KarbiAnglong	27,991	4.22	341,718	51.56
N.C.Hills	3,918	2.60	98,834	65.56
Karimganj	120,602	14.58	1,430	0.17
Hailakandi	54,107	12.05	715	0.16
Cachar	178,624	14.70	16,563	1.36

(xii) Sutradhar

(xiii) Muchi, Rishi

(xiv) Lalbegi

(xv) Dugla or Dholi.

As per 1971 census the scheduled caste population constituted 6.24 per cent and the scheduled tribe 10.99 per cent of the total population of Assam. The total scheduled caste population in Assam as per 1991 census is 1,659,412 and scheduled tribe population is 2,874,441 constituting 7.40 and 12.82 per cent respectively of the total population of Assam. The total scheduled caste population in India as per 1991 census is 1,38,223,277 and scheduled tribe population is 67,758,380 constituting 16.48 and 8.08 per cent respectively of the total population of India. The table shown in the following district-wise distribution of scheduled caste and scheduled tribe population in Assam.[17]

Some Selected Tribal Groups and their Customs

(a) ***The Deori :*** Among the four divisions of Chutiyas i.e, Hindu Chutiya, Ahom Chutiya, Borahi and Deori, the last have been able to maintain their old traditions, religious beliefs and practices intact inspite of various socio-political trials and tribulations as mentioned by Upendra Goswami in his *An Introduction to the Deori Language.*[18] P.N. Bharali describes in his report *Economic Transition of Tribal Society*[19] that the Deoris were the representative priest of the Chutiyas. *Imperial Gazetteer of India*[20] mentions- the Chutiyas are the members of the great Bodo race. They entered through the North-Eastern corner of Assam and established themselves on the upper waters of the Brahmaputra. In 1523 the Chutiyas after some centuries of conflict were finally crushed by the Ahoms.

After the annexation of the Chutiya Kingdom to the Ahom Kingdom as a result of the mixing up and intermarriage between the Ahoms and the Chutiyas a distinction arose between the Ahom Chutiyas and the Hindu Chutiyas. Thus, the Chutiyas were divided into four main divisions-Hindu, Ahom, Borahi, Deori. The following table shows the population of Deori tribe under other religion and persuation having population of 100 or more at state level.[21]

(i) *The People :* The Mongolian characteristics are visible in the Deoris. They are of strong built and possess charming features. They attract the outsiders with their simplicity and hospitality. They are amiable and maintain cordial relation with the non-tribal people of surrounding villages. Deoris are labourious. Except for ploughing, cutting trees and jungles, the womenfolk help their men in all other daily activities. Co-operation among the villages in all spheres is a salient feature of their daily life.

(ii) *Clan System:* There are four broad divisions (khel) among the Deoris namely Dibangia, Tengapania, Borgonya and Patargonya. The last group i.e., the Patargonyas has reportedly become extinct. Each of these originating from a particular place name. Thus Deoris who after coming from the hills lived on the banks of the Dibang. Tengapani and Borgang rivers were known as Dibangia, Tengapania and Borgonya respectively. The Deoris who were living in Patarsal or Patsadia were known as Patargonya as mentioned by Upendra Goswami and Ganak Deori in *Asomor Janajati.*[22] Each of these divisions is composed of a number of exogamous clans called 'Bangshas' (Jakus) as B.N. Bordoloi describes in his book *Tribes of Assam*[23]. Thus the 'Bangshas' of Dibangia are 'Sundariya (Bordeori), Patriya

Table 8. Population of Deori Tribe under other religion and persuation having Population of 100 or more at State Level.

Tribe	*State/Dist*	*Total/Rural/Urban*	*Females*	*Population* *Persons*	*Males*
	Assam	Total	437	216	221
		Rural	429	213	216
		Urban	8	3	5
	Kamrup	Total	4	2	2
		Rural	.....	.....	.....
Deori		Urban	4	2	2
	Dhemaji	Total	4	1	3
		Rural	....	.....	.....
		Urban	4	1	3
	Dibrugarh	Total	429	313	216
		Rural	429	213	216
		Urban	.....	.....	.....

(Sarudeori), Airio (Bharali), Sariya (Bora), Chitikayo (Bhog Randhani), Kontayo, Lagachyo Kaliya-chukoyo', etc. There are altogether 14 numbers of 'Jakus' among the Dibangias. The Bangshas of Tengapania are Machiatika (Bordeori), Bikramiyatika (Sarudeori), Khutiya-Yotika (Bharali), Sakacharutika, Pagimegeratika, Phapariyotika, Chemabariya tika, etc. The Borgonya division too has clans viz., Ikucharu (Bordeori), Chimucharu (Sarudeori), Hizaru (Bharali), Busaru (Balikatia), Lafaru (Bora) and Gosaru. It may be noted that members of the last clans though mentioned in old records are no longer traceable. As regards clans of Patorgonya, the Deoris are not able to locate these.

(iii) *Social Stratification:* Deori society can be broadly divided into two viz, secular and religious. In the former category the Gaonbura reigns supreme who is the head in all socio- political activities. He is the nucleus around whom all the village elders gather for smooth running of the day to day affairs of the village. The assembly of village elders can give judgement in the petty disputes brought before it. Nine office bearers have been assigned specific duties for the smooth functioning of religious activities in every village. Out of these, four important office bearers in the hierarchical order are Bordeori or Baderi, Sarudeori or Saderi, BorBharali and SaruBharali. Generally Bordeoris are selected from Bordeori clans like Sundariya, Machiatika and Ikucharu and they command highest regard from the villagers. It is their custom that a Bordeori must be free from all sins. His main duty is to offer pujas in the 'Than'. The Sarudeori assist, the Bordeori in the Than pujas. The charge of puja paraphernalias remain with Bharali. All the clans have equal status at least theoritically but in practice the Bordeori or Baderi gets high status among the office bearers.

A significant role in the religious life of the people plays by an office bearer called 'Deodhai' which has resemblance with that of Ahom community. While dancing alongwith the beatings of drums he is believed to be possessed by their benign deity and in that mood of transcendantal glory he is able to forecast the fortune of the villagers and about the natural calamities that may occur. The 'Deodhai' should be a person without the slightest blemish and he is considered as a deity in the form of human being while he remains in coma.

(iv) *Customs in Religious Aspect :* The three sections of the Deoris are still maintaining their traditional customs and practices. The common place of worship among the Borgonya and Tengpania sections is known as 'Than' while the Dibangias call it 'Midiku'. All the sections worship Lord Siva and Parvati as chief deities. The Dibangias call this supreme deity 'Kundi Mama'. 'Kundi' is identified as Lord Siva and 'Mama' as Parvati of Hindu pantheon. Another names of this chief deity are 'Gira-Girachi' or 'Burha-Burhi', Pisa-Dema or 'Balia Baba' or 'Balia Hemta' and 'Pisasi Dema' or 'Kesaikhati' or 'Tamreswari'; the son and daughter of Gira-Girachi are two other important deities of the Deoris. They have a good number of household deities also, viz., 'Bakanmak', 'Miruchi, ' 'Kin', 'Dua Chitere', 'Bura Dangaria', 'Mora', 'Chakchik', 'Achira', 'Chanyan', 'Gharar Deo', etc. Sacrifies of animals and fowls, pigeons form an important part of the Deori puja. Rice beer is not offered to the deities but consumption of rice beer after the puja is not forbidden. Wednesday is the most auspicious day for worship and pujas are performed either on Wednesday or on Sunday.

(v) *Marriage :* Marriage is indispensable in case of Deori young boy. Clan exogamy is strictly followed in marriages. After the death of the husband the younger brother of the deceased does not marry the wife of the elder brother. One does not marry the younger sister of his wife. 'Borbiya', 'Majubiya', 'Bhakatbiya' or 'Sarubiya' and 'Gandharba' are the four broad different forms of marriage. The Debangias call these as 'Jonenga Laharuba', 'Bhakat Rupiya', 'Chachibachi' and 'Churubachi'. Borbiya is arranged by the parents and it is continued for three days. 'Majubiya' is arranged by the prospective couple's parents but the duration is two days. 'Bhakat Rupiya' is completed in only one day. In 'Jonenga Laharuba' or 'Gandharba' the couple concerned takes the initiative. The boy with the help of his friends takes away his bride on an appointed day, but no formal ceremony is performed. 'Tamolkata biya' the custom of another type of marriage has now been abolished among Deoris. This type of marriage was solemnised before a girl attains puberity. The 'Pathoria' or a mediator plays important role in a Deori marriage. Both the families i.e., families of bride and groom appoint 'Pathorias'. On the marriage occasion he wears a special dress and he helps in the settlement of bride price and other details in a marriage.

(vi) *Property and Inheritance :* Property such as house, livestock, foodstuff, land, etc. are held jointly by the family. After the death of a father his sons become the rightful owner of his properties which are equally divided among his sons. In case a man dies without any survivor his property goes to the nearest agnetic relations. The wife and daughters are not eligible to share the property unlike the present Hindu Law.[24] The Deoris are patrilineal in descent and they count their relationship through the male line. Children take the clan of the father.

(vii) *Customs at Death and Attendant Ceremonies :* The Deoris generally cremate the dead bodies. Due to certain disadvantages the dead body may be buried. When the dead body is cremated it is customary to keep the pieces of wood or bamboo in seven folds. Dead bodies of persons who die of cholera or small pox are not cremated but buried. If the members of the family desire after decomposition of the body, the skeleton may be brought out and cremated. But the person who brings out the skeleton will have to perform certain rites of purification. If a priest dies it is their custom that all the musical instruments of the place of worship as also of the village should be brought and played on in the funeral procession and all the people of the village both male and female should join and proceed to the cremation ground. In the funeral pyre people will put with the left hand pieces of wood or bamboo, presenting from each family of the village. When in this way the dead body will be completely covered, all will bow down before the pyre. Then the women folk will return home and after that the fire will be lit. In the case of priests the custom is to put pieces of wood or bamboo in nine folds and to move round the pyre nine times. In the case of persons below his rank, the custom is to put pieces of wood or bamboo in seven folds and to move round the pyre seven times. In the case of persons even below that rank pieces of wood are kept in five folds and the move round the pyre five times only. Food, rice-beer, fire etc are carried to the cremation ground and the eldest son offers cooked food and rice beer to the soul of the dead and puts fire in the pyre. After returning from the cremation ground all are purified in the courtyard of the deceased with holy water prepared by a woman of family by adding cowdung, 'Tulakhi' and a copper coin. A ceremony is held on the fourth day. Chicken curry is prepared and selected elderly villagers offer rice beer and chicken curry on the floor and request the soul of the deceased to give up all connection with the inmates of the deceased.

(b) ***The Bodo-Kachari :*** The Bodo-Kacharis of Assam is a branch of the great Bodo group of the Indo-Mongoloid family. Different names are used to designate them. The prominent writers S.K. Chatterji, H.K. Borpuzari, E.A. Gait in their writings mention that in Bengal and in the lower ranges of the Himalayas coming within the territory of Nepal, they are known as Meches. In upper Assam they are identified as Sonowal and Thengal Kachari, while in the western Assam they are more popularly known as Bodo or Bodo-Kachari. In the southern districts of North Cachar and Cachar they are designated as Dimasa and Barmans respectively. *Kalika Purana, Yoginitantra* describe them as 'Kirata'. Chatterji also refers this branch as 'Kirata'[25]. The total population of this tribe in Assam is 6, 10, 459 as per 1971 census which accounts 45.4% of the total state tribal population[26]. They are now largely concentrated in the Kokrajhar district followed by Kamrup, Darrang, Dhubri, Nalbari, Goalpara, Sonitpur, Jorhat district.

(i) *The People :* The mongoloid features are very prominent in the case of Bodo- Kachari. The strong cheek bones, slit eyes, a slight growth of hair in the body and scant beard. They are shorter and more stocky than the Indians of the north-east. Some deviations in the physical features of this branch have of late been noticed under the impact of socio- cultural assimilation as well as marital alliances.

(ii) *Social Life and Institutions :* The improvement of communication, general mobility and intercouse with the people all around have brought some psychological and attitudinal change of all sections of people. To meet this changing situations of life, necessity has arisen to frame some local laws on the basis of customs and traditions as prevailing in the society. These are locally codified, not legally codified, since they have not catered to the norms to be followed for legal codification of the same (as mentioned earlier). These customary usages and practices of the Bodo-Kachari societies came to be followed after approval from the Zonal Council composed of adjacent villages. Some of these local laws are known as *Pandulipis* as they are in manuscripts and hardly printed, and some others are oral in form but socially codified viz. patrilineal in this branch of tribal groups is a custom. Since these are not co-ordinated into homogeneous sets of laws, they differ in content and application from area to area. However, the basic issues pertaining to inheritance of property, succession to office of socio-religious and socio-political nature and liability of atonement on committing unnatural and unsocial offences are more or less identical. As per these customary laws the line of descent is traced through the father who is the head of the family. The eldest male member assumes the charge of the household on the death of the father and discharges his responsibilities in consultation with his mother. The family debt if any is dischargeable from the income of the family and on the event of dissolution of the joint family, the unmarried brothers get double of the family property than the married brothers. The Bodo-Kachari society prescribes atonement proceedings for purification of misdeeds. The 'Deouri' an assistant to the village priest (Oja) usually conducts the atonement proceedings. He is elected on the general consensus of all the villagers on the basis of his characters and ability to guide socio-religious rites. The 'Douri' and the village headman have a distinct place of honour in the estimation of the Bodo-Kachari people. In *Bodo-Kachari Samaj Aru Sanskriti* B.Narji describes that the two important institutions are found in the spheres of customary law, known as 'Hadengoura' and 'Hachangoura'[27]. The former being akin to a judgeship with jurisdiction over twelve adjoining villages and the later with jurisdiction in each such twelve villages, as the subordinate institution to help the 'Hadengoura'. However, the more common institution in the Bodo villages is the villages council. The Gaonbura (village headman) and his assistant the 'Halmazi' (courier of errands) organise village level social works. The clan structure of the Bodo- Kacharis though essentially remind their traditional division of labour yet, in the present day context such divisions are no longer recognised. M.M Brahma in his article *"A brief introduction of the Bodo-Kacharis of Assam"* in the TRI bulletin refers that a clan is known by them as 'Ari'. There are as many as 23 Aries, namely Swargiari, Basumatary, Mosari, Khangkhlari, Doimari, Narzari, Gayari, Mahilari, Ouari, Jojoari, Ishari, Kahari, Sibiugari, Sibiziari/Babaiari, Birgbiugari, Gaujlerari, Fadangiri, Samphrangari/Mao-Marari, Ramsari, Kherkaturi, Thaletari and Borogaori[28].

(iii) *Religious Outlook :* The Bodo-Kachari tribe in their religious philosophy accept the super power of Bathou Barai or Khoria Barai Maharaja which is analogus to 'Sibrai' or Siva of the Hindu trinity. The sizu plant (Euphorbia splendens) is regarded as representing the 'Bathau' - the supreme deity of adoration. Therefore, every traditional Bodo-Kachari household is seen planting a 'sizu' tree along with a sapling of 'jatrasi' and a 'tulsi' in the northern corner of their courtyard. 'Mainao' (also called Buli Buri) is worshipped as the goddess of wealth. Besides these two primary deities, the Bodo-Kacharis worship many other gods and goddesses comprising Agraug, Khoila, Khaji, Rajkhandra, Rajputhur, Buraali, AliBura, Asu-Mainao, Sali Mainao, Bagraja, Basumati and Choudri. Some of these deities (better known as 'Madai') are benevolent and some are malevolent. The malevolent deities are regarded as the originator of all ills including natural calamities and for their propitiation sacrifice and offering of rice beer are invariably necessary.

(iv) *Marriage :* The rigidity of exogamous marriages are gradually on the way to dilution. Marriage among the traditional Bodo- Kacharis is like a civil contract unlike the status of a sacrament in other Hindu marriage alliances. The usual practice of contracting a marriage is by negotiation (Hathachuni[29]). But marriage by servitude (Chawdang-Jagarnay) and widow marriage (Dhaka) do often take place. In marriage by servitude, the would be groom is to render physical labour usually for a period of one year but the period may be extended depending on the degree of satisfaction of the would be father-in-law. But this type of marriage is not seen encouraging nowadays. In the widow remarriage, the widower must cut off his all patrilineal relationship and induct himself to the 'ari' (clan) of the widow. There is another type of marriage known as 'Khar-Chanai'. Here the girl goes voluntarily to a man with the intention of putting up with him as husband and wife and when this unceremonious union is sanctified subsequently in a marriage it is known as 'Khar-Chanai' marriage. In Bodo-Kachari society there is no bar in contacting a junior levirate marriage[30]. But in no case senior levirate marriage can take place. Marriage under junior sorrorate system[31] can take place but not senior sorrorate marriage. Similarly no cross-cousin marriage is allowed in the Bodo-Kachari society. The idea of procuring a bride either by servitude or by elopment has in recent years come to be regarded as contemptuous. Therefore, negotiation marriage (Hathachuni) has become the normal social custom. The system of demanding bride price is still prevalent but in the higher echelon of the society, it is practically non-existent. There is a system under which the co-villagers of the bride may prefer a claim to a certain amount 'Malsa'. This amount when realised is deposited in the village fund to be spent for social purposes. But this amount is liable to be called back by the family of the groom on the event of her becoming widow and prefer to go back to her father's home forever leaving all claims on her husband's property. This counter demand on the 'malsa' is known as 'Khalar-Gothaianay'. Against this custom the court will not accept the case if the bride approaches to the court for regaining the property-subject to the proof of this custom produced in the court and it does not deserve to be codified.

There are fundamental ritualistic differences in soleminising a marriage between the two sections of the tribe, the traditional Bodo-Kacharis and the followers of

Brahmanism. While the traditionalists resort to 'Hathachuni' system, the followers of Brahmans take recourse to vedic rites and perform 'Hom-Yojna' ceremony before the sacred fire. In the traditional system of marriage, the groom instead of going to the bride's house sends a little party to fetch the girl ceremoniously to perform the rituals at the groom's house like Ahom community. Soon after receiving of the bride with benedictory ovation accompanied by her kith and kin, a grand feast is thrown out in honour of the bride and the bridal party by killing a pig and it is customary that a portion of this pork should be kept separately for the next meal of the bridal party to be taken at the bride's house on return. After the cleaning operation of the entire household the bride is asked to make a symbolic cooking like'Saru dhara' of Hindu or other communities and then to offer a little amount of food so cooked to the household deities. Amidst citation of invocatory prayer by the village 'Deori', the bride makes the offering first to Mahadeva and then Mother Kamakhya. The bride is then asked to touch the rice pot kept normally in a corner of the kitchen which she does with her left hand. At this moment the bride is administered an oath of fidelity to her new home. Then both the groom and the bride are given some sermons of married life by one from amongst the elderly persons or by the village 'Deori'. This being over, the bride herself is to distribute the residue of the feast at least once first to her husband and then to the invited guests. This distribution marks the culmination of the 'Hathachuni' marriage. The visit of the groom with his bride to his father-in-law's house on the eighth day of the marriage like other Hindus or general castes 'Athmangala' is a part of the marriage ceremony and until it is done, a 'Hathachuni' marriage is not treated as complete.

(v) *Birth Ceremony :* The traditional Bodo-Kacharis have no sacramentary rites to perform unlike the orthodox Hindus. Here the family makes an offering to the household deities by sacrificing a cock or a hen in the occasion. It is a prevailing custom among the Bodo-Kacharis to entertain the midwives in a feast within a reasonable time. In case the baby is not surviving the mother can discharge her obligation by simply entertaining them with rice-beer and fried chickens.

(vi) *Disposal of the Dead and Death Rites :* Though the Bodo-Kacharis practise both cremation and burial, cremation has come to be the normal practice in these days. The practice of throwing the corpse in the open fields in some interior villages assume that when a corpse is devoured by wild jackals and vultures in open fields, the dead is likely to attain salvation from possible deeds of omissions and commissions done during his or her life time. They believe that human beings cannot escape destiny and destiny is guided by one's own action (karma'). They also believe in transmigration of the soul. The soul of the dead persons may enter into anybody according to the 'Karma' done in the previous birth which custom is practised in case of the Karbi tribe also. It is customary for the members attending a funeral procession to take bath on their return home and drink 'Santijal' (sanctified water) like the Hindu, followed by mastication of a little amount of 'sokota'[32] to carry the idea that from that day onwards the relationship with the dead is finally severed and it is followed by rice-beer drinking in honour of the dead. On the tenth day from the day on which death occurs, the first phase of the funeral rites begins, which is termed as 'Dasa' or 'Dahar', but final sradha ceremony is held either on the 12th or on the 13th day or long thereafter, depending on the pecuniary condition of the household. It also occurs on 10th, 11the, 13th or 30th day in case of Hindus comprising of the Brahmins, Khatriya, etc. and among also the Muslims it is seen.

(vii) *Language and Literature :* Although the Bodo-language has no script of its own, it has been introduced as medium of instruction in the primary level in the Bodo predominant areas of Kokrajhar district with effect from 1963. Subsequently, Bodo medium of instruction was introduced first in the secondary schools of Kokrajhar with effect from September 1968. It has gone upto degree level. The Bodo language has been declared as an associate official language by an ordinance issued on 28th December, 1984[33]. It influences upon the Assamese language also. The present Assamese language possesses a good number of Bodo words. G.C. Sharma Thakur in his article in bulletin published by TRI describes that such as 'Tekeli' (a small earthan jar) in Assamese has been taken from the Kachari word 'Khing Khili'. Assamese 'Dalang' (a bridge) has its root in the Bodo Prakrit. The original word was 'Dau:aang'. Again 'Aapa', Kamrupi equivalent of the Assamese word 'Lora' (Boy) has its root in Kachari 'Aafa' and Chutia 'Appa' meaning boy. There are many Assamese words which have their roots in the Bodo Prakrit.[34]

	Bodo	*Assamese*	*English*
(a)	Naanglaa	Nangalaa	A gate
(b)	Baalandaa	Baralaa	Bachelor
(c)	Aai	Aai	Mother
(d)	Jangkhlaa	Jakhalaa	Ladder
(e)	Gandu	Gaaru	A pillow etc.

Till the mid-nineteeth century, the Bodo literature was composed mainly of oral literature such as folk- songs, folk tales, ballads, proverbs, etc. The written literature emerged first in the wake of the Brahma movement among the Bodo-Kacharis. The subsequent formation of the 'Bodo-Sahitya Sabha' in 1952 is a direct legacy of this literary campaign launched under the Brahma movement. At present the Bodo-literature has been growing rapidly and the 'Bodo Sahitya Sabha' is making considerable effort in publishing Bodo literary work in all fields - short story, fiction, drama, poetry, etc. The source of Bodo literature are mostly indigenous. It has hardly borrowed any legendary or mythological episodes of the old Indian scriptures unlike the literary work in other regional languages[35].

With the beginning of 19th century the trends of social outlook of the Bodo-Kacharis have been changed. The religious philosophy of the Bodo-Kacharis began to change by the preachings of Guru Kalicharan Brahma who was inducted to the Brahma faith by Srimat Paramhangsa Sibnarayan Swami of Calcutta. The Brahma movement was a movement for total change of outlook in all fields, social, religious, political, economic and educational. Apart from the changing trends in socio-religious and socio-political fields, changes have occured in their customs commonly accepted for generation to generation and in oral form as now-a-days written down when commonly accepted and tried in need and the livelihood pattern and the way of life of the Bodo-Kacharis.

(c) ***The Sonowal Kachari :*** The Sonowal Kachari is a large plain tribal group of Assam. They are chiefly found in the district of Dibrugarh. A few Sonowal Kachari villages are in Lakhimpur, Sibsagar and Jorhat. They belong to the great Bodo group and they nostalogically trace their close relationship with the Barmans of Cachar district, Bodo Kacharis of lower Assam districts and Dimasa of North-Cachar Hills district. Like other Mongolian people of these regions the Sonowal Kacharis are short structured, flat nosed, almond shaped eye, straight haired and scanty bearded people. It is believed that the prefix Sonowal in the name of the tribe came to be used during the reign of the Ahom kings when the Kacharis of upper Assam took the trade of gold washers and collectors of gold particles.

(i) *Social Structure :* The Gaonbura or the village headman is the keyman of the village who is entrusted with the day to day village administration. He commands respect from all and presides over the village assembly. Besides the Gaonbura there are other office bearers namely 'Barik', 'Pathek', 'Asirbadia bura', 'Gitghai', 'Medhi', 'Tamuli', and 'Randhani'. There is specific assignment for each office bearer. Thus 'Barik' remains in charge of the namghar. He also acts as the treasurer of the public fund. In some villages separate treasurers are appointed. The 'Pathek' acts as reader of the religious scriptures in public or private functions. Only the 'Asirbadia bura' can shower blessings at the end of the religious ceremonies. The 'Gitghai' is an expert in 'Hurorigit and other religious songs. The 'Medhi' is regarded as the chief in all religious functions. The 'Bayan' is a special instructor who imparts training of others in the art of 'Gayan-Bayan[36]. Similarly the function of the 'Tamuli' is to supply betel leaves and nuts to the audience and participants of a religious function. The 'Randhani' or 'Bilania' is entrusted with cooking and distributing the feast.

(ii) *The Namghar (a centre of solving dispute) :* The centre of solving disputes of the villagers is the 'Namghar'. Complaints regarding anything social or religious are brought before the village elders who deliver judgement and punish the offenders. Punishment depending upon the nature of offence range from imposition of fine in money which is deposited in public funds or in kinds i.e, excommunication (Khutimara). The inter family disputes are amicably settled in the village. No woman will formallly join the 'Mel' (village council) though she does not hesitate in making her voice heard or her opinion felt. 'Gabharu Mel' of Ahom administration is such a 'Mel' where the disputes belonging to 'gabharu' affairs (young girl or woman) are settled.

(iii) *Inheritance :* The system of inheritance of the Sonowal Kacharis is patrilineal which is a custom of this group. The land belongs to the family and the head of the family is the owner of the land is divided equally among the sons. The house is considered as immovable property and after the death of the father generally the eldest son becomes the owner of the house. Every house has its movable property in the form of utensils, implements, livestock and poultries, ornaments, cycles, radios, watches etc. which are owned by individuals.

(iv) *Clan :* The Sonowal Kacharis are divided into seven exogamous clans (Bangshas) viz, 'Bali Khitiari', 'Chiri Puriy', 'Amara bamiya', 'Dhulia', 'Ujani Kuchiya', 'Namani Kuchiya' and 'Tipamiya'. These clans are again subdivided into fourteen subclans ('Khels'). They are 'Hagral', 'Muktal', 'Madani, 'Manikiyal', 'Ahmal', 'Formal', 'Bor Hajoal', 'Saru Hajowal', 'Kumral', 'Dhekial', 'Dingial', 'Lothial', 'Dangral and 'Chetial'. There are again branches of these subclans viz, 'Mukhari', 'Daphlari', 'Nezkatari', 'Daimari', 'Khakhlari' etc[37]. These divisions are not carried to an extent leading to any social disharmony and breach of cohesion. Except on marriage occasion, reference to clans is hardly made. The origin of the clans may be traced to certain characteristics of their ancestors. The members of 'Muktal' and 'Manikial' clan trace their origin to their benign ancestor king Manick and Mukuta.

(v) *Religion :* The Sonowal Kacharis are the devout followers of 'Mahapurushia Baishnav dharma'. All the Sonowals are the disciples of 'Auniati Satra' with the only exception of a few Sonowal Kacharis of Lakhimpur district who owe allegiance to the 'Checha Satra'. Among the villagers there are two broad religious divisions namely 'Sarania' and 'Bhajania'. Those who are on the other side of the fifties follow the strict rules of dharma known as 'Bhakats'. These 'Bhakats' have various grades and the senior may be a 'Medhi'.

(vi) *Marriage :* The sonowal Kacharis consider the marriage as indispensible for the adult boys and girls. A boy usually marries at the age of 22-25 years while the marriageable age for girl is 18-22 years. Marriage in the same clan is strictly prohibited. Marriage ceremony takes place at the girl's house. Monogamy is the general rule and the second wife is taken only after the death of the first wife. In case of second wife, permission from the first wife is essential. If a second wife is taken without prior permission from the first wife then later can file a case before the assembly of village elders. In such cases the second wife have to live in a separate house.

The Sonowal Kacharis have four distinct forms of marriage viz. (a) 'NowaDhowa' or 'Bor Biya', (b) 'Hom Diya' (c) 'Gandharba' and (d) 'Churchuria' or 'Rabha sarakai diya'. Non tribal influence is noticed in their marriages particularly in the former two types which entail huge expenditure and long drawn formalities. These are usually arranged by the parents of the respective couple. Only in the 'Homdiya' marriage they may employ Brahmin priests. The widely prevalent form of marriage is 'Gandharba' where the couple concerned takes the initiative. Generally, 'Gandharba' marriage is the outcome of love at first sight and the boy and the girl decide this course as they apprehend doubt about their parent's agreeableness to the formal marriage. The socio cultural occasions provide ample scope to the young boys and girls to develop love at first sight. If the boy is uncertain about the acceptance of the marriage proposed from the parents of the girl as well as from his own parents, then one night he takes away his sweetheart to his residence with the help of his friends. After three days, the parents of the girl are to be imformed which is called 'Jananidiya' or 'Chordekhadiya'. The boy is required to bear the incidental expenses, information must be sent at the expenses of a feast culminating the marriage. The 'Rabha sarakai diya' or 'Churchuria Biya' is also a popular type of marriage where the run away couple is formally recognised as married couple, with a unceremonious feast to a few village elders.

(vii) *Bride Price :* Nowadays, brideprice is charged only in 'Gandharba' form of marriage. There is no fixed bride price. It may vary according to the status of groom and the goodwill of the girl's parents towards the groom's family like Muslim society who call it 'Mohrna'. In some Sonowal Kachari villages a nominal price (Rs5.00) is given. It is reported that in no case does the bride price exceed Rs 300.00 even in the case of 'Gandharba' marriage.

(viii) *Death and Attendant Ceremonies :* The deadbodies among the Sonowals are cremated. In the past the 'Behari' section practised 'Peradiya' (Coffin system). But since 1921 the system has been abolished[38]. In this type of burial a coffin was made of two beats specially prepared for the occasion. One beat was used for the corpse while the other served the purpose of a cover. Deadbodies of children below the age of five, pregnant woman and epidemic cases are burried. Purificatory ceremonies are almost similar to those of the neighbouring non tribals with exception that the Kacharis generally do not employ a Brahmin to preside over the purificatory ceremony. The 'Medhi' presides over all the functions in connection with death. They observe a three tier purificatory ceremony namely 'Tilani' on the third day, 'Dahdinia daha' like the Hindus or Muslims and on the 20th day the 'Kuridinia Kaj' 'Namkirtan' and a general feast for the villagers are held in the purificatory ceremony.

(d) ***The Karbis :*** The Karbis constitute an important ethnic group in the hill areas of present Assam. The term 'Mikir' according to them is given by the neighbouring people. J.Gogoi in his article *Mikir in Asomor Janajati* by P Bhattacharya refers that they never call themselves 'Mikir' but call themselves Karbi and sometimes Arleng which literally means 'a high slopping land'[39]. In their folk-lores and folk tales the term 'Mikir' occurs nowhere. Besides the Karbi Anglong district at present they reside at North Cachar Hills, Golaghat district, Nagaon district, Kamrup, Sonitpur and also Darrang district. Racially the Karbis belong to the Mongoloid group and linguistically they belong to the Tibeto-Burman group. North-East India, specially Assam, was subjected to successive waves of migration from the central Asia beginning from several hundred years of B.C. B.K. Baruah in his book *A Cultural History of Assam* mentions that the original home of the various people speaking Tibeto-Burman languages was in Western China near the Yang-Tee-Kiang and the Howang-ho rivers and from these places they went down the courses of the Brahmaputra, the

Chindwin and the Irrawaddy and entered India[40]. The Karbis along with others entered Assam from Central Asia in one of the waves of migration.

(i) *Administrative and Regional division :* Each village (Arong) under the Karbi kingdom was headed by village headman called Sarbura. Several Karbi villages constituted one longri and the administrative officer of a longri was called Havai. The Kingdom had 12 (twelve) such longris and these longris constituted into four Artus and each Artu was governed by an officer called Lingdok. And at the apex of the four Lingdoks was the king called Recho or Lingdok po.

From the point of view of habitation, the Karbis are divided into three groups namely, Chinthong, Ronghang and Amri. These groups are otherwise known as Chinthong, Nilip-Ranghang and Amri-Marlong. Those who live in plains districts are called Dumrali.

(ii) *Clans :* B.N. Bordoloi and others have mentioned in their *Tribes of Assam* as like in *Asomor Janajati* described by J. Gogoi that the Karbis have five clans called 'Kur'. These are Terang, Teron, Enghee, Ingti and Timung. Each of the five clans has a number of sub-clans. While Enghee and Timung have 30 (thirty) sub clans each, Terang and Teron have 6 (six) sub clans each and remaining clan Ingti has only 4 (four) subclans[41]. These clans are completely exogamous and marriage between a boy and a girl belonging to the same clan can never take place since the children of the same clan are considered as brothers. Violation of this customary law obviously leads to ex-commumication of the couple involved. Even in the cremation ground called Tipit or Theri, area is kept demarcated for each clan.

Although all the five clans are socially equal, Ingti being a priestly clan was supposed to have a higher status in earlier times.

(iii) *Religion :* From the point of view of religion the karbis can be regarded as animists[42]. Hinduism in its crude form finds manifestation in their worships of gods, goddesses and deities. They believe in the immortality of the soul, life hereafter and reincarnation. Among the innumerable deities some are considered to be benevolent and some malevolent like the Bodo-Kacharis. Each disease is associated with a presiding deity. Hemphu and Mukrang are two benevolent household gods. For the appeasement of the deities the karbis observe many religious rituals throughout the year where the sacrifice of pigs and birds and use of rice beer are indispensable. A smaller section of the Karbis has embraced Christianity.

(iv) *Marriage :* Monogamy is the prevailing practice among the Karbis. There is no bar to polygamy and the cases of polygamy are very rare. Widow remarriage is allowed by the Karbi society and the unmarried younger brother is required to marry the widow of his elder brother like the Bodo-Kacharis. But under no circumstances the elder brother is allowed to marry the widow of his younger brother. Cross-cousin marriage is a preferential one. Marriage by negotiation and marriage by selection of life partners are prevalent among the Karbis. In case of marriage by negotiation the consent of the girl is a must since a karbi damsel can not be forcibly married to a boy of her disliking. Marriage by capture is also found to be present to a limited extent and in this case the formal marriage has to be solemnized after the birth of the first child at a convenient date. Divorce is rare in the Karbi society. It can be obtained through the approval of the village council and the council gives its approval only when it finds that the separation between the husband and wife is absolutely essential.

Like other tribal societies, the Karbis do not have the system of bride price. After marriage the wife continues to use the surname of her father. But the children assume the title of their father.

(v) *Traditional institutions and the legal aspects :* The Karbis like the other tribes have some traditional institutions which have been continuing from time immemorial. While some of the institutions are socio-political in nature, some are of economic character.

The traditional village council of the karbis is called 'Mei' and this council is composed of all the elderly male members of the village. The council is presided over by the gaonbura, the village headman. All the village disputes which are not of very grave or serious nature are settled by it. In addition to this the village council decides if the village is to be shifted to new jhum sites and it distributes jhum lands to be cultivated in a particular year to the families of the villages. However, the 'Mei' has lost its original footing in the present context. Now people prefer to go to the law courts instead of referring the disputes to the village council.

'Farla' the bachelor's dormitary of the Karbis is also known as 'Jirkedam'. In the plain area of the Karbi Anglong district where there are no bachelors' dormitories, the Risomar or the youth club, serves more or less the same purpose although the functionaries are different. The dormitary is constructed in a central place of the village with locally available construction materials. All the unmarried boys of the village from the age of 10 are the members of the dormitory. The farla or Jirkedan has 10nos. of office bearers like Kleng serpo (king), Klengdum (Chief Minister), Sunderkethe (Commander), Sundersu (Prince designate), Barlanpo (Surveyor), Motan Are and Motan Arbe (Guides), Chengbruk Are and Chengbruk Arbe (small drumbeaters), Than Are and Than Arbe (convenors), Mei Apai(Fire keeper) and Lang Apai (water keeper). This dormitory can be regarded as an institution for social work. It performs all sorts of social services for the village in general and families in particular as and when such occasions arise. The members of the Farla donot claim any monetary remuneration from the concerned family for the services it has rendered. The spirit of offering a helping hand to the needy by the youths of a Karbi village has not yet been eroded even by the absence of the building of the bachelors' dormitory.

The Karbis inhabiting the Karbi Anglong district has a very interesting traditional institution which caters to the needs of the poor families specially during the lean months of the year. It is an economic institution, pure and simple, based on fellow feelings and co-operation. It is the traditionally maintained grain bank called Kerung Amei.

(vi) *Birth and death :* The birth of a child whether male or female is an occasion for joy in the family in the sense that a person died earlier in the family is supposed to be reborn in the same family which is a customary to the Bodo-Kacharis also. In other words, the Karbis believe in rebirth as human beings and not in the form of animals, birds or other creatures. Hence for a new born child the name giving ceremony where the maternal uncle of the child takes the leading part is the most important one. The maternal uncle taking a very small quantity of rice beer called Horlang in a small container pours it to the mouth of the new born

> child drop by drop. If the baby is a female one she will utter the names of all the dead females one by one associating a name with each drop. The name that will be associated with the last drop will automatically be the name of the female child. Similar procedures of associating each drop of rice-beer with the names of each dead male in the family are followed in case of name giving ceremony of a male child and the name associated with the last drop will determine the name of the newly born male baby.

For the cremation of the deceased the Karbis observe some specific rules and regulations and they believe that the non-observance of them might lead the family to great troubles in near future. Although they perform the funeral ceremony at the time of the cremation of the deceased, they also perform the death ceremony called Chomangkan at a later date for the eternal peace of the deceased.

(e) ***The Miris (Mishings) :*** The Miris are also known as Mishing. They are mainly concentrated in the riverine areas of Lakhimpur, Dibrugarh, Sibsagar, Jorhat and Sonitpur districts of Assam. This colourful ethnic group living amidst the Assamese people for many centuries has been able to maintain its traditional socio-cultural traits inspite of the changes that have taken place in the socio-political-religious life of Assam.

The Miris were originally a hill tribe within the ranges of the Abor, Miri and Mishimi hills of the erstwhile North-East Frontier Agency, now Arunachal Pradesh and they came down to the plains before the reign of the Ahom Kings and since then began settling in the riverine areas of the Brahmaputra and Subansiri rivers of Assam.

In the Assam District Gazetters, B.C. Allen[43] has given an account of the Miris.:

> The Miris or as they style themselves Mishings were originally settled in the hills to the north of Lakhimpur between the Dafla and the Abor territory. They are thought to be members of the Tibeto Burman family and the Chutiya Miris claim kinship with the Chutiyas. According, to their own account they descended from the hills with the Chutiyas when first they conquered Lakhimpur and retired again with them into their mountain fastnesses, when they were finally defeated by the Ahoms in the 16th century. On the advent of the British the Miris again began to settle in the plains, a process which has been in steady progress ever since.

However, they belong to the Tibeto Burman family of the Mongoloid group, physical features analogue to them.

(i) *Clan :* The Mishings are broadly known by two sections namely 'Borgam' and 'Dahgam'. Amongst these two sections of clans, there are many other sub clans namely as mentions by B.N. Bordoloi and others in his *Tribes of Assam* that amongst the Dahgam-Moying, Chayang, Taye, Pamegam, Murung, Bori, Pangging, Yein, Panchang, Noroh, Koman, Pogag, Paow, Bosing, Ayan, Padun, Saro, Nagate, Regon, Darik, etc. and amongst Borgam-Doley, Kutum, Kuli (Kouli), Pait, Patir, Basar, Pasar, Kardong, Misong, Pegu, Kumbang etc[44]. Knowledge of clan is very important for solemnising marriage ceremony. In their day to day life, however, clan distinction is never taken into account. Marriage must not take place in the same clan.

(ii) *Property and Inheritance :* The Mishings are patrilineal and the descent is through the male line. After the death of a father the property is divided equally among the sons. The sons can demand a partition of the family property during the life time of a father provided they have attained a matrimonial status. In the event of such a partition the father may not keep a share for himself. He can choose to remain with any of his sons he likes. Daughters are not entitled to share the property. But if a man has no son, his daughters may share the property, provided they bear the funeral expenses at their father's death. If a man has no son but his son-in-law lives in the father-in-law's house till the latter's death, he may inherit the father-in-law's property.

(iii) *Kebang, a legal court:* In this tribe every village has a 'Kebang' which can be aptly compared with a legal court of the village. The elderly men of a village constitute the 'Kebang' which is supreme in all matters within a village. The head of each 'Kebang' is called a 'Gam' who conducts the proceedings of the 'Kebang'. The 'Gam' is selected by the members of a 'Kebang'. The complaints whether social or religious are brought to the notice of the 'Kebang' which delivers judgement and punishes the offenders. Of late 'Kebang's position has been considerably eroded due to the existence of the Gaon panchayat. The role of Gaonbura or the Panchayat President has been felt more than that of the 'Gam'. But 'Kebang' is still a living institution and the people still regard the decision of the 'Kebang'.

(iv) *Marriage :* The two forms of marriage formal and informal are found to be prevalent among the Mishings. The former is an expensive affair and it is usually planned and arranged by the parents. In a formal marriage at first boy's parents or his close relatives would send information to the proposed bride's parents expressing the desire for the marriage proposal and as soon as the parents of the girl indicate their consent, the boy's party makes necessary arrangements for the formal proposal. A certain date will be fixed for the purpose and in the stipulated date the boy's party approaches the girls parents with presents like 'Apong' and betel leaves and nuts and formally announces the marriage proposal. On this day a date is fixed for the visit of the would-be-bridegroom. On the date fixed the would-be-bridegroom is led by his parents or relatives to the girl's house and he would be formally introduced to the parents and other relatives of the girl. Customarily the boy has to stay at the residence of the girl's parents for five days and during this period the boy is required to help the girl's parents in the field. This is called 'Magbo Ginlink'. After some months or a year the date of marriage is fixed and on this occasion also the boy's parents along with some of the relatives come to the girl's parents with 'Apong', fish and betel leaves and nuts. The Mishing marriage continues for two days. On the first day the bridegroom is led to the bride's house and he stays at the bride's house for the night. The ceremony takes place on the next day when all the villagers gather in the girl's house where a grand feast is arranged. The elderly persons give advice to the couple and the couple returns to the groom's house. With this the formal marriage comes to an end.

The payment of the bride price is known as 'Alig'. Formerly a 'mithun' or its equivalent of a fixed amount was charged as bride price. Today the amount has been considerably minimised.

'Duglalanam- besides formal marriage which is beyond the reach of the poor, runaway and kidnapping for marriage purpose are also popular among the Mishing which are socially recognised. In most cases elopement or runaway is resorted to mainly due to dissent of either of the party's parents or due to poverty. The boy takes away the girl with the help of his friends on an appointed date and the bride is received in an unceremonious function. The girl's parents are informed on the following day and the father of the girl along with a few co-villagers starts for the boy's house. The elderly people of the boy's village receive the girl's father and a meeting is held where the bride price is fixed. In such cases a higher bride- price is demanded (generally Rs. 100.00 or more and 'Apong' jars). The boy is allowed to pay the bride price in instalments.

Kidnapping is also not a rare occurence amongst the Mishings. Cases of such incidents are decided by the 'Kebang' concerned. The 'Kebang' inflicts penalty upon the offender who has to pay the fine in cash to the girls parents. Sometimes penalty is imposed in kinds also. The amount of such penalty ranges from Rs 50 to Rs. 2000 depending upon the whims of the girl's parents.

(v) *Religious beliefs :* The Mishing religion is based on the belief on supernaturalism and animison. They believe that spirits which they call 'Uie' are the guiding factors of their life and there are spirits everywhere. The spirits if not properly worshipped, cause sickness misfortune and death. The 'Mibu' or the village expert is the only person who can appease these spirits. Pigs, fowls, apongs etc. are offered in the name of the spirits. The 'Mibu' possesses super-natural power of finding the cause of illness and offers remedies. 'Urom uie', 'Taleng uie', 'Dabur Uie', 'Gumin Uie' etc are the various kind of 'Uie'. 'Urom Uies' are the spirits of the ancestors who are appeased by sacrificing two or three large pigs and supplying 'apong'. Offferings are not made to the 'Yalos' (souls) of unnatural and premature deaths. Thunder, lightening, storm, drought etc are worshipped with occasional offerings of fowls, pigs, and apong. These spirits are called 'Taleng Uies'. Dabur Uies are the spirits which cause flood, other natural calamities and diseases. It is performed at an interval of three to five years. 'Gumin uies' are worshipped along with pujas meant for other spirits at an interval of five years or so.

Now Mishing prefer to introduce themselves as Hindus and they are followers of the Bhakata-cult, a doctrine having Mishing and Baishnavism cum Tantricism mingled together[45]. The 'Bhakats' of this cult are generally old persons of both sexes who woe allegiance to the 'satras'. The 'Bhakats' preside over the religious ceremonies who are assisted by the junior 'Bhakats' called 'Sadhu'. Mishing 'Bhakata pantha' contains elements of Tantricism because recitation of verses from the 'Kirtana' or 'Bhagawata' and propitiation of the spirits by offering rice, meat, etc go together. There are now a good number of Mishings who are strict believer of Baisnava faith.

(vi) *Customs in the disposal of the dead :* The prevailing practice among the Mishings is buried. The deadbodies are buried irrespective of age, sex, and nature of death. The dead body is taken out to the courtyard not by the usual door but by a special door made for the purpose in the rear wall of the house. The corpse is bathed and kept in a log coffin called 'Rung Kung'. Like Hindus 'Tilani', 'Mahekia', and 'Daha' are the three parts of the purification ceremony of this society. Tilani, on the third day is the religious ceremony without feast and fun. The

> persons who attend the burial are invited. 'Mahekia' is the important purification ceremony observed after a month. A feast is arranged where all the villagers take part. The most important ceremony is 'Daha' which is held after one year or so unlike the Hindus who observe it in ten days. Feast with pork and apong is arranged for the villagers. If there is any pending cases in the clan then joint 'Daha' is observed.

It appears that the brideprice is still prevalent amongst the Deori tribes though it is in considerable amount. The wife and daughters are not eligible to share the property unlike the present Hindu law. These prejudicial customs should be abolished. The saivism of Hindu trinity has been reflected in the religious philosophy of Bodo-Kachari. It can be witnessed from the fact that Bathau Barai is analogous to 'Sibrai' or 'Siva' of the Hindu trimity. Junior levirate marriage held among these tribes. The position of women in these societies can be supposed to be high from it. Influence of Hinduism upon this tribe has also been observed in case of the marriage ceremony and death rites. Instituting of 'Mel' giving much freedom to the women shows the freedom, status towards the females of Sonowal Kacharies. Nominal bride price indicates the status of women in that society. Non-tribal impact on this tribe has been noticed in case of the two type of marriages e.g., 'Borbiya' and 'Hom Diya' and death ceremonies to some extent. In the Karbi societies liberal attitude has been noticed in case of widow remarriage, selection of groom and no system of bride price has been observed. A modern practice has also been noticed in relating to the use of surname. After marriage the wife continues to use the surname of her father, but the children assume the title of their father. The distribution of Jhum land is similar to that of co-operative and paik system prevailed in Ahom period that cultivated land is not permanantly given to the cultivators. The formal type of marriage of the Mishing tribe is analogous to the Hindus to some extent. The customs of traditional system of marriage depicts the influence of Hindu castes upon this tribe. Consideration of nominal brideprice indicates the status of this tribal women.

The tribal societies are mostly liberal and akin to socialistic pattern of society. They donot have much discrimination in case of caste, religion and women except that of Deoris.

Modern legal system is based on concept of democracy and the concept of sociolism. The two concepts developed in the modern society. So, unless the tribal society is made literate functionally and enlightened with all modern concepts they will not be able to appreciate the implication of modern legal system bringing justice to the society.

Thus, the different types of customary laws and practices of aforsaid tribal groups have been depicted in their literature relating to traditional behavioural pattern of socio-cultural, religious, legal as well as administrative aspects of life. These unwritten literature of customs and tradition reflects their style and way of living. Though the people of these tribal groups have started to be enlightened to some extent due to educational, socio-cultural upliftment, much of the customary laws stated here are still continuing at the backward areas of respective tribal societies in Assam for which these type of people have been deprived of the opportunity made by Article 21 of the Indian Constitution, which declares that nobody will be deprived of his life or liberty except according to procedure established by law. There can be no liberty without an exercise of will. Since a custom is not law itself, so the village elders and Chiefs should come forward to take steps for doing analysis upon them at their respective areas. It has been observed, that some of the customary practices have been recorded by few of the tribal societies like Tengapania Deori society located at Sibsagar district. If others too make the similar effort, it will be easier to analyse their traditional beliefs and practices at different aspects so that this will pave the way for modification through abandoning the bad effecting customs and making codification of the customs which should be codified for the greater benefit of their respective societies.

An Analysis of the Surveyed Tribal Areas in Respect of Impact of Customs in Law Courts

Singiani Village of Panidihing Mouza in Sibsagar District : All the people of this village are comprised of Deoris. The villages under Rajabari Gaon Panchayat of Panidihing mouza shows the following numbers of population:

It has been studied that the main tribal inhabitants except those of few, i.e., Dehing Kalghar, Rangadaria, Teteliguri, Khalihamari are Deoris. The social customs, religious beliefs and other practices of Deoris have depcited evidently in Singiani gaon. In Singiani gaon almost all the peoples are the Tengapania Deoris (494) where only one Lower Primary School and High School are there. The perchantage of literacy is 30. The secular as well as the religious stratifications are apparent in this society as mentioned earlier. Sri Rampal Deori, the present Gaonbura of Singiani village has been working since 1980 and performs his duty in five villages. He has not found the cases of heinous nature since long, which can not be settled locally but to be referred to either the police or the court. It can be witnessed from the record collected from Asstt. Sessions Judge court, Sibsagar, because they use to send these type of cases to the police or court of concerned jurisdiction.

It has appeared from the information that the Deoris are less entitled to heinous type of crimes and considerably less criminal offences are found sent to either police or respective court of concerned jurisdiction. The petty disputes

Table 9. Population of Villages under Panidihing Mouza in Sibsagar District.

Gaon Panchayat	*Villages*	*Total Population*	*S.T.*	*S.C.*
Rajabari	Dehing Kalghar	485	160	306
	Rangadaria	248	70	81
	Teteliguri	701	86	50
	Chelgheli	28	—	—
	Khalihamari	151	7	13
	Nemuguri	445	276	—
	Jamira	577	573	—
	Rajabari No.1	240	79	—
	Rajabari No.2	295	212	56
	Khenajan	1041	996	—
	Katiari	681	611	—
	Barpathar	301	301	—
	Singiani	507	494	—
	Samaguri	274	223	—

brought before the village elders along with Bordeori and his subordinates are disposed of according to some definite rules and regulations i.e., prescribed customary laws and these have been stated in a document which can be referred to as a legal literature of Tengapania Deori society in Sibsagar district. In this document the penances to be done by the accused are being stated along with other rules of conducting committee of Tengapania Deori society. For instance, few sections of the 20th schedule of this document have been mentioned below-

20th Schedule : Penance

Section-1: In case of killing a cow by infliction of blow or such other cruel means one shall have to undergo penance as follows:

(a) 1 duck, 9 hens, Rs 51/- as community fine.

(b) 1 pig for members of the communion.

(c) Cost for sacred water, Rs 20/-

Section-2: In spite of penance as above the concerned person will be considered to belong to second grade forever.

Section-3: In case a cow, in the condition of tied up, dies by falling down to the drain well or pond dug by self, the concerned person (whoever the owner it does not matter) shall have to do penance by offering 1 duck, a pair of hen and Rs 5/-, being the cost for the refreshment, that he will have to collect from temple. If a cow does not die due to a sudden attack or assault, then the section 3 will be applicable, etc. However, the offence appears to be considered more on religious ground as sacred water is required for purifying the person from guilt of cow slaughter and community fine charged. As such these customs do not deserve to be codified as laws, although it has been practised as customary laws.

Table 10: A List of Cases Disposed at Court, Sessions Judge Sivasagar (Only of tribal people)

Session Case No.	*Nature of Crime*	*Documents Used*	*Address*	*Dates*	*Judgement*
13 (S-C) 87	Kidnap	Sec. 366 of Indian Penal Code	Ramakanta Mili, Saraideo, Sonari	07-11-87	Acquitted
4 (S-C) 90	Kidnap	Sec. 360 of Indian Penal Code	VijoyMili, Sivasagar.	16-06-90	Acquitted
20 (S-C) 90	Rape	Sec. 376 of Indian Penal Code	Kang Kanyak, Soraideo, Sonari.	25-07-92	Convicted
30 (S-C) 95	Rape	Sec 376 of Indian Penal Code	Jati Sonowal, Soraideo, Sonari	08-01-97	Convicted
35 (S-C) 95	Rape	Sec. 376 of Indian Penal Code	Ghanasyam Mili, Sivasagar.	02-09-97	Convicted
28 (S-C) 96	Theft	Sec. 436 of Indian Penal Code	Diiip Mess, Sivasagar	07-08-97	Acquitted
26 (S-C) 97	House trespass, Kidnap, Criminal Break of trust	Sec. 448/366/477 of Indian Penal Code.	Siva Kanyak and others.	18-03-98	Acquitted

Saguri Sapari, Banhguri and Taung Mishing Gaon of Dergaon Mouza in Golaghat District : This Mishing gaon is situated on the bank of the river Brahmaputra and twelve kms from Dergaon in north. The whole area consists of six villages. Few information related to the aforsaid three villages are given in Table 11.

The present gaonbura (headman) Sri Boloram Taut has been working since 1986. No specific literature relating to their administration or justice is followed. In case of trying the offences by the village authority they follow their consented judgement what they decide at their panchayat meeting. On the otherhand, they follow customary laws. In case of theft the elderly persons use to give punishment by ordering the thief to lift that stolen aminal on his soulder, cutting heir and on his back with some colourful sentences he moves the entire village. A marriage dispute in 1997 had to be disposed of by insisting fine only, the headman said for peaceful living and for the later followers. No, other offences like rape, adultery, dacoity, murder, gambling etc. have been taken place since long. If any offence or case of heinous nature is found, they use to send them to the police and the court that follows the laws as in case of general. Elopement has not been recognised as an offence if it is not within the prohibited degree and it is their custom to make relation between the parties after the elopment is completed. The 'Kebang' is not found to be active in these villages to administer the social, legal as well as some religious activities. The customs followed in the disposal of the dead are apparantly depicted in these villages. The sub clans i.e., Doley, Tahir, Pegu, etc are existing and follow common customs in diferent aspects of social, legal and religious activities of their daily lives. It has been observed that due to lack of knowledge and education a large number of family members are seen in each family, e.g., the number of family members of the cultivator Sri Kamal Patir is 15, but formal education undertaken by them is nil. According to the headman the

Table 11. Literature, Literacy and Population at few Villages of Dergaon Mouza in Golaghat District

Sl.No.	*Name of Villages*	*Population*	*Literacy*	*No. of 1zSchool*	*Literature relating to Administration/Religion*
1.	Saguri Sapari	2,000	20%	L.P.=1 M.E=1	Customary/'The Kirtana'.
2.	Banhguri	1,200	25%	L.P=1 M.E=1 High=1	-do-
3.	Taung	400	20%	L.P.=1 M.E=1	-do-

females of this tribe are afraid or ashamed of or do not like to live on the floor of ground constructed home, they only like to live in the 'Changghar'.

Karbi Gaon of Duarbagari Mouza in Karbi Anglong District: The area surveyed comprised of gaons namely Rongbong ghat, Poisaingti gaon, Langkhang gaon and Volunteer gaon. This village is situated on the bank of the river Kaliani and 30 kms from the N.H. 37 besides the Numaligarh Refinary Limited, Numaligarh. The area consisting of the four small gaons with total population of 650. 150 numbers of people Rongbangghat, 100 numbers at Poisaingti gaon, 200 in LangKhang gaon and 200 numbers in Volunteer gaon have been living unitedly. Sri Dygroon Ingti, the gaonbura over these villages administer the social, legal situation with the help of elderly persons. The name of the headman itself is an example of custom of beliving in rebirth. The members of the family and others believe that the present Dygroon Ingti is none but his grandfather who died at Dygroon, the place beside the river Dygroon, that is why the headman named by this nomenclature when born, of course somebodies use to give name by the exact name of dead persons who were relating to them. Elopement is occured now and then among them which is recognised as their custom, if it is not within the prohibited degree. The elderly people of the Karbi desire that their offences or crimes should not be lighted out the outside of their jurisdiction. The cases like marriage dispute, , bride dispute, cattle trespass, land dispute, simple hurt, illicit sexual cases the headman along with the village authority try to dispose of by mutual understanding at first, otherwise by insisting compensation in kind or fine. The Karbi people are eager to have education and knowledge which is observed from the fact that there are three numbers of schools, Lower, Middle and High. It is found that unlike the Deoris no specific document is followed for the administration of legal as well as religious aspects. As mentioned earlier, serious offences are not tried by village authorities. Sex-offences though they may appear serious, are treated as violation of customary laws and are therefore tried generally by the village authorities. Below is a case of illegal sex —

Sum Milik, aged 30 years and Kareng Milik aged 25 years of Doloi Milik gaon of Amri block had a love affair and as a result Kareng Milik conceived. But they belonged to the same clan and were cousins by relation. In January 1986, the father of the girl brought the case before the Lyndokpo of Amri region, who referred the matter to the Havai of the area. The Havai called both the parties and heard them. They confessed the illicit sex-relationship. But as they belonged to the same clan, the sex relationship could not be regularised by marriage. Since they were within the prohibited degree, marriage was taboo. The Havai and his council ordered separation of the two lovers and a fine of Rs 225/- on the boy. The fine was realised on the spot and divided among the persons present in the Mei. The father of the girl was advised to marry away the girl to any person of a different clan to which the child, when delivered would belong.[46]

Dimasa Gaon Studied in North Cachar Hill District

(i) *Traditional Justice administration among Dimasas* : The Kachari King was the fountain head of justice and all major offences were punished under his orders. The punishment were extremely harsh. Murder- convicts were beheaded, right-hand of a thief was chopped off and a person convicted of adultery or rape lost his ear or nose.

(ii) *Village Gaonbura and Council tried minor offences:* Minor offences were tried by the village headman or Gaonbura with the help of the village elders. The traditional village headman who is at the top of the village administration was called Khunang. He had both executive and judicial powers. His judicial powers consisted of trying cases, maintenance of law and order in village. In discharging his duties he was assisted by another official called Dilek (assistant headman). In the traditional village organisational set up the Dimasas had eight officials, five, including the Gaonbura & his assistant belonged to the senior group and three to the junior group.

The traditional village council with the eight sets of officials headed by Khunang settled disputes, tried cases of thefts, elopements, etc. and the judgements delivered were binding on the concerned parties. When women were involved the elderly women were also invited to participate in the trials. Khunang and other functionaries of a few villages met and sat together to settle the inter-village disputes.

(iii) *Mouzadari system :* After the British came, they abolished the harsher punishments like beheading, chopping, mutilation, etc. and introduced the rules like '1906-set of Rules', '1937 set of Rules', '1955-set of Rules'. In the rural areas, they introduced, the Mouzadari system according to which the Mouzadar not only collected house tax and land-revenue but also settled disputes as per customary laws. The Mouzadar held a course with at least three Gaonburas in attendance and the members of the public at large. He heard both parties and their witnesses. Sometimes, parties were required to go through the ritual of oath taking by holding the tiger's tooth. The Mouzadar was empowered to pass a sentence of fine only and not of imprisonment. Out of the fine money realised, one-third was distributed among the persons present in the trial including the Mouzadar himself and the balance two-thirds went to the complainant as compensation.

Umanand Langmailai was the first Mouzadar of the entire N.C. Hills area. Now the number of Mouzas and of the Mouzadars has gone up to fourteen.

The Gaonburas settled petty disputes with the help of the village elders while the Mouzadars tried more serious offences and disposed of inter-village disputes.

(iv) *Types of offences and punishments :* Murder, hurt, rioting, theft, assault, adultery, incest, rape, illicit sex and elopement were the common offences among the people. Civil cases arose out of land-disputes, divorce, defamation, insult, succession-disputes and disputes over bride-price.

Corporal punishments were abolished by the British soon after they annexed North Cachar Hills. Fine and compensation were the usual penalties imposed by the traditional village councils. The amount of fine or compensation was calculated on the basis of member of clans of the Dimasa tribe. Now, the Dimasas tribe had 40 male clans and 42 female clans. A male clan was called Sengphong a female clan Julu. A guilty person was fined either Rs 40/- or Rs 42/- or Rs 40/- + 42/- or Rs 40x2 or Rs 42x2 or Rs 82x2 and so on. If fines were not paid by the guilty, he was ex-communicated or sometimes even banished.

a. Some offences and their customary punishments:

(i) *Murder :* Punishment for murder in pre-British period was imposed by the Raja. The murderer was beheaded. During the British period murder cases were not allowed to be tried by traditional judiciary, but were disposed of at the level of Deputy Commissioner and Asstt. to Deputy commissioner.

(ii) *Hurt :* Punishment for hurt was fine. Minimum fine was Rs 40/- i.e., Rs1/- for each male clan.

(iii) *Theft :* In theft case, the guilty person was made to return the stolen property or if that was not available, then its value. Besides, he was also liable to pay a fine which varied according to the gravity of the offence, the minimum being calculated on the principle of one rupee for each clan.

(iv) *Marriage or illicit sex within prohibited degree :* If marriage or illicit sexual connection took place within the same clan (what was prohibited by customs), then under no circumtances was their marriage accepted as valid by the society. Incest was the highest social offence. The married couple was forced to separate, and fine was realised from both the male having to pay at double the rate. If illicit connection took place between members of the same clan, both were fined. The rate of fine was double for the male partner. If any child was born as a result of marriage within prohibited degree or of illicit sexual connection, it would have to be maintained by the male. The marriage would be abrogated and the parties separated. If the fine was not paid, the accused male would be excommunicated and might even be banished.

(v) *Elopement :* In case of elopement, fine was imposed on both boy and girl. But if they were not within prohibited degree, they might be allowed to marry. Otherwise they would be separated.

Village court of Dimasa gaon at N.C.Hills even now follow the above mentioned customary laws. According to the traditional system of settlement of disputes, the cases at the village level are being tried also by the present-day village courts.

The following is a case decided by the village court of Gunjung at Haflong, presided over by the Mouzadar.

Incest : Sri Hamigendra Haflongbar had a love affair with Srimati Darbi Haflongbar, and as a result the latter conceived. But the boy happened to be her own cousin-brother of the same male clan (Sengphong). Sexual relationship between members of the same clan was prohibited by customary laws. The father of the girl complained before the village court against the boy, Hamigendra. The village court heard the case twice. The boy denied causing the pregnancy.

No direct evidence of such offence can be obtained. Hence, the village court on the circumstantial evidence was satisfed that Hamigendra was responsible for the pregnancy. Both the boy and the girl were found guilty and both were fined. The boy was fined Rs. 300/- and the girl 150/-. Against this decision, the boy appealed to the Subordinate District Council Court which directed the girl to take oath as there was no adequate evidence of the culpability of the accused. Against this decision of S.D.C.C. the girl's father appealed to the District Council Court. The District Council Court held that it was not necessary for the girl to take oath. Demand for such oath could be considered only when there were doubts about the person who caused the pregnancy. In this case, there was no such doubt as the accused himself could not think of any other person who might be involved in illicit connection with the girl. The District Council Court set aside the direction of the S.D.C.C. and upheld the decision of the village court. The District Council made clear exposition of the customary law. Since marriage within the clan could not take place, the illicit connection between boy and the girl which might have been regularised by marriage was culpable too. Both were liable to pay fine, since the girl was a willing partner.

(i) *Theft :* In 1982, one Jaypal Langthasa lifted a buffalo from a grazing field of village Gurubari and sold it to a buffalo trader of Maibong at Rs 840/-. Owner Julideo Thaosen after search, found it at Maibong Rly station and collected the name of the seller from the trader. He then complained against Langthasa before the Mouzadar who promptly went to Rly station and seized the buffalo and kept it in the custody of the trader till disposal of the case. After one week trial was held. Both parties with witnesses were present. The Mouzadar in the presence of Gaonbura ordered the accused to return the sale-price to the trader who, on receipt of the same returned the buffalo to the owner Julideo. The accused was fined Rs. 200/-. One third of the fine went to the Mouzadar and the rest to the Gaonburas and the other members present[47].

Attabari Sonowal Kachari Gaon of Lengeri Mouza and Dainijan Gaon of Dibrugarh at Dibrugarh District

The Attabari Sonowal Kachari gaon is situated on the bank of the Khowang river. The entire area comprised of 5 villages with 5000 population where almost all the people are Sonowal Kacharis. This Kacharigaon seemed to be as developing area in different aspects of their daily life. The following information regarding education assists in knowing about their scope for further development.

Table 12. Information Regarding Education and Literature in the Kacharigaon of Lengeri Mouza and Dainijangaon of Dibrugarh District

Name of the Village	*Population*	*Academic institution*	*Literature/Document followed in disposing the cases*
Attabari Sonowal Kachari Gaon	5000	L.P.=3nos M.E. 4 nos High=4 nos Higher Secondary =2nos College =2nos Basic Training Centre for Primary School=1no	No specific document is available.

So far the education is concerned the way of living, economic condition, their knowledge in different aspects of social and relegious life have been depicted at an developing stage. According to Sri Fanindra Das, the headman, he has not found any case since long except one cattle trespass, which was disposed of by insisting a fine of Rs 200/- and a feast with 'Khaj' which was provided by the accused. Now-a-days in case of offences of grievous nature the village authority like to send the cases to the police. They do not want to follow the custom of providing feast or the like in the cases of like this nature.

2, 000 people are there in Dainijan gaon with 1, 000 at Duliagaon which is an adjacent to Dainijan gaon comprising of all the Sonowal Kacharis. Among this male dominant tribe, literacy is found 40% in this area, 70% of the educated persons are known as service holders. They are Baishnava sect of Hindu religion. The Bhakatial and Non-Bhakatial groups are observing their customary practices. Sri Jagal Saikia, the headman of Dainijan gaon described that the feast with 'Khaj' is accepted by the Non-Bhakatial elderly persons for the offences like bride dispute, marriage dispute and other non-serious cases. The value of the stolen objects or animals along with the traditional feast is the usual punishment for theft or the non-serious cases. In the cases of illicit affair or the like ex-communication seldom takes place if not the accused person directly comes to understanding with the judgement of the village authority.

Survey of Religious Literature dealing with Customary Laws

Before going to describe the religious literature dealing with custom it is important to analyse the religious composition in Assam. The religious composition of Assam has been closely influenced by historical, social, political and cultural factors. The minorities have high concentration in some of the districts, though Hindus dominate the cultural land scape. The districtwise distribution of different major religious groups of Assam has been given: (Census of India-1991, see also. Encyclopaedia of N.E. India, vol-II Majid Hussain, ed., Delhi, Rima, 1998, pp. 58-59).

It has been observed that the Muslim is the second largest religious group amongst other existing religious groups in Assam.

Though the Shunni and Shiya the two sects of the Muslim inhabitants are in Assam as in other states of the country, they follow their traditional legal practices according to the holy Qur'an and Hadith, the two basic sources of Muslim laws.

Questions relating to family relations and status, namely marriage, divorce, maintenance and guardianship of minors, succession and inheritance, religious usages and institutions and dispositions of property by hiba, will and waqf are governed by the present Muhammadan law so far as the Muhammadans are concerned. Of course, the different sects have their own rule as their caste, custom and follow with respect to litigants of that sect. But the entire Muhammedan what they follow as Muhammedan law is basically based on the Qur'an and Hadith.

(a) ***The Islamic customary practices :*** an instance of general caste's tradition.

(i) *The Al-Qur'an and Hadith:* The two prime sources of Muslim law:

The name *Al-Qur'an*, the proper name of the sacred book of the Muslims occurs several times in the book itself. The word *Qur'an* as an infinitive noun from the root qura'a meaning primarily collected things together and also be read or recited. It is stated to be a revelation from the Lord of the World. It was sent down to the prophet Mohammed having been revealed to his heart through the Holy spirit (7th century A.D.).

The whole Qur'an is divided into 114 chapters each of which is called Surah. The chapters of the Qur'an are of varying length, the largest comprising 286 verses and the smallest containing only three verses. The longer chapters

Table13. Distribution of Population of Different Major Religious Groups in Assam

	District	*Hindu*	*Percentage*	*Muslims*	*Percentage*	*Christians*	*Percentage*
1.	Dhubri	382, 817	28.73	938, 789	70.45	7, 539	0.56
2.	Kokrajhar	531, 477	66.38	154, 801	19.33	78, 586	9.82
3.	Bongaigaon	516, 830	64.00	264, 393	32.74	17, 890	2.21
4.	Goalpara	266, 499	39.88	335, 275	50.18	52, 745	7.89
5.	Barpeta	557, 929	40.26	776, 974	56.07	3, 558	0.25
6.	Nalbari	787, 485	77.47	202, 653	19.93	10, 988	1.08
7.	Kamrup	1, 486, 526	74.32	467, 544	23.38	31, 820	1.59
8.	Darrang	786, 332	60.54	415, 323	31.98	81, 952	6.31
9.	Sonitpur	1, 142, 228	8.20	189, 859	13.33	85, 427	5.99
10.	Lakhimpur	598, 946	79.70	109, 010	14.51	30, 401	4.05
11.	Dhemaji	449, 492	93.87	7, 114	1.49	4, 891	1.02
12.	Marigaon	348, 989	54.56	289, 835	45.31	147	0.02
13.	Nagaon	979, 395	51.73	893, 222	47.18	15, 704	1.87

(Contd.)

(Table 13 Contd.)

14.	Golaghat	713, 131	86.12	58, 859	7.12	51, 897	6.26
15.	Jorhat	815, 320	93.59	37, 651	4.32	13, 287	1.52
16.	Sivasagar	810, 445	89.25	67, 260	4.32	21, 108	2.23
17.	Dibrugarh	951, 763	91.29	46, 816	5.16	35, 682	3.42
18.	Tinsukia	867, 825	90.18	30, 095	3.13	47, 526	4.94
19.	Karbi Anglong	562, 102	84.82	10, 421	2.89	82, 709	12.48
20.	Karimganj	414, 731	50.15	405, 706	61.37	4, 774	0.58
21.	N.C.Hills	109, 959	72.92	3, 340	0.34	36, 911	24.48
22.	Hailakandi	196, 269	43.70	246, 016	54.79	5, 677	1.26
23.	Cachar	770, 803	63.42	419, 150	34.49	23, 148	1.90
	Assam	**15, 047, 293**	**67.13**	**6, 373, 204**	**28.43**	**744, 367**	**3.32**

are divided into Rukus or sections, each section generally dealing with one subject, the different sections being interrelated. Again each section contains a number of Ayats or verses. The total number of verses in the Qur'an is 6247 or 6360, if the common opening verse is added to each chapter. For the purposes of recitation, the Qur'an is divided into 30 parts (jur). Most of the verses, which embody rules of law, were revealed to settle questions that actually arose for decision; some in order to repeal objectionable customs like infanticide, gambling, usury and unlimited polygamy; some for effecting social reforms such as by raising the legal status of women, settling the question of succession and inheritance on an equitable basis, providing protection for the right of minors and other persons under disability, and some layed down principles of punishment for the purpose of securing peace and order. All these were prevailed as the revealed order from the Lord, then converted into customary practices and have been established as Mohammadan law with many other laws promulgated through tradition or the *Hadith*. The aforesaid rules principally occur in the 'Suratu'l-Baqara, 'Suratu'n-Nisa', Surat-Al'Imran, Suratu'l Ma'ida, Suratu'n-Nur, Suratu'l-Talaq and Surat Bani-Isra'il. It also contains general injunctionswhich have formed the basis of important juristic inferences.

For instance 'Suratu'n-Nisa' in the 4th chapter of part-iv contains about orphan's guardians, law of inheritance, treatment of women, women who may be married; part-v in the same chapter (surah) includes- women's rights over their earnings, disagreement of husband and wife etc.

In the 2nd section of 'Suratu'n-Nisa' describes about the duties of guardians to orphan wards —

> *"Wa at-l-yatama amuwalahum waa la tattabaddalu-l-Khabicha bitwataiibi, wala ta-kulu amwalahum ilaamaalikum. Innahu kana huban Kabir."*[48]

i.e., give to the orphans their property, and substitute not worthless (things) for their good ones and devour not their property adding to your own property. This is surely a crime and great sin ...

Again in the same section it has been stated that-

"Wa inkhiphtum alla tukk chittu filyatama fankihuma twa-ba lakum mina-nichai, machna wa chulasa waa ruba-a; fa-in Khiftum ala ta-dil fawahidatan aoma malakat aimunukum, Jalika adana ala-tau-lu."[49]

i.e., if it feared that he cannot do justice to orphans, it is advised to marry such women as seem good to him, two or three or four[50], but if it is feared by him that he will not do justice, then it is advised to marry only one or that which his right hand possesses. It has been said that it is more proper that he may not do injustice.

Section 1 of the chapter 65 the Surah Al-Talaq (Divorce) describes-

Ya aiyuhannabiyun irjatwalaqtumunnisa fatwalikuhunna li-iddafihinna wa ahswul iddata; wattakkulaha rabha kum; lar-tukhriju hunnamin buyutihinna wa-r la yakh rajuna illa an yatina bi-far-hiswatim mubaiyinah.

Watilka huddulah. Waman yata-ada hududa-larhi fakkad jwalama nafsahu. Lartadri la-all-daha yuhudisu ba da-jalika amara[51]

i.e., it has been said, when divorce is done he should divorce her for her prescribed period (Iddat) and calculate the period. Not to turn out of her house, nor should she herself go forth unless she commits an open idecency. It has been observed that these are certainly the sources of the present Muhammadan laws prevailing in the country.

Section 6 in the chapter 5 mentions about punishment of offenders. According to this section the punishment is of four kinds, which clearly shows that the punishment to be inflicted in any particular case would depend upon the circumstances of the case, as well as the time and place where the crime was committed, viz., if murder has been committed in the course of dacoity the punishment would include the execution of the culprit, which may take the form of crucifixion; if the offence is so heinous or the culprit has caused such terror in the land that the leaving of his body on the cross is necessary as a deterrent. In other cases, the punishment may be imprisonment, where the severe punishment of cutting off of hands is deemed unnecessary. The Judge would take all the circumstances into consideration and inflict such punishment as he thought necessary. A particular case dealt with under this verse was that of a tribe called 'Urainah' Some men of this tribe came to the Prophet and accepted Islam. They fell ill and were sent by the Prophet to a place at a little distance from Modinah for change of climate and recovery of health. But when they regained health, they killed the very people who had served them and went off with their camels. Then they committed dacoities and violated the chastity of women, and they were severely punished.

Besides these in the *Qur'an,* many other aspects embodied with the customary practices or laws which make the Muslim societies ordered and peaceful, viz., trials and tribulations, remarriage, contracts and evidence, the drought (lighter punishment followed by severer), women's right over their earnings, etc. Traditions or the Hadith are the inspired precepts of Muhammad in matters of law and religion. The another legal literature which is a preliminary one is in the shape of this Hadith, which depicts the force of customs and usages in establishing rules of law in Islamic societies.

Traditions are grouped into three classes according to the nature of their proof. Such of them as have received universal publicity and acceptance, having been related by an indefinite number of men in each one of the three ages[52] and of different places are called continuous. Traditions of this class, like a verse of the Qur'an ensure absolute certainty as to their authenticity and demand implicit belief. The next class of traditions are regarded in law as carrying conviction of their genuineness into a man's mind, though not absolute certainty like the first.

These were reported by a limited number of companions in the first instance, and thereafter, i.e., in the two successive preiods, fulfilled the conditions of continuous tradition. They are called well known traditions (mashhur). The third class are designated, isolated traditions (ahad). These latter neither insure certainty of belief like the continuous, nor carry conviction like the well known traditions, but their genuineness in the opinion of generality of jurists is so far guaranteed, that it would be justifiable to base a rule of law thereupon. Traditions which rest upon the testimony of one or more narrators, limited in numbers and not fullfilling the conditions of either of the other two classes, fall within this category.

The Hadith compiled by Bukhari[53] is supposed to be the most popular and rightful document relating to tradition and customary laws for Islamic societies. The conducts embodied with the laws for Muslims for smoothly running the every step of their daily life have been scattered in this legal document. Suicide, theft, mortgage, judgement and witness, marriage and divorce, murder, will, succession, inheritance, conducts towards the servant, slave, self-defence, women education are some of the legal matters amongst the other important laws of Muslim social life. The section regarding the suicide states that those who commit suicide will have to be committed suicide by obstructing the respiration amidst the fire in hell. If he/she commits suicide with any weapon, will have to be committed suicide at the same manner amidst the fire in hell[45]. In connection with theft it mentions here that those who are accused of theft are punishable with cutting their hands, whatever may be the amount of material theft. Precedent should be followed, in the case of judgement, that class of judges will fly to heaven if they do justice, those judges must go to the hell if injustices have been done knowingly and also those who are doing injustice without conscience, etc, are some of the examples of laws which have been customarily followed in the Muslim societies.

(b) The Bhagavadgita, an example of sources of Hindu customary practices :

This is the aggregated revealation of the Lord Krishna to Kuntiputra Arjuna at the battle field of Kurushetra. Hence, the time of this work cannot be separated from that of the Mahabharata (i.e., 4th century B.C. to 4the century A.D.). The work comprises though the many aspects for salvation of the human life and dharma, these are meant to lead the men through lawful activities laid in the traditional scriptures. These have been depicted that the dharma or law flourished through the ages customarily practised. In the *Bhagavadgita*, Krishna, who himself said to be the Supreme authority of the universe said to Arjuna-

"Yah sastravidhim utsrjya
vartate Kamakaratah
na sa siddhim avapnoti
na sukham na param gatim"[55]

i.e., he who discards the scriptural law and acts as his desires prompt him, he does not attain either perfection or happiness or the highest goal.

"Tasmac Chastram pramanam te
Karya Karyavyavasthitau
jnatva sastravidhanoktam
Karma Kartum iha'rhasi."[56]

i.e., therefore, let the scripture be the authority for determining what should be done and what should not be done. Knowing what is declared by the rules of the scripture, should do the work in this world.

Regarding the laws of Kshatriya in the battlefield *Gita* mentions —

Svadharmam api ca' veksya
na vikampitum arhasi
dharmyad dhi yuddhac chreyo'nyat ksatriyasya na vidyate.
...
atha cet tvam imam dharmyam
Samgramam na Karisyasi
tatah svadharmam Kirtim ca
hitva papam avapsyasi[57]

i.e., Having regard for own duty, the Kshatriya should not falter, there exists no greater good for a Kshatriya than a battle enjoyed by duty. Swadharma or law of action, requires the Kshatriya to engage himself in battle ... If he does not do this lawful battle, then he will fail from his duty and glory and will incur sin.

On the version of Arjuna it is emphasisd on the laws inherent to the families which is utmostly required to attaining the ultimate goal.

"Kulaksaye pranasyanti
Kuladharmah sanatanah
dharma naste Kulam Krtsnam
adharmo bhibhavaty uta"[58]

It has been stated that in the ruin of a family, its ancient laws are destroyed and when the laws perish, the whole family yields to lawlessness. Again here it is stated —

"Adharmabhibhavat Krasna
pradusyanti Kula striyah
Strisu dustasu varseneya
jayate varnasamkarah."[59]

i.e., when lawlessness prevails, the women of the family become corrupted and when women are corrupted, confusion of castes arises.

Besides these, it is observed that many of the present country laws had been delivered by Krishna, viz., he said about the self defence, when Arjuna hesitated to fight against his relatives and honourable warriors in the battlefield.

The Bhagavadgita is a religious book not only for a single sect of Hindu religion but also for the many castes and tribal groups under Hinduism. Punjabi, Marathi, Bengali, Oriya, Bihari, all are the followers of this great work. In Assam along with the general Assamese people other tribals and castes have been following the saying of this book.

Like the *Bhagavadgita, the Kirtana,* although is the basic religious book of the Baishnava sect of Assamese people, it is also followed by some of the tribal groups besides the general Assamese community as a whole in Assam.

The Kirtana is a 15th century work by Srimanta Sankaradeva the propounder of Baishnava religion in Assam. In this book, also there are many versions involved with laws which have been customarily practised by its follower. *The Kirtana*- describes about the punishment to be done in hell for those who have the sinful eyes towards the Bishnu or Baishnava.

"Bisnu-Baisnavak kare dhikkar katibe antil jihbak tar..."[60]

As such this book can be regarded as an essential source of laws regulating for Baishnavites as well as other Assamese social, religious life, where practices are being embodied fearing the version laid in *the Kirtana.* In this way the literature, pertaining to the socio-religious with political purpose throw light upon the legal system and customary practices which have been prevailing since the ancient periods in the country as well as in Assam. In case of Assam the customary laws and practices have been well depicted specially through the behavioural pattern and socio-religious activities of tribal groups.

Customs in the Folk-Literature of Assam : Assamese folk-literature is rich in proverbs, rhymes, aphorisms and practical maxims like 'Dakar bachans' etc. The customs and practices of Assamese people have been reflected in these folk-literature. Many of them have socio-economic and literary values with apt references to works in agriculture etc. But it is observed that these folk literature do not convey any legal message. Few of them have been mentioned below with brief analysis —

"Sate patal panchat ghon
Chayat tamol nadan-badan."

i.e., to get good production of nut it is essential to keep in mind, between two plants of nuts there should be only six feet distance, not seven or five. The proverb indicates the practice of Assamese people in farming embodying with social lives. This type of proverbs is literary composed in such a way, which could be easily kept in mind.

In 'Dakar bachan' values of medical science are also apparent thus —

"Ji khai tini khilikha
Tar manot rog tilika."

i.e., some aboriginal fruits are very useful for the people. The myrobalam nut is helpful to keep abdomen clear and hence it thus saves the people from several diseases.

The Assamese people are habituated with these folk-literature and the custom of quoting these proverbs and maxims are still prevailing in Assam.

Now it made to have the comprehensive knowledge about the customary laws and practices merged in legal system, ancient scriptures, to some extent in folk-literature and different socio-religious, behavioural pattern developed throughout the ages in the country, specially in Assam.

Instances of Some Acceptable and Non Acceptable Customs of General Communities and Other Tribal Groups

(a) Muslim Personal Law

So far, the character of the customs and practices are concerned, these have been prevailing without proper reasoning or scientific basis to the concerned group of people in the societies. Some of them have been practised against the public policy and their welfare whereby conflicts are arisen and approach to the court for disposal of the cases. If such types of cases have been codified since early locally or by the court, then it disposes of the cases litigated as per laws adopted by the local panchayat or by the court, i.e., according to customary laws for that particular group of people. It has been observed that the personal laws of this type of customs particularly amongst the Muslims have effected the progress of that particular group of people. The Islamic countries mostly have been victimised by these types of personal laws and these should be abolished by law. For instance, in *The Eastern Clarion,* a local English daily news paper, a news was published on 21st sept 1999"... under Islamic sharia laws (personal), a marriage is annulled if the husband utters the word 'talaq' thrice before his wife... Khatoon, 28, reportedly told police that she saw an uncertain future for her and her daughters after her husband made the divorce declaration ... Khatoon was infuriated as she picked up an axe and killed all the four daughters. It may be mentioned herewith in context with the personal law of Muslims i.e., about the origin of the custom of divorce among them. The custom that was prevailing in the Arab society was to divorce wife by triple talaq in one occasion. During Prophet's time, during the time of first and second Caliphs, Hajrat Abubakkar and Hajrat Omar, such three utterances of talaq on any one occasion was considered to be one talaq only. It was only during later part of the regime of Hajrat Omar, such triple talaq was ordered to be final and irrevocable. This was only to punish the husband who ignores the *Quranic* rule of divorce. Prophet Mohammad seeing use of such triple talaq during his life time lamented that his followers had started playing with The Book of God even during his life time. People used to divorce at whims, or get back his divorced wife at ease with the help of this custom. At a later stage, the Hanafi School of law gave its approval to this custom. Hanafi School had to accept the custom as a historical necessity as this school developed during the reign of Ommyyad dynasty without any royal patronage. Therefore, it is rightly declared by the Muslim Personal law Board of India that the utterance of three talaqs in one occasion is a criminal act. However, the actual law of divorce as laid down in the Holy Quran is not at all oppressive for women. The guiding principle of this law is that among all the evils disliked by God, divorce is the worst, and may be used only to ward off a greater evil than divorce that may happen in the married life of a couple, i.e., when conjugal life has become hell than heaven for them. It is seen that it overrides the saying of 'Clear proof of Written text of the law will outweigh the usage or customary tradition' of Islamic view.

(b) Tribal Customs

Superstition breds inhuman attrocity even in the society of this 21st century. From time immemorial irrationality and inhuman behaviour of a section of people have always retarded the upcoming civilization of mankind. Civilization doesnot make any sense to them who are blind followers of the tenets of the dark work.

Witchcraft had become a topic of stories and legends for years. In prejudicial world man had to take recourse to such black art as a means of acquiring 'Superhuman' quality and also to fulfill own urges and interests. Even in the present age of 21st century some people have been victimised due to such superstitious believes.

Recently, such an incident took place in Adabari Tea Estate of Sonitpur district of Assam. According to sources on May 14, 2000 some tea garden labourers charged an woman called 'Sukuwara' of 30 years of age of the same tea estate to be the root of all evil mainly due to the sudden death of one Suresh Praza of 28 years of age who succumbed to death after two days of mental derangement. The labourers accused her of his death and considering her to be 'witch' (an evil power) assaulted her publicly and later killed her with inhuman torture and ablazing her by pouring kerosine! They even didnot spare her at her death bed when they pinned sharpened bamboo sticks into severed parts of the body! Another shocking incident took place in Erasuti Kaweimari village under Thelamara Police Station of Sonitpur District of Assam in January 2000. In the sensational incident under the influence of superstitious belief some tea garden labourers killed 4 fellow persons. In the sameway a woman was also brutally murdered accusing her to be witch in Borjuli T.E under Rangapar Police Station of the same district.

Along with the tribal people of Assam the tribal groups of N.E. Region have also got victimised by their prevailing customs. Reference may be made about the news which was published in the 'Times of India' on Oct 3, 1998. The news said. "... After a spate of shocking robberies in Shillong some months ago, the "dorbars" started night-time community policing by "volunteers," who are reported to have caught suspects and handed them over to the dorbars... The village "dorbar" (Committee), a traditional institution very dear to the Khasis in Meghalaya, has come under severe scrutiny lately due to its alleged involvement in some lynchings. ... Eleven of these suspects, tribals and non-tribals were killed and 71 were injured. The deaths shocked the state and created a general sense of insecurity. These fears were reportedly fuelled by police inaction. .... The involvement in lynchings has raised certain questions about the dorbars. Are they above the law? Though elected bodies, are they truely representative as women (of the Khasi tribe) and non-tribals don't have voting rights?" Such types of customs should be abolished by law. Similarly, the innumberable brides victimised from 'Dowry' are the common news today.

In *the Eastern Clarion,* 17th sept'99 published "...Urmilla Sahu of Jamugurihat ... was married to Ghiladhari Sahu 7 years back. Urmilla's parents gave costly materials and Rs 20, 000 as dowry. But the pressure for dowry was kept up. .. Urmilla's father said that she was killed by her husband, and his family for not bringing enough dowry..." Such types of customs and practices which are practised by the group of people intervene the development of societies as well as the nation belonging to these group of people. This custom should be abolished by implementing 'Anti Dowry Law'.

Now-a-days there are many such unwholesome stories of brutal murder of death due to dowry that we read in print media. Recently, one Bornali Rai of Guwahati was suspected to be murdered by her husband's family only due to dowry. Mostly women are victimised in such cases. The inhuman exposition of animal wrath and inordinate greed of material property always lead to tragic end of one or other. The weaker section sustain the suffering or consequence inevitably.

But the point, here to be noted is that the evil customs and superstitious beliefs should be logically verified and stringent legal measures should be evolved to obstruct and annihilate such unforturnate incidents. On the otherhand, the truth in cases like the wonderful marriage between a 3yrs girl and a dog in West Bengal should also be examined. Female indignities, mostly among the tribals should be critically studied so that no more precious life should go wasted.

It may also be mentioned, here that the customary practices customs which are good and healthy for the people should be brought out and carefully accepted for benefit of the people.

Among the people of general communities it has been observed that besides the degradation of the status of women, the caste discriminations have come to prevail amongst the Vaishnavs and the other Hindu religious people when few of them undergo with strict rules prescribed by their

'Satradhikar' of concerned satras in Assam. Even the two bhakatas who have taken saran at two separate 'Gosai' or Satradhikar hesitate to take food cooked in the same vessel. Although the remarriages among the widows according to their own will have come to prevail gradually at few places of upper and lower Assam, but it is not so in most of the places of the region. But the religious custom of caste discrimination evolved through 'satriya principles' have been found rigid every where in Assam. These types of customs should be abolished interfering by the satras itself or through socio-cultural movement of the people in Assam.

Of course, some practices have been observed as neither good effected nor bad affected. Keeping in view of these character the matter of codification or repealation or modification should be taken into consideration. Instances of such types of customs and practices and customary laws prevailed in Assam are laid down-

(1) An age-old custom has still been going on in Doobi-near Pathsala of lower Assam.This custom is called 'Notydance'. The 'Noty' are a group of Hindu girls who are offered by their parents at the service of the temple. The very word Noty is now understood in a derogatory sense. The girls are socially underestimated and not provided with any status. It should be stopped by government interference by law.

(2) In some rural areas surrounding Nalbari, widows are not allowed to accompany the bridal party even now. This inhuman conduct is a matter of shame for modern society. This practice should be abolished by Non Government Organisation, resolutions and implimentation.

(3) The utter dismay 'Satidah' is still a system in some remote parts of this country. As far as information put in, the last 'Satidah' took place in Assam in 1936 when the wife of a teacher of Cotton Collegiate

School of Guwahati Sri Jajneswar Sarmah put an end to her life following this superstitious rite.

(4) The stratification still shown in Namghar on the basis of caste and creed is not at-all a healthy sign. Such is the custom of Rati Sewa Samaj which deserves abolition.

(5) Some matrimonial customs in no sense should not be transmitted into socially adopted law or codified customary laws. As for instance among the Kalitas, Keots getting married to a lower caste like Sudra mainly in lower Assam, both the spouses have to become disciples (to take'saran') of a 'Satradhikar' who is also called Gosain Prabhu by his Bhakatas. There is of course slightly different custom in this regard in upper Assam. Either of the spouse may take 'Saran' before the marriage ceremony in this part of the state.

(6) Likewise, untouchability is more prominent in the districts like Barpeta, Nalbari, in lower Assam. Brahmin, Koch, Kalita donot in general consider, Muslim, Bodos and other tribal people at par with their rank and prestige socially. This type of practice should be abolished.

(7) Even after much movement of the progressive women for the equal rights with men and the much talk to this end has been done, nothing of that sort has been achieved particularly in the religious area. A known fact is that women are still not allowed to enter the Namghar in Barpeta of lower Assam whereas a quite reverse picture is seen in upper Assam. Similarly in case of Muslim, the custom of interference in entering the women into the Idgah should be abolished. In the eye of law, there is no distinction between castes, creeds, sex, etc. So in public place this distinction is not tenable.

(8) To stay empty-stomach during the marriage day for both the bride and groom is a social custom mainly among the Hindu communities. From the scientific point of view this may be alarming for both the persons who have to undergo a good amount of mental pressure and tension for the reason best known.

(9) Even now among Koch, Kolita, Kaibarta of Hindus the father-in-law or mother-in-law do not take food offered or cooked by their childless bride. These practices should not be socially adopted so far the discrimination are concerned. This custom should be abolished.

(10) 'Dheki geet' (or Dhekisong) and 'Naokhelia geet' are the songs, sang at lower Assam like Nalbari, Rangia. These signify the intrinsic zeal and spirit of the ceremony through the melodious tune of expression that is specific to the region only.

(11) Unlike in upper Assam, 'Dhoti' (a kind of indigenous wearing that originally be longed to Hindus) is a garment to be put on in a wedding among lower Assam's Muslims. 'Chaygaon' is an instance of this.

(12) Bhaona- the religious play with originality of Sankardeva is not in vogue in lower Assam, like Nalbari, Rangia, Mongoldoi except instituted in 'Rakhleela'.

(13) Bridegrooms generally set off their journey towards the house of the bride at night in lower Assam for 'Nikah'-the matrimonial sacrament among Muslims. They do so keeping in mind the relation of luner calender with the house of 'Nikah'.

(14) The Assamese Muslim community by and large is influenced by prevailing customs of Hindus in some social aspects, e.g, the sanctification of both the

bride and the groom, with pulses and turmeric in their bathing is such a custom which was abolished in 1950 considering it as antishariat. Quazi Atiqur Rahman of Dibrugarh was instrummental in this.

(15) Inspite of movement undertaken by the progressive women, the dissolution process of marriage through 'Talaq' system has been prevailing in Assam along with other parts of India and abroad, which is an easy process for dissolving the long marriage tie among them. These codified personal law of Muslim should be repealed.

(16) Qabin-nama of Muslim community is a documentary statement given by the bridegroom at the time of 'Nikah' which strengthen the bond of marriage to the bridal side. The custom has been practised particularly in lower Assam which should also be prevailed equally in Upper Assam.

(17) Among the Muslims the practice of polygamy in the case of marriage has been prevailing. This codified customary law should be abolished and emerged with the law of the land, thereby the parties committing this crime should be punished under section 494 and 495 of Indian Penal Code so far as the economic and overall development of the population as well as of the nation is concerned.

(18) According to the prevalent social custom in the Khasi tribal group any one of the divorced couple cannot remarry. Another irrational custom among the Khasi people is that the youngest daughter gets the largest quantity of her maternal poperty. Here law can interfere for equal right and justice among all children.

(19) The Dafala women donot generally enjoy much freedom in different aspects of society. They cannot take part in any religious ceremony except

preparing wine. They donot have any position in any institutional or social function, they can only be onlookers. They donot enjoy at all freedom out side their homes. These should be brought into notice and reformed.

(20) The locally codified laws or customary laws in the case of property and inheritance of Deoris, Boro-Kacharis, Dimasa-Kacharis, Mishings, etc differ with that of Hindu succession Act 1956. which provides uniform system of law, equal property right to female, etc. The unequal separation system of succession and inheritance under the customary laws of these tribal groups should not be codified and can be merged with the uniform Hindu Succession Act, 1956.

(21) The system of bride-price is prevalent among the tribal groups like Deories, Mishing, Dimasa-Kachari etc. except Karbis. This customary law of system of bride price among them should be abolished or should not be codified so far their economic condition is concerned.

(22) The functional aspects of the bachelor's dormitory-'Nodrang' of Dimasa kacharis have almost lost their significance, but in order to develop the socio-cultural aspect, it is important to revive this traditional institution.

(23) The traditional bachelor's dormitory Farla or Jirkedam or Risomar (youth club) among the Karbis have been regarded as an institution of social work and their original footing should remain the same.

(24) The system of traditional 'Kerung Amei' the grain bank, an economic institution among the Karbis

should not lose their original significance, it caters to the needs of the poor families specially during the lean months of the year.

(25) Among the Bengalis an irrational practice has been prevailing at marriage ceremony. The bridegroom has to offer a fish to the bridal party on that very ring ceremony day of wedding. The bridal party measures the groom his capacity, rank and status by considering how much big is that fish. The custom should be abolished.

(26) Futwa, which is a judicial decree or judgement done by religious heads. Though it has not arisen in case of state like Assam, Govt. interference is essential if it is occured to intervene in destroying freedom of thinking and speaking, approved by public movement.

Inummerable customs and practices being followed in Assam of which the legal or scientific value is nil. The customary laws which have been socially or locally codified but not legally codified so far, should be brought to the notice, if it is fit for the same. The court should interfere in practising the harmful custom. A custom that overrides personal law grounded upon religious consideration, in effect overrides religion itself. A custom that overrides religion itself cannot be called a just custom. Therefore, the custom at its inherent nature should be brought by the concerned learned persons so as to make the proper analysis and comparative study with religious, legal and scientific aspects at present value. A seperate branch of Law Research Centre embodying customs and practices of different tribal groups should be established for this purpose specially in upper Assam besides that of Guwahati High Court so as to gather systematically and make analysis upon them along with the study and research of the traditions of local inhabitants in the same line.

Table 14 : Development of Legal Literature embodying the Customary Laws in Assam at a Glance (shows basic information sources and somewhere only instances of the presented literature in a consecutive order since the Vedic period)

1.	The Rigveda	10th Century B.C.	Documentary (Earlier oral)	Rishis	The whole Veda is the first source of sacred law, traditions and customs. It deals with various aspects of law viz., marriage, theft, burglary, robbery, cheating etc.
2.	Smritis:				
(A)	The Dharmasutras (i) Gautama (ii) Baudhyana (iii) Apastamba and (iv) Vasistha	7th century B.C. to 2nd century B.C.	Documentary	Respective Smritikars.	All the Dharmasutras mention about the marriage system, succession, inheritance, adoption, widow's right etc., but different laws have been observed in different sutras.
(B)	The Metrical Smritis:				
	(i) Manusmariti	2nd century B.C. to 2nd century A.D.	Documentary	Manus	The basic source of Hindu laws relates to the laws of kingship,castes, land, marriage, punishment, breach of cdontract, boundary dispute, cattle trespass theft etc.
	(ii) Yajnavalkya Smriti	1st century B.C. to 3rd century A.D.	Documentary	Yajnavalkya	Deals with the laws more systematic and concised than Manus, relating to the right to women, inheritance, Vyavahara Partnership, Kings duties etc.
	(iii) Narada Smriti	2nd century A.D.	Documentary	Narada	It deals with positive law or Vyavahara, marriage system, customs and the laws mentioned in the Manusmriti, but it is an abridgement

(Contd.)

(Table 14 Contd.)

					of the larger work of Manu. He is the first to give a legal code unhampered by the mass of religious and moral teaching. He prescribes the remarriage system of widow.
3.	Arthashastra	4th century B.C. to 3rd century A.D.	Documentary	Kautilya	It is a treatment of entirely different branch of law viz, rights, duties, responsibilities of the king, revenue system, marriage, divorce, partition, contract; criminal laws for theft, robbery, defamation, assault, gambling; spy. slavery warfare etc.
4.	The Mahabharata	4th century B.C. to 4th century A.D.	Documentary	Vyas	The great epic provides the information relating to polygamy, caste system, marriage system, kings duties, land system, laws of warfare etc.
5.	The Bhagavadgita	4th century B.C. to 4th century A.D.	Documentary	Vyas	A part of the Mahabharata concerned with the laws of Kshatriyas, customs relating to marriage, women's right, king's duties, laws of selfdefence etc.
6.	The Ramayana	3rd century B.C. to 2nd century A.D.	Documentary	Valmiki	Deals with the customary system of marriage, Swayambara system; custom of maidens sale, polygamy, war system like 'Ashwamedh', kings duties, spy system etc.

(Contd.)

(Table 14 Contd.)

No.	Source	Period	Type	Author	Contents
7.	Two other Metrical Smritis:				
	(a) Parashara Smriti.	5th century A.D.	Documentary	Parashara	The document includes the subjects of Prayashchitta, caste system, it omits the discussion on Vyavahara. It emphasizes that some positive laws are to be determined by the decisions of a parishad or an assembly of the learned.
	(b) Katyayana Smriti	3rd century A.D. to 6th century A.D.	Documentary	Katyayana	This literature contains many important branches of laws i.e., law and procedure, rights of women, stridhana, rule of bailment and liability of the bailee, widow's right of inheritance etc.
	The two basic literary sources of Muhammedan laws including customs:				
8.	(A) The Qur'an	7th century A.D.	Documentary	The Lord	The basic source of Muhammedan law embraces the laws of marriage, orphans and their property, divorce, laws of inheritance and customary Law son bridal dispute, illegal relationship, women's right, education, punishment for the crimes like theft, robbery, murder etc.
	(B) The Hadith	7th century A.D. to 9th century A.D.	Documentary	The Prophet Muhammad and his Chief	Deals with conducts and rules for running the social life, religious life, tradition relating to the cases of

(Contd.)

(Table 14 Contd.)

				followers	suicide, theft, mortgage, marriage, divorce, women education etc.
9.	Harshacharita	7th century A.D.	Documentary	King Bana	Deals with the then existing laws and practices prevailed in Assam covers the laws of land, kings duties, marriage etc.
10.	Kalika Purana	10th to 11th century A.D.	Documentary		It indicates certain deals for the king to administer the country. Different 'Rajnitis' have been described, Information on spy, slave etc. are also included.
11.	Inscription and Epigraphic grants: Umachal rock inscription (Kamakhya hills, Kamrup district)	470-490 A.D.	Documentary	Surendravarman	Deals with the information of the king, his work, prevailing rules etc.
	(b) Nagajari fragmentary stone inscription (Sarupathar, Golaghat district)	5th century A.D.	Documentary	Bhaskaravarman	Concerned with the title of the king and the hints of locality etc.
	(c) Barganga rock inscription (Doboka, Nagaon district)	518-542 A.D.	Documentary	Bhaskaravarman	Indicates the king's name, his work, rules etc.
	(d) Doobi copper plates (Barpeta district)	600-650 A.D.	Documentary	Bhaskaravarman	It gives light on the administrator, his acts etc.
	(e) Nidhanpur copper plate (Sylhet, Bangladesh)	600-650 A.D.	Documentary	Bhaskaravarman	Deals with activities of the king, rules etc.
	(f) Hayungthal copper plate inscription (Karbi Anglong district)	815-832 A.D.	Documentary	Harjaravarman	Describes the title of the king, shows his activities with customs etc.

(Contd.)

(Table 14 Contd.)

	(g) Nagaon copper plates (Puranigodam, Nagaon district)	860-880 A.D.	Documentary	Balavarman	Indicates the king's name, his duties etc.
	(h) Guakuchi copper plates inscription (Nalbari, Nalbari district)	960-990 A.D.	Documentary	Indrapalavarman	Deals with the king's title, his activities etc.
	(i) Kamauli copper plate (Varanasi, U.P)	1126-1140 A.D.	Documentary	Vaidyadeva	Indicates the then existing custom, kings name, work etc
12.	Yoginitantra	16th century	Documentary	Tantrik	It describes about the funeral oblation, sacrifices, customary practices embodying rites and ritual etc.
13.	Buranji:				
	(a) The Assam Buranji	13th century A.D. to 20th century A.D.	Documentary	Edited by S.K. Bhuyan	Deals with the information about administration, judicial procedure, social custom, procedure, social custom, crime and punishments etc., provided by earliest kings to Gadadhar Singha (1681-96)
	(b) The Satsari Assam Buranji		Documentary	Edited by S.K. Bhuyan	It is a collection of information relating to political history, and legal system of defferent Ahom kings. Pratap Singha, Swarganarayan, Pramatta Singha, Gaurinath Singha, Jayadhawaj Singha and Chakradhawaj Singha etc.
	(c) Deodhai Assam Buranji		Documentary	Edited by S.K. Bhuyan.	Describes the information about the earlier period of Ahom history and the relation with Koches, Jayantias, Kacharis, Mikirs, Chutiyas, Naras

(Contd.)

(Table 14 Contd.)

					with the Mughals which depict the social custom and legal aspects of those days.
	(d) Tungkhungia Buranji		Documentary	By Srinath Barbarua Edited by S.K. Bhuyan.	This literature belongs to a clear account of administrative machinery in legal aspect of Tungkhungia dynasty of Ahom Kings (1681—1826 A.D.)
	(e) A history of Assam	20th century	Documentary	Edward Gait	It deals with the matters like judicial administration of Ahom Kings, Tribal Kings, Mughal relation with subjects of Assam, about the British rule, custom and traditon, Codes, Acts etc.
(f)	The Comprehensive History of Assam	20th century	Documentary	Edited by H.K. Borpuzari (vols-5)	It deals with the annals of ancient Assam, medieval Assam and the modern Assam. It is authoritative work of 20th century for research and study.
14.	Persian chronicles Account of foreign travellers:	13th century A.D. to 19th century A.D.			
	(a) Tabaquat-i-Nasiri	1260 A.D.	Documentary	Minhaj-ul-Siraj.	Relates to Mughal's conduct and practices, depicts the relation of Muslim and Ahom, etc.
	(b) Ain-e-Akbari	16th century	Documentary	Abul Fazal	Deals with the administration of Emperor Akbar and Muslim culture and custom.

(Contd.)

(Table 14 Contd.)

	(c) Fathiya-i-lbriyah	16th century	Documentary	Shihabuddin Talish	It indicates the legal system and traditions of medieval Assam.
	(d) Accounts of a Portuguese traveller	16th century	Documentary	Ralph Fitch	It throws light on the legal adminis-trative set up of KochBehar with Assam.
	(e) Account of an English traveller	18th century	Documentary	Captain Welsh	Deals with an account on the working of the Ahom administration and the traditions of Ahom society.
15.	Numismatical Sources:				
	(a) A silver coin of 173.2. grams	17th century (1648 A.D.)	Documentary	King Jayadhwaj	It indicates the name of the ruler, idea of religious custom etc.
	(b) Three silver coins weighting 172,171.5 and 171.1 grams.	17th century	Documentary	King Gadadhar	It deals with king's name, his works traditions etc.
	(c) Gold coins	18th century	Documentary	Harish Chandra Narayan	It indicates the relation between Koch, Kamrup and Mughal and their traditions.
16.	The Kirtana	15th century	Documentary	Srimanta Sankardeva	It includes along with Lord's 'name', the hints of custom, practices and legal aspect like punishment for theft, prohibition, etc.
17.	Jikkir and Jari	17th century (1635-1650 A.D.)	Documentary	Shah Millan (Ajan peer)	Indicates about the Ahom legal administration and Muslim customary practices in Assam.
18.	Acts II, IV of 1835	19th century (1835 A.D.)	Documentary	British government	Deals with the rules and administra tion of districts-Goalpara Kamrup, Darrang, Nagaon, Khasi and Jayantia hill and their customary laws also.

(Contd.)

(Table 14 Contd.)

19.	The Special Assam Code of 1837	1837 A.D.	Documentary	British government	Relates to the laws of Civil and Criminal aspect held in Assam
20.	Act. XXVI of 1850	1850 A.D.	Documentary	British government	Deals with the laws regarding commissions to municipal affairs etc.
21.	Reports on the Province of Assam	1853 A.D.	Documentary (Report)	A.J. Moffatt Mills	It deals with various letters and accounts which provide the information about the judicial administration and traditional practices of early British days in Assam.
22.	The Civil Procedure Code, 1859	1859 A.D.	Documentary (Code)	British government	Deals with the laws regarding crime and punishments in civil litigations of British administration.
23.	The Indian Panel Code	1860 A.D.	Documentary	British government (Code)	It includes crimes like abetment, criminal conspiracy, offences relating to religion, against property, theft, robbery etc. and punishment for these and many other subjects adhered with law.
24.	The Scheduled District Act. XIV of 1874	1874 A.D.	Documentary	British government	Deals with the laws relating to the backward areas or scheduled districts in Assam, their customary practices.
25.	The Laws of Local Extent Act of 1874	1874 A.D.	Documentary	British government	It describes the laws about the hill areas and scheduled district of Assam.
26.	The Frontier Tracts Regulation II of 1880	1880 A.D.	Documentary	British government	Deals with the laws of hill districts in Assam.

(Contd.)

(Table 14 Contd.)

27.	The Assam Land and Revenue Regulation, 1886	1886 A.D.	Documentary	British government	It belongs to the land law and revenue system in Assam.
28.	The Government of India Act, 1919	1919 A.D.	Documentary	British government	Concerned with the laws in relation to Governor in Assam
29.	The Government of India Act, 1935	1935 A.D.	Documentary	British government	Deals with the laws of Indian administration and federal system.
30.	The Indian Independence Act, 1947	1947 A.D.	Documentary	British government	It deals with the laws relating to India, Pakistan, new Constitution, crown Independence, legislature etc.
31.	The Constitution of India.	1950 A.D.	Documentary	Government of India	It is concerned with the laws relating to the union and its territories, citizenship, fundamental rights, laws for scheduled tribes, schedule castes, election, finance, property and all other social, political, economic aspects of the citizen of India.
32.	The Assam Land (Requisition and Acquisition) 2nd amendment Act, 1950	1950	Documentary	Government of Assam	Deals with the laws of requisition and acquisition of land in Assam
33.	The Municipal Act, (amendment) 1958	1958	Documentary	Government of Assam	Concerned with the laws of Municipality in Assam
34.	The Assam Legislative assembly members salaries and allowances (amendment) Act, 1965	1965	Documentary	Government of Assam	It deals with the laws relating to the Salaries and allowances of MLA in Assam.
35.	The Assam Fixation of Ceiling on Land Holdings (amendment) Act, 1972	1972	Documentary	Government of Assam	Concerned with the laws relating to the fixation of ceiling on land holding in Assam.

(Contd.)

(Table 14 Contd.)

36.	The Assam Schedule Caste and Schedule Tribe (Reservation of vacancies in services and posts) Act, 1978	1978	Documentary	Government of Assam	Concerned with the laws regarding the S.C. and S.T. in case of reservation of vacancies in services etc.
37.	The Customary Laws and Practices of the Pati-Rabha of Assam.	1979	Documentary (Report)	The Law Research Institute, High Court Guwahati.	This report deals with customary law and practices of Pati-Rabha society i.e., social background, the family, marriage system, divorce, adoption, fostering, minority, guardianship, gifts, will, debts, etc.
38.	A Study of the Land System of North Eastern Region.	1982	Documentary (Report)	The Law Research Institute, H.C.	It describes the evolution of tenures which deals with integration disintegration of Assam, evolution of tenures in Brahmaputra valley, Barak valley, Tribal belt, Char areas, land system in Autonomous hill districts, land reforms etc.
39.	The Assam Panchayati Raj (amendment) Act	1990	Documentary	Government of Assam	Concerned with the laws relating the Panchayat system in Assam.
40.	The Boroland Autonomous Council Act.	1992	Documentary	Government of Assam	It deals with the laws relating to the land for Bodo tribe in Assam.
41.	Criminal Justice System in Assam.		Documentary (Report)	The Law Research Institute, H.C. Guwahati	This seminar report contain the outcome of a seminar organised by the LRI. It highlighted and discusses the various problems faced by the judiciary in the state of Assam.

(Contd.)

(Table 14 Contd.)

42.	Drug Abuse and its Statutory Control.	1993	Documentary	The Law Research Institute, H.C. Guwahati	It deals with the profiles of the drug abuses, social background of the drug abuses, cases of drug abuse, traditions and relevant statutory laws etc.
43.	Tribal Traditions and Development in Relation to Hill Areas of Assam.	1996	Documentary (Report)	Tribal Research Institute, Guwahati.	The seminar report includes the customary laws of the hill tribes Karbi traditions, tribal traditional institutions in Assam etc.
44.	Tengapani Deori Deva Mandir Parichalana aru Samajik puja patolor niyamaboli.	1998	Documentary (book form)	Edited by Khagendra Nath Deori.	It describes the rules for maintaining the social, religious rites and customary laws of Tengapani Deoris in Sivasagar district of Assam.

References

1. Tassadque Hussain, Customary Law and Indian Constitution, 1st ed. New Delhi, Rima Publishing, 1987 p. 3.

2. Jeuti Barooah, Customary law of the hill tribes and their relation to development in the hill areas of Assam. A semmier on 'Tribal traditions and development in relation to hill areas of Assam' held at TRI, Ghy, (19th Sept-21st Sept.' 96).

3. B.S. Sinha, Jurisprudence, Allahabad, Central law 1987, p. 220.

4. R.R. Maurya, Hindu Law, Allahabad, Central law, 1985, pp. 29-30.

5. The other sources of Hindu Law are-1.Veda, 2. Smriti, 3. Legislation and 4. Precedent.

6. *Ibid*. p. 24.

7. Encyclopaedia Britannica, Vol. 3, 15th ed, Chicago, Ency. Brit. Inco, 1985, p. 871.

8. In considering whether a custom is reasonable or unreasonable one should not be influenced or guided by modern ideas, for that which appears to be unreasonable to us now may have been considered as eminently reasonable and necessary for the growth and well-being of a community in the by-gone ages.

9. Vide clause 5 (3) of the sixth schedule of the Constitution.

10. L. Collingwood, ed. 21st Century Universal Encyclopaedia, Sydney, Regney Publishing, Vol. 28, 1996, pp. 284-285.

11. David G. Mandelbaum, Society in India, Vol. II, Bombay, Popular Prakashan, pp. 1-2.

12. Webster's Comprehensive Dictionary, A.H. Marckward and Cassidy, ed. Vol. I, Chicago, J.G. Ferguson, Publishing, 1997. p. 207.

13. Ram Ahuja, Indian Social System, New Delhi, Rawat pubn, 1994, p. 239.

14. Census of India 1991, Directorate of Census Operation, Assam p. IX (introduction).

15. Directorate of the Tribal Research Institution, Ghy, Government of Assam.

16. *Ibid.*

17. Directorate of Census Operation, Ghy, Assam, Census of India. 1991.

18. Upendra Goswami, An Introduction to the Deori Languages Ghy, ABILAC, 1994. p. 1-3.

19. P.N. Bharali, Economic transition of tribal society: a report In. Bulletin of TRI, Vol. I, No-III, 1985, p. 65.

20. Imperial Gazetteer of India, Eastern Bengal and Assam, 1909, pp. 590. See also Asomor Janajati, ed. by P. Bhattachaarya, Ghy, Lawyers book stall, 1962, p. 87.

21. Directorate of Census operation, Assam, Census of India, 1991, p. 113.

22. Upendra Goswami, Deori-Chutiya', In: Asomor Janajati, ed. by P.C. Bhattacharya, 2nd ed., Guwahati, Lawyers book stall, 1991, pp. 86-102. See also Ganak Deori, Deori Sakalar atit aru bartaman, In: Asomor Janajati.

23. B.N. Bordoloi and others ed., Tribes of Assam Part-I, 1st ed., Guwahati, TRI, 1987, p. 27.

24. The Hindu law enactments passed in 1955 and 1956 lay down that their provisions will not apply to the members of the scheduled tribes coming within the meaning of clause (25) of Article 366 of the Constitution of Indian unless the Central Government by notification in the official Gazette directs that any of the enactments shall apply to them also.

    In Satish Chandra Vs. Bagram-

    Parties belonged to the Bodo-Kachari caste which is ST in the state of Assam. Two brothers A and B formed a joint Hindu family. A died leaving his widow and his brother B (Bagram), Widow's name was mutated in revenue records in place of A. In 1962 widow made a gift of property in favour of Satish Chandra who filed a suit for declaration of his title and recovery of possession.

It was held that the provision of Hindu Succession Act would not be applicable to them, as no notification to this effect has yet been issued by the central Govt. Under the prior Hindu law the daughter was not entitled to get a share in her father's property in the presence of a son, grandson or greatgrandson. The Hind succession Act 1956 makes both son and daughter as heirs. The daughter has been given share equal to that of a son, she takes now simultaneously with the son. R.R. Maurya, Hindu Law, pp. 8 and 275.

25. S.K. Chatterji, The Place of Assam in the History of Civilisation of India, Deptt of pubn, University of Gauhati, 1970, pp. 6-7.

26. The Tribal Research Institute, Bulletin, Vol. I, no-II, 1984, Ghy, p. 39.

27. B.Narzi, Bodo Kacharir Samaj aru Sanskriti, Guwahati, 1966, pp. 139. See also- B.N.Bordoloi and others ed., Tribes of Assam, T.R.I, Guwahati, 1987, pp. 5-7.

28. Mohini Mohan Brahma, A Brief Introduction of the Bodo Kacharis of Assam, In: Bulletin of TRI., Assam, Vol. I., no-I, 1983, pp. 52-53.

29. The word 'Hathachuni' literally means distribution of rice by the bride with a wooden ladle. *Ibid.*

30. Junior levirate marriage i.e., the younger brother marrying the wife of his elder brother on the event of his (elder brother's) death. The senior is the converse.

31. i.e., on the event of death of one's wife, the younger sister of the deceased wife (if not married till then) can be taken as a wife. Senior is the vice-versa.

32. a bitter tasting dried leafy substance.

33. B.N. Bordoloi and others, Tribes of Assam, Part-I, Ghy, T.R.I, 1987, pp. 15-16.

34. G.C. Sharma Thakur, The Autochthones of the Brahmaputra Valley and their contributions towards the Cultural Heritage of Assam, In: Bulletin, Vol. I, no-II, 1984, TRI, Guwahati, p. 41.

35. D.P. Mukherjee and S.K. Mukherjee, Contemporary Cultural and Political Movement among the Bodos of Assam. A Seminar paper included in 'Tribal movement in India', Vol. I, ed. by K.S. Singh and published by Monohar, 1982, p. 235.

36. Gayan-Bayan- is a religious dance sequence propounded by Mahapurush Srimanta Sankardev.

37. B.N. Bordoloi and G.C. Sharmah Thakur, Tribes of Assam, Part-II, Guwahati, TRI, 1988, pp. 85-86. See also Labhit Saikia, Sonowal Kacharir Sonskriti, Dibrugarh, Labhit Saikia, 1981, pp. 6-7.

38. *Ibid*. p. 91.

39. J.Gogoi, Mikir, In: Asomor Janajati, ed by Promod Bhattacharya. Lawyers book stall, Guwahati 1991, p. 126.

40. B.K. Baruah, A Cultural History of Assam (early period), Guwahati, Bina Library, 1969, p. 6.

41. B.N. Bordoloi and others, Tribes of Assam, 1st ed. Ghy, TRI, 1987, pp. 56. See also J. Gogoi, Mikir, In: Asomor Janajati, p. 119.

42. belief that all objects (trees, stones, the wind etc. have souls).

43. B.C. Allen. 1906, Assam District Gazetteers, Vol. III, Lakhimpur, Chap. IV, p. 118.

44. B.N. Bordoloi and others, Tribes of Asam, Part-I, p. 109.

45. *Ibid*.

46. Based on the statement of Sri Anjan Teron the Lyndokpo of Amri.

47. The above account on offences are based on the statements made during the interviews.

48. The Holy Qur'an, trans. by Muhammad Ali, Lahore Ahmadiyyah Anjuman Isshaat Islam, 1st ed., 1996, pp. 186-187.

49. *Ibid.*

50. i.e., this section permits polygamy under certain circumstances. Polygamy is in Islam is both in theory and in practice an exception, not a rule and as an exception it is remedy for many of the evils. Prostitution, the great evil of civilization caused the polygamy to be allowed as a remedial measure.

51. *Ibid*, p. 1069.

52. The first in the period ending with the lives of those Muslims who had lived during the lifetime of the Prophet and these men, those who had the previlege of meeting and coming into contract with him, are known as Companions of the Prophet or briefly speaking Companions. The second age covers the lives of persons who not being Companions themselves, lived during the lifetime of and came into contract with any of the Companions. These were known as successors of the Companions or successors (taba'un). The third age is Conterminous with the lives of persons who not being successors themselves, lived during the lifetime of and came into contract with any of the successors, called succcessors of the successors of the companions. (taba 'taba' in) See A. Rahim, Muhammedan Jurisprudence, Allahabad, Allahabad law agency, n.d., p. 47.

53. The Hadis Sharif, Edited by Rafiqueullah, 1st ed., Calcutta, Haraf Prakashani, 1979.

54. *Ibid.* pp. 18, 62, 114.

    See also Hadish Shangraha Compiled by Jalil Ahshan Nadbhi, 2nd ed., Guwahati, Asomiya Islami Sahitya Prakashan Samity, 1995, pp. 45, 56, 143.

55. S. Radhakrishan, the Bhagavadgita, 2nd ed., New Delhi, Blackie & Son, 1977, p. 340.

56. *Ibid.*, p. 341.

57. *Ibid.*, pp. 112-113.

58. *Ibid.*, p. 92.

59. *Ibid.*, p. 93.

60. Kirtana-Ghosa aru Nama-Ghosa, by Srimanta Sankaradeva, Srimanta Madhavdeva, Dibrugarh, Basudev Chutia, 1985, p. 21.

5

Conclusion

Introduction

Jonathan Swift said in his novel *'Gulliver's Travels'* man is a social animal[1]. Yes, even the modern and enlightened man cannot but realize the truth behind the statement when the society is constrained by all the laws, rules and regulations that are prevailing. Common practices have been adopted and been customarily formalised for man and from time immemorial and they have remained the controlling and guiding force in various aspects of man's life. In ancient time, untill these controlling rules were codified as laws in the present time in personal matter, customs were the guiding rules. Laws have also been amended time to time according to the need of the hour. The instance is the forming of a committee to review the Indian Constitution.

I am stating below in brief the observations recorded in detail in the chapters on the basis of thorough study of the legal literature as well as analysis of the survey reports in this work.

Findings

(a) *The legal system and its development throughout the ages :* In the eye of justice based on modern law, all are treated equally whether he or she is high or low either in caste or status or education etc. But both in ancient and medieval legal administration and social custom in India much discrimination was made between high and low caste and between men and women.

In ancient time religion was more powerful than the sovereign and king's power was dominated by religious thinking. As regards to legal system in medieval period of Assam, with the help of council of ministers, the king administered the provinces where severity and retaliation were the guiding principle of the panel code. But, the Muslim legal administration was based on religious tradition and scripture or shariat. The 'paik' and 'khel' system of Ahom administration depicts the picture of the practices prevailed among the people in Assam. Unlike the ancient and medieval period of Assam, in the modern period, law is based on the concept of democracy, liberty and equality. Modern laws provide constitutional rights to the citizens of the country. At present, daughter can inherit the property, widow can marry under Hindu Family Law. But, in respect of civil code, the distinction has remained same among the Hindus and Muslims. This should be constitutionally amended for uniform civil code. This common or uniform civil code would help and accelerate national intregation.

(b) *Customs and original literature of modern law :* The dimension of the society is too big to be managed without rules, regulations, statutory laws and government notifications. The societies of general communites and some other tribes and castes of developed areas in Assam have been involved with the country laws in case of disposing their legal matters. It has been found that there are some sources of these laws which had existed in ancient and medieval periods in the form of non-documentary or informal form e.g., *The Veda,* in the oral form and the *Hadith* as tradition. Gradually this had been transformed into documentary forms. But some of them remained in the original form. Traditions and customs represent such abiding laws among different communities and social groups. The customary practices or customs and tradition relating to different fields are more in quantities in case of tribal people compared to other groups of people due to apparent reasons i.e. lack of education, religious faith, conservativeness etc. It is also remarkable that the same sources may be the origin for general laws as well as customary laws. For instance, the two literary documents, *the Qur'an* and *the Hadith* are the sources of present general laws and customary laws derived for Muhammedans in there personal laws.

A development of literature related to law embodying customs and traditions is now evident as laid down specially in the fourth chapter of this report (pp. 195-208, Chap-IV).

It has been observed that the existing laws in different fields of activities are not of recent origin. The origin of these had evolved in the ancient time. The Section 100 of Indian Penal Code, 1860 describes 'the Right of Private Defence' of the body extends to causing death, origin of which may be traced from the revelation of the Lord Krishna in the battlefield of Kurukshetra, when Arjuna hesitated to fight and kill his relatives and other known honourable warriors. The present civil and criminal aspects of law have been found in the literature originated centuries ago in the form of *Manusmriti* and in the later publications like *Arthashastra, Narada smriti,* etc. (pp. 80-83, chap-III). It is seen that the definition of partnership given by *Yajnavalkyasmriti* is same as provided by the Indian 'Partnership' Act, 1932 in section

4. The concept of divorce, or remarriage on the grounds of impotency of husband, death, etc. have been found in the *Narada smriti,* which is a chapter under present Hindu Marriage Act, 1955. The rule embodied in *Katyayana smriti* is similar to the rule of constructive res-judicata contained in Explanation IV to section 11 of the Civil Procedure Code 1859 (pp. 86-87, Chap-III). It has been found that Brihaspati was the first jurist to make clear distinction between civil and criminal justice with legal procedure as examination, cross-examination and re-examination of the witnesses as found today. *Brihaspatismriti* provides the right of inheritance of the widow i.e., freedom of women, 1800 years back from today (pp. 84-85, chap-III). The idea of inclusion of learned and educated persons in the Ministry could be found in *Kalika Purana* (pp. 96, chap-III). Notwithstanding these, the origin of these laws as well as the Smritis, Digests, Commentaries have been influenced by the customs. Similarly the existing laws are also influenced by the customs. During the nineteen-fifties the parliament passed four Acts relating to Hindu law. These are -

(i) The Hindu Marriage Act, 1955;

(ii) The Hindu Succession Act, 1956;

(iii) The Hindu Minority and Guardianship Act, 1956

(iv) The Hindu Adoptions and Maintenance Act, 1956.

In all these Acts a section has been introduced which lays down the overriding effect of these Acts. The provision is thus stated:

> "Save as otherwise expressly provided in this Act .... any custom or usage as part of that law in force immediately before the commencement of that Act, shall cease to have effect with respect to any matter for which provision is made in this Act."[2]

The section clearly indicates that untill the above mentioned four Acts have been passed, matters were settled based on customs and traditions.

Like the above, the provisions of customary practices have been followed traditionally age after age. The existing personal laws of the muslims have been being followed traditionally by the Muhammedans, the basic source or the literature of which are the Qur'an and the Hadith (pp. 177-179, chap-IV).

The customs of giving punishments in various ways in the Ahom administration are evident in the literature like Buranji (pp. 100-102, chap-III). The traditional punishment of extracting eyes had been continuing throughout the Ahom period and took place when the accused was found to be against royal policy. The Jikkir composed in the 17th century describes —

> *"Jetia najar dikhout pelai*
> *ubhati daria boihe*
> *Jetia najarak dikhout pelale*
> *nagarat sara khelai he"*[3]

i.e., as the eyes of Ajan Peer was extracted out and thrown down into the river 'Dikhou', immediately it began to flow in the opposite direction...

Similarly, in case of other offences the punishments had been given according to the traditon or 'Purbanyayik' system i.e., the 'Res-judicata', which being laid in the laws of the country today. Many customs and traditions of general communities gradually have been transformed into the laws so as to follow commonly them after proper codifications Practise of marrying four spouses one after another during their life time in the muslim societies even now has been codified into personal laws, is an instance in this respect.

(c) *The customs and the law in different periods of the country and Assam :*

(i) *In ancient period :* It appears that the religion was more powerful then the sovereign in the country in ancient time. The fact is clear from the statement in *The Veda* that the first source of sacred law is the whole *Veda,* next the traditions and conducts of those who know the *Veda* (pp. 68-79, chap-III). Although justice was administered according to the Dharmashastras, Vedas etc., sources of these were the case- law or vyvahara along with code of sacred laws of the country and king's order. These laws were expounded by the Brahmanas and followed customarily throughout the ages (pp. 47, chap-II). Laws were based on religious scripture and spiritual thinking in this period. The caste prejudice in matters of legal dealings and prejudice against women have been found in the country including Assam in ancient and even at present time also (pp. 188-193, chap-IV).

(ii) *In the medieval period :* The laws were reformulated and modified according to the tradition, convenience and religious fanaticism. Application of laws and traditions by Muslim rulers in the country and Ahom rulers in Assam have been witnessing the fact. Customs and traditions were followed in the 'khel' and 'paik' system in Assam. The king who administer the justice with the help of council of minister was the fountain head of justice. In this period law is not based on democracy, liberty and equality. Prevailing practice of untouchability among the high castes and restriction of widow re-marriage among the Hindus specially in case of Brahmins indicate the existence of caste prejudice on the one hand, and lesser freedom of Hindu women than the social groups like Muslims and tribal groups on the other hand.

(iii) *In the modern period :* In the modern peroid, law is based on justice on the concepts of democracy, liberty and equality in the democratic countries like India. Most of the legal matters prevailing in the present legal system are found to be the derivation of Smriti age (pp. 80-84, chap-III). Most of the present laws are found as religious customs of ancient time, e.g. as regards to women in the *Bhagavadgita*, it is stated that when lawlessness prevails, the women of the family become corrupted and when women are corrupted confusion of castes arises (pp. 183, chap-IV). It clearly indicates that the ancient society was regulated by laws in the form of religious customs found in the religious scriptures. Kautilya accorded equal status to men and women in contrast to later development in Hindu law through customs (pp. 91, chap-III).

Though the Buranjis and informal types of literature like epigraphic sources, inscriptions and some reports of foreign travellers have been given enormous information in relation to legal aspects in medieval period of India including Assam, still many others have to be searched for study and research.

(iv) *Customs and socio-legal aspects in the tribal and hill areas of Assam :* While disputes were resolved according to the principles laid down in the Smritis and the Dharmasutras in the rest of India in the ancient time, in the tribal and hill areas of Assam these were settled on the basis of perennial customs which are still prevailing. However, the influence of Hindu religious philosophy is found in most tribal customs.

The saivism of Hindu trinity has been reflected in the religious philosophy of Bodo-Kachari. Influence of Hinduism upon this tribe has been observed in case of marriage ceremony and death rites. On the other hand, more freedom and status to women amongst the Sonowal Kacharis have been found in comparison to Hindu women. The liberal attitude in case of widow remarriage, freedom in selection of groom and no system of brideprice amongst the Karbis are praiseworthy. Although, consideration of nominal bride-price rather indicates the status of Mishing women. All these tribal groups do not have much discrimination in case of caste, religion and women except that of Deori people who have been found discriminating in case of castes.

The different tribal groups in Assam have their own customs and traditions which are more in quantities than the general communities or the castes. Some of them are transformed into codified laws after analysis in the courts. These tribal groups which are inhabitants of backward areas in several respects like communication, education, pecuniary position, etc. are still themselves away from the jurisdiction of the laws of the country.

Though under the provisions of the Sixth Schedule, the Regional Councils and District Councils of the tribal areas are empowered to make laws with respect to land, forest, water course, inheritance of property, marriage and divorce and other social customs the councils have not achieved proper measures to enlighten these people.

Deoris : It has been found from the investigation that the Deori people are still expected to follow what the Bordeori says like the king. Nobody is allowed to protest or raise objection to his judgement. The Dibangia Deori sect has their own language, they have their counting book in own language which is known as "Jimsoyan Jugiba" published by Deori Sahitya Sabha. The Tengapania Deori sect has their legal literature in written form to dispose of the cases as referred, to in appropriate page in this report. The pioneer person of Deori society, and culture, Bhimbor Deori made efforts to step with equal footing of the developed societies. Nevertheless, their traditional beliefs and practices have stood on the way in the present age of information technology also to have information and knowledge from outside world.

Karbis : During the recent years the Karbi society has undergone transformation and changes. The grip of inertia in which this society was found in the past, has now been slackened. In this connection, the pioneering leadership was given by late Khorsing Terang who was not only the first Chief Executive Member of the Karbi Anglong District Council but also the first Member of the Assam Legislative Assembly from the Karbi community.

From the point of view of folk-lores and folk-songs, the Karbis are very rich. They have their own version of the *Ramayana* called *Sabin Alun* which has been handed from generation to generation orally and it is certainly a source of legal information as mentioned earlier. In the literary field prof. Rangbang Terang, Mr. Longkam Teron, Mr. Samsing Hanse, Mr. Lunse Timung, Mr. Song Bey, Mrs. Sathi Teronpi have made significant contributions for the development of Karbi literature. The Karbi women have also been coming up to accept the challenge of transition. Mrs. Banali khongman, the first Karbi women graduate, had not only headed Assam Public Service Commission but headed later on the Union Public Service Commission too. Even accepting the traditional beliefs and customary practices now the Karbi people, even the girls are now coming forward for higher education in greater numbers.

The Karbis living within the jurisdiction of the Karbi Anglong District have their own District Council which is managed by their own people. In the Karbi villages, the receipt of less number of cases by the headmen have been witnessing the existence of peaceful life in their own places. But the presence of several extremist groups and activities of anti-social elements is an another chapter attached to the history of the peace loving community.

Bodo-Kacharis : In case of Bodo-Kacharis recently, the government of Assam has announced the demarcation line for Bodo land comprising the major Bodo predominent areas in Assam. The Bodo Autonomous Council will have the right in law to administer the concerned people of the said areas. Nevertheless, the traditional institutions like 'Raijani Metheng' have the important role in legal administration so far. It is presided over by the village headmen petty cases, social crimes arising out of disobedience to customary rules and rituals are tried by this institution like the Kebang of Mishing tribe. Since they have their own language, in Bodo dominant areas like Kokrajhar and areas in Dhubri district instruction in the primary schools is given through the medium of mother tongue. The Bodo Sahitya Sabha have been playing a significant role in promoting Bodo literature and culture. Several literature like *Bodo-Kacharir Jana Sahitya, Bodo-Kacharir Samaj aru Sanskriti* by Dr Promod Chandra Bhattacharya, etc. have drawn the vivid picture of Bodo-Kachari culture and customs. The government of Assam has made efforts for their development in some aspects, specially in the Bodo-dominant areas. Even the solar energy centres to support the technology like Television. has been set up in these areas. Nonetheless the traditional, social and religious life which embrace the legal aspects also, are still on vogue with all their traditional beliefs and customs in the same areas.

Mishings : In respect of Mishing societies, although the Mishings are maintaining the traditional or customary cultural pattern, some changes have been noticed in their life and culture which are affecting the core of their culture.

Changes are noticed in respect of religious beliefs and customary practices as Baishnavism has penetrated into their culture. Due to large scale contact with the non-Mishings, the Mishings are gradually entering into avocations which were till recently non- existent among them. Like the Karbis the educated sections in this group also are hankering after government and professional jobs and today the number of employees like doctors, engineers, teachers among them are not negligible. The Mishing villages like in Dishangmukh are located in far flung riverine areas and one will find medical dispensary, development block office in the central place of the villages. The villagers are adopting allopathic treatment but a large section are still depending upon the indegenous treatment because of poverty. Sri Atul Taye, the headmaster of local Lower Primary School had informed that a lot of scholars have surveyed their society, even someone came from Italy recently to their place and the people of Mishing society are eager to enlighten about their culture to the outside world. It is observed/that lower primary schools have been established in almost all villages; and the grammar like *Mishing Grammar* written by Bal Ram Prasad, edited by G. Devi Prasad Sastry and P.T. Abraham has assisted in promoting their language. Recently Mishing language has been accepted as a medium of instruction in Lower Primary schools in Mishing dominated areas.

Sonowal Kacharis : The socio-economic set up of the Sonowal Kacharis has undergone tangible changes. There have arisen a number of semi urban growth centres due to infra-stractural developments in the post independent period. The people are more conscious about economic and educational development. The roads connecting the villages, as observed in different districts like Dibrugarh, Jorhat, Sibsagar, etc/served as catalyst in spreading the modern cultures and value systems generated in towns into their society. Change is also noticed in the material culture including dress and food habits. The people prefer to build up modern Assam type houses. The religion and culture of the neighbouring non Sonowal Hindus has made tangible impact on their socio-religious life and the process of assimilation is visible. However, customary practices are still followed in social, religious and legal aspects. Like the other Hindus, this tribal group also regards the Namghar as the centre for solving disputes arisen out of local matters. Excommunication is noticed similarly as occured in the Hindu societies like Koch, Kalita, Kaibarta, etc. as a social practice.

Dimasa Kacharis : The Dimasa Kacharis are a peace loving tribe. Being cut off from the main stream of national life for generations, the culture and traditional customs of the Dimasas have remained more or less unaffected. But this does not mean that changes are not coming to them. Because of the expansion of education and development activities in different spheres changes are gradually coming to their life and culture. Among the prominent personalities mention may be made of late Joybahadur Hagjer and late Surath Chandra Daulagopu who were Ministers of Cabinet Rank. The Dimasa living within the jurisdiction of North Cachar Hills district have an Autonomous District Council under the Sixth Schedule of the Constitution of India. They are now managing their own affairs. Nonetheless, due to following, still some of the customary practices as in case of marriage disputes, bride disputes etc., they are suffering much without their knowledge of it. The same consequences has been observed from performances of the traditional institutions like 'Kebang' and 'Salis' the village council of Dimasas.

(e) *Adoptable, non-adoptable customs and prejudicial beliefs at present in Assam:* (i) Among the general communities: In spite of freedom givren by the Hindu Marriage Act, 1955 to Hindu windows for remarriage, society yet doesnot approve it practically. Inspite of willingness by some of the widows they donot dare to remarry in fear of social taboo. There are rare cases of widows marrying again only falling in love either with approval or without approval from the families concerned.This social practices should be abolished and freedom should be given to the Hindu widows.

The practices of non-permission to the Muslim women to join the Idd-gah and Friday prayers (Jumma namaz) should be legally and socially abolished. It is good sign that about 500 Muslim women have completed their Namaz at Maj gaon Idd-gah field at Dol gaon constituency of Darrang district in the year 2000, daring to break the social custom, for the first time in Assam.This social and religious custom of depriving the Muslim women should not be adopted in the rest of the country also.

The dowry system prevailing among the general communities in the different states of India still followed by the people inspite of Anti Dowry Act passed by the Parliament.The social practice of demand of dowry in marriages could not be prevented by the Anti Dowry Act, although the Act has helped the concern parties against the torture and death of the bride after marriage. This social practice should be condemned by each and every responsible citizen of India and no responsible people should make neither any dowry demand nor accepting the dowry demand. In the North Eastern States fortunately there is no social custom of dowry demand, although parents are giving whatever they like to their daughters. Strong punishment should be given so that dowry demand may totally disappear form the society.

The practice of three talaqs which gives immense freedom to the menfolk amoung the Muslims is very much prejudicial against the existence of women which should be legally abandoned. It is unfortunate that the practice is still legally accepted as Muslim personal law, although there are much controversies and objections against this socio-religious practice. All these prejudicial social and socio-religious practices should be abolished by the proper interference and public movement.

(ii) *Among the tribal people in Assam:* A traditional co-operative system of Karbis is 'Kerung Amei' the grain bank, now almost lost their original significance. Karbi should move to revive its original significance. The customs of secrecy i.e., keeping silent about the socio-religious practices and beliefs amongst the Deori people which have been observed in Tengapani area of Sibsagar district should be abolished by a movement of educated people of concerned areas.The customary law of junior levirate marriage (i.e., the younger brother marrying the wife of his elder brother on the event of his elder brother's death) of Bodo-Kachari, Dimasa-Kachari, which is a prevalent practice among them may be approved in case of other communities also.

The system of succession and inheritance depriving the womenfolk under the customary practices of Deoris, Bodo-Kacharis, Dimasa-Kacharis, Mishings should be abolished by government interference and public movement. This may be replaced by an Act like Hindu Succession Act, 1956. This custom in Hindu society has been abolished legally by Jawaharlal Neheru the then Prime Minister of India, with the above mentioned Act. The prejudicial beliefs and practices like 'Santi Deo Sakam' of Deoris, which is performed in order to getting relief of disease should be abolished and analysed logically.The Mishing people of Daibari Lakhimi pathar Mishing gaon of Sibsagar district and the people of Mishing gaon near Gelabill of Golaghat district have been found blindly worshipping various types of spirits for getting relief of diseases as they are ignorant of scientific reasons of their ailments. A Mishing woman namely Panimola Pegu of Lakhimi pathar Mishing gaon stated with grief that she has lost five young sons and daughters without knowing about the diseases they had suffered from.The reasons behind these types of victimisation should be brought into notice and traditional practices of blindly worshipping behind these types of sufferings should be abolished through public movement and interferences undertaken by the educated youths. On the otherhand, some people have been victimised specially in the tribal areas of Assam due to superstitious beliefs about 'witchcrafts', which should be logically varified and abolished through public movement and made legally punishable (pp. 186, Chap-IV).

It has been found from the present study that the oral or non-documentary or informal literature comprising the customary practices in each tribal group are enormous, but in recorded form are negligible. It is a difficult work to collect information of entire tribal groups and local inhabitants of Assam, about their legal aspect and customary practices and literature. Particularly, the tribal people of backward areas of plain and hills have been lagging behind in socio-economic and cultural aspects than other communities in Assam. They have not been able to enjoy the opportunities offered by the Govt. The justice which are available in the courts of law have not been availed of due to their traditional beliefs on customs. Besides, these people have been suffering from many problems and grievances along with the general people of backward areas in Assam. With these end in view the following recommendations have been made in order to meet the aforesaid problems :

Recommendations

(1) Every aspect of the tribal and backward communities in the region should be taken into account when we talk and wish to develop their present socio-economic status along with the other developed societies around them. Their social,

economical, cultural life must be upgraded in order to enable them to take the challenge of the modern age so as to be able usher in a new and healthy outlook for themselves. In this case the prevailing harmful or non-harmful customary practices must be abolished or modified locally, if not, by government interference. On the whole, the enlightened world must realise its responsibility towards the backward communities which exist in both the plains and hills.

(2) Education with the philosophy of selfreliance must be given to the tribal children whose personalities must be oriented towards high degree of achievement in all-round welfare. Through education, efforts must be made to do away with their superstitions merged in customs and traditions with regard to human destination. As such, science educational programmes for the tribal communities may suit well for the purpose.

(3) Institutional frameworks must be provided to the tribal youths in particular for special incentive programme for diversified modern occupation involving science and technology. Government machineries, banks, corporations and voluntary organisations should participate with more liberal attitude in implementing the various developmental schemes for the tribals. The government agencies have to play the leading role in true implementation of the development programmes.

(4) Of all the developmental programmes, priorities must be given to development of roads and communications, improvement of public health, development in agricultural production and

availability of capital through bank and corporation for undertaking small scale industries. The tribals, particularly the educated youths must be induced to take up non-agricultural occupations such as business enterprises, agro-industries, manufacturing industries, and other types of trades and commerce. The present socio-economic conditions of the tribal people of Assam are such that most of them cannot afford to borrow from the commercial banks for business undertakings. The tribal development commission of government of Assam, therefore, must act as substitute of the banks for the tribal enterpreneurs.

(5) The permanent legal information centres should be set-up at first for two areas namely at Dibrugarh for Upper Assam and Guwahati for lower Assam so that the research scholars, aspirants and the common people can acquire the necessary information they seek.

(6) The literary documents regarding socio-cultural, religious, economic information as well as non documentary information specially of all the tribal groups, along with castes and other communities should be documented and preserved and made available through machine readable system.

(7) The office for case-study records and related information should be set up in every concerned court so as to get benefit by the research scholars and concerned personnel for legal settlements.

(8) The meetings, seminars should be organised highlighting the matter relating to harmful traditional practices and the grievances in other aspects like water, communication, medical treatment in the backward plains and hills of

Assam. Ofcourse, seminars, conferences on the customary laws of the tribal groups in North Eastern Region are being held in place like Guwahati!

(9) The legal literature in English should be translated into the local languages to carry the message in its proper perspective to the common people - the legitimate beneficiary of democracy. The government monopoly in publications should be withdrawn in the greater interest of the people.

(10) Keeping in view of the importance of the Mishing and Karbi weaving Industry for the development of their economy, the authorities concerned should pay more attention to the problems pertaining to revival, çombination of traditions with modern technology, popularization of their products, promotion of internal and external marketing, availability of raw materials, for a faster pace of development of their cottage industries.

(11) In this age of population explosion it is essential to prevent the laws like personal laws of Muslims by which maximum four spouses are allowed to marry by a person one after another during the life time. Besides, there is no family planning among the Muslims in plea of religious taboo. Both these customs have given rises to unplanned big family resulting into economic hardship. Therefore, uniform civil code for both Hindu and Muslim should exist and the harmful socio-religious customs should not be allowed to stand in the path of modernization on scientific line.

Coming towards the conclusion of this research work, the points to be emphasised have been mentioned below.

It is found that there are more to learn from the ancient as well as the medieval administrative rules or strategies including the legal aspects laid down in the literature. The *Arthashastra* of Kautilya dealing with the matter of law and procedures, the instances of justice; the efficient administration under uncorrupted Ahom Kings, Chao-Lung-Siu-Kapha to Purandar Singha in medieval period are worthmentioning. The calm and charm in the life of mostly unpolluted rural tribal people are still found through the customary systems governing the tribal societies, many of which are adoptable in even changed situations. Proper status given to womenfolk, absence of rigid caste, spirit of socialism enabling everyone to share benefits are found due to the customs and traditions prevailing in most of the tribal societies.

Last but not the least It must be mentioned here that though customs, customary practices and traditions and related legal literature have been surveyed for its historical development, it may be concluded bringing into the fact that there are innumberable social customs and traditions which deserved to be codified legally and socially and if necessary, modified according to the prevailing laws of the land. On the otherhand, there are few which are hurmful to the society.

Inspite of my hard labour devoted to this work, I donot claim that the work has been exhaustive. The areas which I could not cover may be taken up by further researches in order to complete the work to the full satisfaction of the society and mankind.

References

1. J. Swift, Gulliver's Travels, 7th ed. New Delhi, Arti Books Centre, 1981, p. 185.
2. R.R.Maurya, Hindu Law, 3rd ed. Allahabad, Central Law Agency, 1985, p. 30.

3. A.Malik, Ajan Fakir Aru Suria Jikkir, 3rd ed.Guwahati, Students Stores, 1999, p. 31

APPENDIX

An Alphabetical List of Indian Legal Periodicals and Law Reports:

Sl. No.	*Title of the Periodicals and Reports.*
(1)	Academy Law Review (Kerala law agency, Trivandraum)
(2)	Accident and Compensation Cases (Delhi)
(3)	Accidents Claims Journal (12, Malkaganj, Delhi) (1966-)
(4)	Accident Judicial Reporter (1992-)
(5)	Administrative Tribunal cases (Eastern book co., Lucknow) (1986-)
(6)	Administrator (Lal Bahadur Shastri National Academy of Administration. Aligarh)
(7)	Agra High Court Reports (1866-1868)
(8)	Ajmer-Merwara Law Journal (1927-1956)
(9)	Aligarh Law Journal (Faculty of law, Aligarh Muslim Univ., Aligarh)
(10)	All India Civil Law Journal (1980-)
(11)	All India Criminal Law Cases (1980-)
(12)	All India Land Law Reporter (1975-)
(13)	All India Land Law Reporter (1979-)
(14)	All India Rent Control Journal (1969-)

(15) All India Reporter (A.I.R Ltd., Nagpur) (1914-)

(16) All India Service Law Journal (1973-)

(17) All India Service Law Reporter (1967-)

(18) All India Transport Accident Cases (1983-)

(19) All India Tribunal Cases (1958-1961)

(20) Allahabad Civil Journal (1978-)

(21) Allahabad Criminal Cases (1964-)

(22) Allahabad Criminal Reports (1953-)

(23) Allahabad Criminal Rulings (1977-)

(24) Allahabad Law Journal (A.I.R. Ltd., Nagpur) (1904-) Vol. 1 to 26 till 1928 after which citation by year.

(25) Allahabad Law Reporter (1920-1947)

(26) Allahabad Law Reporter (1975-)

(27) Allahabad Law Reporter (1920-1947)

(28) Allahabad Law Reporter (1975-)

(29) Allahabad Law Times (1923-) Acts etc only.

(30) Allahabad Rent Cases (1977-)

(31) Allahabad Weekly Cases (1975-)

(32) Allahabad Weekly Cases (1881-1908)

(33) Allahabad Weekly Cases (1935-1977)

(34) Andhra Law Times (Dilsukhnagar, Hyderabad0 (1954-) citation by year.

(35) Andhra Pradesh Law Journal (1969-)

(36) Andhra Pradesh Law Journal (criminal)

(37) Andhra Pradesh Sales Tax journal

(38) Andhra Weekly Reporter (1955-)

(39) Annual Survey of Indian Law (Indian Law Institute., New Delhi)

(40) Arbitration Quarterly (Journal of the Indian Law of Arbitration, New Delhi)

(41) Asian Labour (ICFTU Asian Regional Organisation, New Delhi)

(42) Assam Law Reports (1960)

(43) Awards Digest (Journal of Labour Legislation, National Labour Institute, New Delhi)

(44) Banaras Law Journal (Law School, Banaras Hindu University, Varanasi)

(45) Banker's Journal, Bombay

(46) Bengal Law Reports (1868-1875) except for 1868 other years 2 volumes per year H.C.& P.C rulings

(47) Bengal Law Reports (Full Bench Rulings) 1855

(48) Bhagirath (Business Manager, Publications div. New Delhi)

(49) Bihar Bar Council Journal (1971-)

(50) Bihar Criminal Cases (1975-)

(51) Bihar Law Journal Reports (1953-) citation by year.

(52) Bihar Law Judgements (1978-)

(53) Bihar Law Times (1963-)

(54) Bihar Reports (1935-1947)

(55) Bombay Cases Reporter (1978-)

(56) Bombay H.C Reports (1862-1875)

(57) Bombay H.C. Criminal Ruling (1869-1907)

(58) Bombay H.C. Printed Judgements (1868-1900)

(59) Bombay Law Reporter (Old City Civil Court, Fort, Bombay) (1899-) (Irregular)

(60) Bombay Rent Cases (1979-)

(61) Bombay Unreported Printed Judgements (1872-1900)

(62) Bourke's Reports (Calcutta) (1865-76)

(63) Burma Law Journal (1922-1927)

(64) Burma Law Reports (1948-)

(65) Burma Law Times (1908-1920)

(66) C.B.I. Bulletin (R.K. Puram, New Delhi)

(67) Calcutta H.C. Notes (1974-)

(68) Calcutta Law Journal (1905-) 1905-1959-100 vols. Two vols. per year, later citation by year.

(69) Calcutta Law Reports (1878-1883)

(70) Calcutta Weekly Notes (1897-)

(71) Central Province, Law Reports (1888-1904)

(72) Chandigarh Criminal Cases (1978-)

(73) Chandigarh Law Reporter (1973-)

(74) Chandigarh Law Review

(75) Chartered Secretary (I.C.S.I. House, New Delhi)

(76) Civil and Military Law Journal (Rajouri Garden, New Delhi)

(77) Co-operative Law Journal (1964)

(78) Cochin University Law Review (Dept. of Law, Cochin Univ., Cochin)

(79) Cochin University Law Review (Dept. of Law, Cochin Univ., Cochin)

(80) Company Cases (Company Law Institute of India Ltd, Chennai) (1931-)

(81) Company Law Journal (1963-)

(82) Company News and Notes (Deptt. of Company Affairs, New Delhi)

(83) Company News Reporter (1976-)

(84) Comparative Law Review (Comparative Law Association, Law College, Pondicherry)

(85) Consumer Protection Reporter (1991-)

(86) Crimes (1983-)

(87) Criminal Law Journal (AIR Ltd., Nagpur) (1904-) citation by year after 1951)

(88) Criminal Law Reporter (S.C. & Rajasthan) (1973-)

(89) Criminal Law Reports (S.C. & Madhya Pradesh) (1973-)

(90) Criminal Law Reporter (S.C.& Gujrat & Madhya Pradesh) (1973-)

(91) Current Central Legislation (Eastern book co., Lucknow) (1975-)

(92) Current Civil Cases (1985-)

(93) Current Civil Law Judgements (M.P) (1983-)

(94) Current Criminal Law Judgements (M.P.)

(95) Current H.C. Notes Reports, Calcutta.

(96) Current Indian Statutes (1923-)

(97) Current Labour Reports

(98) Current Law Journal (Civil & Criminal Punjab & Haryana) (1961-)

(99) Current Law Journal (Tax Laws) (1961-)

(100) Current Taxation Reports (1972-)

(101) Cuttack Law Reports (Criminal) (1972-)

(102) Cuttack Law Times (Law Times Press, Cuttack) (1939-)

(103) Cuttack Weekly Reporter (1970-)

(104) Decisions of Sadar Dewani Adalat (1818-1862)

(105) Delhi Law Review (Faculty of Law, Univ of Delhi., Delhi)

(106) Delhi Law Times (Delhi Law Times Office, Delhi) (1965-)

(107) Dominion Law Reporter (DLR) 1943-1953 all courts

(108) Drug Cases (1975-)

(109) Education Cases, Allahabad

(110) Election Law Reports (1951-)

(111) Essential Commodities cases

(112) Excise and Food Adulteration Reports (1982-)

(113) Excise Law Times (1982-)

(114) Factories Journal Reports (1949-)

(115) Federal Court Reports (1939-1949)

(116) Federal Law Journal (1938-1949)

(117) Foreign Trade Review (quarterly journal of Indian Institute of Foreign Trade, New Delhi)

(118) Gandhi Marg (Journal of Gandhi Peace Foundation, New Delhi)

(119) Gujarat H.C. Reporter (1960-1977)

(120) Gujarat Law Herald, Ahmedabad (1981-)

(121) Gujarat Law Reporter (Gandhi road, Ahmedabad) (1960-)

(122) Hindu Law Reporter, Chandigarh

(123) Hydes E. Reports (Bengal H.C. 1862-1863)

(124) Hydes Reports (1897)

(125) ILR (Allahabad) (1875) 58 vols till 1936 citation by year 1937.

(126) ILR(Andhra) (1955) citation by year

(127) ILR (Assam) (1949-)

(128) ILR (Bombay) (1875-60vols. till 1936) citation by year 1937

(129) ILR (Calcutta) (1875 till 1936, 63 vols. till 1936) citation by year from 1937.

(130) ILR (Cuttack) (1949-) citation by year

(131) ILR (Hyderabad) (1951-1956)

(132) ILR (Karachi) (1939-1946)

(133) ILR (Kerala) (1957-)

(134) ILR (Lahore) (1920-1947) from 1936, citation by year

(135) ILR (Lucknow) (1926-1948)

(136) ILR (Madhya Bharat) (1952-1956)

(137) ILR (Madhya Pradesh) (1957)

(138) ILR (Madras) (1876) from 1937 citation by year

(139) ILR Mysore (1951-) followed by ILR Karnataka

(140) ILR (Nagpur) (1936-1956)

(141) ILR (Patiala) (1952-1955)

(142) ILR (Patna) (1922)

(143) ILR (Punjab or East Punjab) (1948-1957)

(144) ILR (Rajasthan) (1951-)

(145) ILR (Rangoon) (1923-1936)

(146) ILR (Travancore- Cochin) (1951-1956)

(147) Income Tax and Tribunal Cases (1963-)

(148) Income Tax Cases vols.1 to 10 (1886-1937)

(149) Income Tax Journal (1963-)

(150) Income Tax Reports (Company Law Institute of India Ltd., Madras) 1933-)

(151) Income Tax Tribunal Decisions (1982-)

(152) Index to Indian Legal Periodicals (ICI)

(153) Indian Advocate (Bar Association of Indian, S.C. of India, New Delhi)

(154) Indian Appeals (L.R. 1872-1950)

(155) Indian Bar Review.

(156) Indian Cases (1909-1947) vols. 1-231

(157) Indian Decisions (Bombay H.C. & P.C., 1875-1878)

(158) Indian Decisions- New Series- (1862-1875)

(159) Indian Decisions-Old Series (O.S.) (1774-1858)

(160) Indian Economic and Social History Review (Delhi School of Economics, Univ. of Delhi, Delhi)

(161) Indian Factories Journal and Factories Journal Reports (Laws of India Pvt. Ltd, Madras) (FJR) (1960-)

(162) Indian Factories Journal Report (1949-)

(163) Indian H.C. Reports (Bombay-1901-1906)

(164) Indian H.C. Reports (Cal-1901-1906)

(165) Indian Journal of Industrial Relations (Shri Ram Centre for Industrial & Human Resources, New Delhi)

(166) Inian Journal of International Law (Indian Society of International Law (Indian society of International Law, New Delhi)

(167) Indian Journal of Legal Studies (Faculty of Law, Univ. of Jodpur, Jodpur)

(168) Indian journal of public administration (Indian institute of public administration, New Delhi)

(169) Indian Journal of Social Works (Deptt. of pubns. Tutu Institute of Social sciences, Bombay)

(170) Indian Jurists (1877-1893)

(171) Indian Labour Journal (Labour Bureau, Simla)

(172) Indian Law Index, Monthly (1990-)

(173) Indian Police Journal (Indian Police Journal, New Delhi)

(174) Indian Quarterly (Indian Council of World Affairs, New Delhi)

(175) Indian Rulings (IR) (1929-1947)

(176) Indian Socio-Legal Journal (Indian Institute of Comparative Law, Bikaner)

(177) Islamic and comparative Law Quarterly (Deptt of Islamic & Comparative Law, Indian institute of Islamic Studies, New Delhi)

(178) Jabalpur Law Journal, Gwalior (1957-)

(179) Jaipur Law Journal (JLT Studies in Law, Univ. of Rajasthan, Jaipur)

(180) Jammu and Kashmir Law Report (1948-)

(181) Johnston & Co Reprint. Selection from Reports on Civil Cases in Punjab Record 1886-1900 (Lahore-1915)

(182) Journal of Islamic and Comparative Law (Delhi)

(183) Journal of Parliamentary Information (Lok Sabha Secretariat, Parliament House, New. Delhi)

(184) Journal of Shipping Customs Law (1974-)

(185) Journal of the Bar Council of India (Bar Council of India, New Delhi)

(186) Journal of the Constitutional & Parliamentary Studies (Institute of Constitutional & Parliamentary Studies, New Delhi)

(187) Journal of the Indian Law Institute (ILI, New Delhi)

(188) Journal of the Indian Society of Criminology.

(189) Journal of the Indian Society of International Law.

(190) Judgements on Hesman Rights Indian Social Institute, New Delhi)

(191) Karnataka Law Chronicle (1982-)

(192) Karnataka Law Journal (1923-)

(193) Karnataka Law Journal (Shankarapuram, Bangalore)

(194) Kashmir Law Journal (1962-)

(195) Kerala Law Journal (1957-)

(196) Kerala Law Reporter (1959-)

(197) Kerala Law Times (1949-)

(198) Knapp's Reports (P.C.) 1829-36 (1829-31, 1831-34, 1834-36)

(199) Kurukshetra Law Journal (Faculty of Law, Kurukshetra Univ. Kurukshetra)

(200) Labour and Industrial Cases (AIR Ltd. Nagpur) (1968-)

(201) Labour Appeal Cases (1954)

(202) Labour Law Journal (1949)

(203) Lahore Law Journal (1919-126)

(204) Lahore Law Times (1922-)

(205) Law Quaterly (ILI, West Bengal State Unit, Calcutta)

(206) Law Reporter (by J.G. Shome Judgments of Cal. H.C. & P.C) 1878-1881

(207) Law Reporter Allahabad (1920-1936)

(208) Law Weekly (1914-)

(209) Law Weekly (criminal) (1968-)

(210) Lawyer (Journal of the ILI, Madras State Unit, Madras)

(211) Lawyers Collective (Bombay)

(212) Lok Udyog (Bureau of Public Enterprises, Ministry of Finance, Govt of India, New Delhi)

(213) Lower Burma Rulings (1900-1922) 1 vol. for 2yrs.

(214) Lucknow Law Times (1960-) (Eastern Book co., Lucknow) Reports, Statute Law of U.P. & Central.

(215) M.P. Law Times (1959-)

(216) Macnaghton W.H. Reports of Sadar Adalat (1831-1840)

(217) Madhya Bharat Law Reporter (1952-56)

(218) Madhya Pradesh Cases (1957)

(219) Madhya Pradesh Law Journal (1956-)

(220) Madhya Padesh Law Times (Allahabad Law Pubns, Allahabad)

(221) Madhya Pradesh Rent Control Journal (1978-)

(222) Madras Criminal Cases (1914-1950)

(223) Madras High Court Report (1862-1875)

(224) Madras Caw Journal (1891-)

(225) Madras Law Journal. (Criminal) (1957-)

(226) Madras Law Limes (1906-1924)

(227) Madras Law Weekly (1915-)

(228) Madras Weekly Notes (1910-)

(229) Maharashtra Law Journal (1963-)

(230) Maharastra Law Reporter (1947-)

(231) Marshal W. Reports Civil Cases H.C. of Bengal 1862

(232) Matrimonial Law Reporter (1978-)

(233) Moore's Indian Appeals (1836-72)

(234) Molay's Digest (Cases of S.C. of Judi. India & P.C) (1849-60)

(235) Municipal Corporation Cases (1973-)

(236) Mysore Chief Court Reports (1896-1930)

(237) Mysore H.C. Reports (1931-1950)

(238) Mysore Law Journal (1923-1970)

(239) Mysore Law Reports (1878-1895)

(240) Nagpur Law Report (1905-1935)

(241) National Law Review (LIPS, New Delhi)

(242) North West Provinces H.C Reports (1869-75)

(243) O'Kinealy & G.S. Henderson Cal. H.C. Report Cases and P.C. Judgments.

(244) Orissa Judicial Decisions (1959-70)

(245) Oudh Cases (1898-1926)

(246) Oudh Law Journal (1914-1926)

(247) Oudh Law Reports (1934-1946)

(248) Oudh Weekly Notes (1924-1946)

(249) P.C. Judgements (Not Reported in ILR (1876-1897) by B.R. Dave.

(250) P.C. Judgements (P.B) 1930-33 by & lyer and A. Swarmi Nath Iyer.

(251) P.C. Judgements on Appeals from India (Saraswati & Banerjee) (1826-1886)

(252) Patna H.C. Cases (1917-1926)

(253) Patna Law Journal (1916-1921)

(254) Patna Law Journal Report (New) (1957-)

(255) Patna Law Report (1923-1925)

(256) Patna Law Report (New) (1957-1977)

(257) Patna Law Times (1920-1949)

(258) Patna Law Weekly (1916-1918)

(259) Patna Weekly Notes (1936-1977)

(260) Pepsi Law Reports (1949-1951)

(261) Prevention of Food Adulteration Cases (1971-)

(262) Prevention of Food Adulteration Journal (1975-)

(263) Punjab Law Journal (1967-)

(264) Punjab Law Reporter (1900-)

(265) Punjab Law Reporter (Delhi Section) (1968-)

(266) Punjab Law Reporter (P.L.R, Chandigarh)

(267) Punjab Records (1866-1919)

(268) Punjab University Law Review (Deptt. of law, Punjab University, Chandigarh)

(269) Punjab Weekly Reporter (1905-1922)

(270) Rajasthan Criminal Cases (1976-)

(271) Rajasthan Law Weekly (1950-)

(272) Rajdhani Law Reporter, New Delhi

(273) Rangoon Law Reports (1937-1947)

(274) Ratan Lal's Unreported Cases (1889-98)

(275) Rent Control Journal (1981-)

(276) Rent Control Reporter (1969-)

(277) Reserve Bank of India Bulletin (R.B. of India, Bombay)

(278) Revenue Decisions (1951-)

(279) Sales Tax Cases (Commercial law of India Pvt. Ltd. Madras) (1938-)

(280) Saurashtra Law Reporter (1948-1956)

(281) Seminar (New Delhi)

(282) Service Cases Today

(283) Service Law Cases, Delhi

(284) Service Law Reporter

(285) Simla Law Cases (1977-)

(286) Sind Law Reporter (1907-1938)

(287) Social Action (Indian Social Institute, New Delhi)

(288) Social Defence (National Institute of Social Defence, New Delhi)

(289) Southern India Sales Tax Cases, Madras

(290) Srinagar Law Journal (1979-)

(291) Suddar Dewani Adalat Decisions 1792-1855

(292) Supreme Court Appeals (1952-1970)

(293) Supreme Court Cases (Eastern Book Co, Lucknow)(1969-)

(294) Supreme Court Cases (Criminal) (Eastern Book Co., Lucknow) (1973-)

(295) Supreme Court Cases (Taxation) (Eastern Book Co., Lucknow) (1973-1990)

(296) Supreme Court Criminal Rulings (Allahabad) (1970-) .

(297) Supreme Court Journal (1950-)

(298) Supreme Court Reports (1950-)

(299) Supreme Court Weekly Reporter

(300) Sutherland's Full Bench Rulings Sup. 40 (1862-1864)

(301) Sutherland's Judgements of P.C. on Appeals from India (1838-1867)

(302) Sutherland's Reports of Appellate Decisions of H.C. of Calcutta, Jan. to July 18640

(303) Sutherland's Reports on Special Number July 1862 to July 1964

(304) Sutherland's Weekly Reporter (1864-1870 1 vol. for 1864, 1876 and 1877, 3E vols. for 1865, 2 vols for other yrs.

(305) Tamil Nadu Law Notes Journal (1975-)

(306) Tamil Nadu Law Notes Journal (Cri), Madras

(307) Taxation (Jor Bagh, New Delhi) (1948-)

(308) Taxation Law Reports (AIR Ltd., Nagpur) (1971-)

(309) Taxman (1978-)

(310) Travancore Cochin Law Report

(311) Travancore Law Journal (1911-1947)

(312) U.P. Criminal Cases (1974-)

(313) U.P Criminal Law Reporter (1968-)

(314) U.P. Criminal Times (1937-1941 & 1947)

(315) U.P. Law Trit une (1979-)

(316) U.P. Local Bodies & Educational Cases (1981-)

(317) U.P. Sales Tax Journal (1982-)

(318) U.P. Tax Cases (1974-)

(319) Un- Overruled Civil Cases of Punjab (1866-1880)

(320) United Provinces Law Report (1919-1921)

(321) Unreported Judgements (S.C.) (1969-)

(322) Unreported Printed Judgements of Bombay H.C. (1869-1898)

(323) Upper Burma Rullings (Civil & Cri) (1892-1922)

(324) Weir's Criminal Rullings vols. 1&2

(325) Writ Law Reporter Madras.

The aforesaid law reports include cases decided by the superior courts which have value as precedents and may be said to have as such the traditional or customary implied nature.

An Index to some Indian Legal Reference Materials :

(A) Well-Known Digests:

(1) All India Rent Control and Eviction Cases (from earliest time to 1976 -Eastern Book Company, Lucknow)

(2) All India Rent Control Digest (1969-1990) Vinod Pubns.

(3) Complete Digest of Supreme Court Cases (since 1950, Vols I-XVI each volume up to the date of pubn, Eastern Book Co., Lucknow)

(4) Complete Supreme Court Criminal Digest (1950-1992, Eastern Book Co., Lucknow)

(5) Consumer Protection Digest (Vinod Pubns)

(6) Digest of Income Tax Cases-3 Vols.-1933-1985 (Central Law Agency, Allahabad)

(7) Digest of Labour Cases (1960-)

(8) Fifteen Years Digests (1901-1965(AIR Ltd., Nagpur)

(9) Fifty Years Digests 1901-1950 (Digest Pubns, Madras/Nagpur)

(10) Income Tax Digest 1886 to 1978 (AIR Ltd., Nagpur)

(11) Index to Case Law & References on Criminal Law 1983-1993(Vinod Pubn., Delhi)

(12) Key to Supreme Court Judgements 1950-1992 (AIR Pubn, Nagpur)

(13) P.J. Patel's Supreme Court Reference Citations 1950-1977, (Legal Research Bureany, Jamnagar)

(14) Quinquennial Digests 1966-1970 (AIR Ltd., Nagpur)

(15) Quinquennial Digests 1971-1975 (AIR Ltd., Nagpur)

(16) Quinquennial Digests 1976-1980 (AIR Ltd., Nagpur)

(17) Quinquennial Digests 1981-1985 (AIR Ltd., Nag / Mad)

(18) Quinquennial Digests 1986-1990 (AIR Ltd., Nag/ Mad)

(19) Sales Tax Digest (S.V. Aiyar, Commercial Laws of India Pvt Ltd., Madras)

(20) Supreme Court Civil References, 1950-1993

(21) Supreme Court on Constitutional Law (Eastern Book Co., Lucknow)

(22) Supreme Court Decennial Digest (1981-1990 in 5 vols, Eastern Book Co., Lucknow)

(23) Supreme Court on Essential Commodities Act (Eastern Book Co., Lucknow)

(24) Supreme Court Labour & Services Digest (1950-1993 vols. I-VI, Eastern Book Co., Lucknow)

(25) Supreme Court on Public Servants & Disciplinary Action (1950-1987) Vinod Pubn.

(26) Supreme Court on Law Relating to Motor Vehicles (1950-1980, Eastern Book Co., Lucknow)

(27) Supreme Court on Preventive Detention (1950-to date, Eastern Book Co., Lucknow)

(28) Supreme Court Yearly Digest Series (1977 Onwards Eastern Book Co., Lucknow)

(29) Yearly Digest (MLJ Ltd., Pubns) (Discontinued)

(B) Well-Known Legal Dictionaries

(1) A Concise Law Dictionary (5th ed. 1954)-P.G. Osborne.

(2) A Dictionary of Legal Terms- N.M. Dani

(3) A Dictionary of Legal Terms-(1st ed., 1975) Vinod K. Agarwal

(4) A Selection Legal Maxims by Herbert Broom

(5) American Jurisprudence (70 vols.) and Corpus Juris Sceundum (72 vols) (West Publishing Co.)

(6) Black's Law Dictionary

(7) Biswas Encyclopedia 1979 Law Dictionary

(8) Dictionary of American Penology (1st ed, 1919)-Williams.

(9) Dictionary of Legal Police Terms & Phrases (English- Hindi)-R.C.Puni

(10) Dictionary of English Law by Charles Sweet (1882)

(11) Dictionary of English Law by W.G.Byrne (1923)

(12) Dictionary of English Law by Jowitt (1959)

(13) Dictionary of Laxation (1st ect., 1981)-Garry Hart.

(14) Dictionary of Statutory Terms...(1972)-BR. Beotra.

(15) Direct taxes Law Lexicon (1st ed., 1982)-G.S. Agarwal

(16) Glossary of Judicial & Revenue Arms (2nd ed., 1968)-H.R. Willon

(17) Glossary of Legal Words, Terms, Phrases, Maxims & Doctrines (2nd ed., English-Gujarati)-A.N. Karia.

(18) Glory of Term and Expressions Sales Tax, (1977)-S.P.Singh.

(19) Income Tax Dictionary (1st ed., 1982)-R.N. Lakhotia

(20) Judicial Dictionary (8th ed., (1980)- K.J. Aiya

(21) Law Dictionary (English & Hindi), 3rd ed., - Kamlesh Chopra.

(22) Legal Dictionary (1st ed., 1981)- Sinha & Narula.

(23) Law Dictionary(1st ed., 1982, Eng-Guj)-A.N. Karia, 2nd ed., 1976

(24) Legal Glossary (4th ed., 1988, Govt. of India, Ministry of Law & Justice) English-Hindi, Hindi-English, Latin-Hindi, with a list of Central Enactments)

(25) Legal Thesaurus (1980)- William G. Borton

(26) Maxims of the Law (1616) by Francis Bacon

(27) Mitra's Legal & Commercial Dictionary (2nd ed., 1976)- A.R. Biswas

(28) Mozley & Witecley's Law Dictionary Part I- (1970)- John B. Saunders

(29) Mozley & Whiteley's Law dictionary Part II- (1970)- A.C.Sen.

(30) Oxford Companion to Law (1980)-David M. Walker.

(31) Stroud's Judicial dictionary (1890, 3rd ed., 1952)

(32) Supreme Court on Words & Phrases (1993 R/P 1995)-Surendra Malik (Eastern Book Co., Lucknow)

(33) Terminology in Land Reforms (1st ed., 1982)-P.T. George

(34) Trilingual Administrative Dictionary (1st ed., 1988)-Govt. of Gujarat

(35) Venkata Ramaiya's Law Lexicon (Vol.I and II)- M.C. Desai

(36) Wharton's Law Lexicon (1848 and many later editions)

(37) Dhitherly's Dictionary of Insurance (1980-) Hugh Cockdrell

(38) Words and Phrases Judicially Defined by Ronald Burrow

(39) Words and Phrases Legally Defined (Ronald's ed., rev.,) by Sounders.

Bibliography

1. Ahmed, M.B. (1995). The Administration of Justice in Medieval India. 1st ed. Lucknow, Eastern book, pp. 104-125.

2. Ahuja, R. (1994). Indian Social System. 1st ed. New Delhi, Rawat Publication, p. 239.

3. Ali, M. trans (1996). The Holy Quran. 1st ed. Lahore, Ahmmadiyyah Anjuman, pp. 186-187.

4. Allen, B.C. (1906). Assam District Gazetters, Vol. III, Lakhimpur, Govt of Assam, Chap. IV, p. 118.

5. Ansari, M.S. (1987). Assam & Meghalaya Pension Code. 3rd ed. Allahabad, Orient Law House, pp. 20-25.

6. Ansari, M.S. (1992). General Provident Fund. 2nd ed. New Delhi, Orient Law House, pp. 30-31.

7. Ansari, M.S. (1992) Assam and Meghalaya Service Code.1st ed. Allahabad, Orient Law House, pp. 210-215.

8. Barpuzari, H.K. ed. (1990). The Comprehensive History of Assam. 1st ed. Vol. I. Guwahati, Publication Board of Assam, pp. 173-194.

9. Barpuzari, H.K., ed (1992). The Comprehensive History of Assam. 1st ed. Vol. IV. Guwahati. Publication Board of Assam. pp. 2-34.

10. Barua, B.K. (1986). A Cultural History of Assam. 3rd ed. Guwahati, Bina library, pp. 43-44.

11. Baruah, S.L. (1985). A Comprehensive History of Assam. 1st ed. New Delhi. Munshiram Manoharlal, pp. 135-413.

12. Basu, D.D. (1972). Commentary on the Constitution of India. Calcutta, S.C. Sarkar & sons., pp. 30-35.

13. Bhatnagar, J-P. (1993). Assam Financial Rules. 3rd ed. Allahabad Orient Law House, pp. 150-152.

14. Bhattacharya, P.ed. (1962). Asomor Janajati.1st ed. Guwahati, Lawyer's Book Stall, pp. 87-126.

15. Bhuyan, S.K. (1985). Studies in the History of Assam, 2nd ed., Guwahati, Omsons, pp. 229.

16. Bandopadhyay, A. trans (n.d.) Brihat Kalika Puran. Calcutta, Benimadhav Children's Library, Chap. 95, pp. 233.

17. Bordoloi, B.N. and Others ed. (1987). Tribes of Assam. Part-1. 1st ed. Guwahati, TRI, pp. 27.

18. Brahma, M.M. (1983) A Brief Introduction of the Bodo-Kacharis of Assam, In: Bulletin of TRI, Assam, Vol. 1, No. 1, pp. 52-53.

19. Brihaspati smriti, n.d., Gacward's Series, vol-XXVI, Delhi, Banarsidas, pp. 92-93.

20. Brown, C.J. (1922). Coins of India. p. 69.

21. Chatterji, S.K. (1970). The Place of Assam in the History of Civilisation of India.1st ed. Deptt. of pubn., University of Gauhati, pp. 6-7.

22. Choudhury, P.C. (1966). The History of Civilisation of the People of Assam to the Twelfth Century A.D.

2nd ed. Gauhati, Deptt. of Historical and Antiquarian Studies in Assam, pp. 8-50.

23. Collingwood, L.ed. (1996). 21st century universal encyclopaedia, 1st ed. Sydney, Regney Publishing, pp. 75-105.

24. Das, J.N. (1985). An Introduction to the Land Laws of Assam. 6th ed. Guwahati Bookland, pp. 62-67.

25. Dayal, R. (1984). An outline of Indian History and Culture.2nd ed. NewDelhi, Orient Longman, pp. 20-29.

26. Devsharma, R. ed. (1977). Kautilya's Arthasastra. Vol. IV.1st ed. Asom Prakashan Parishad, p. 10.

27. Dewan, V.K (1991). North-Eastern Region education code. 3rd ed. Allahabad, Orient law house, pp. 1-10.

28. Dewan, V.K. (1985). Fundamental Rules and Subsidiary Rules (Assam & Meghalaya) 3rd ed. Allahabad. Orient Law House. pp. 10-12.

29. Doloi, S.N., tran. (1994). Yoginitantram. 4th ed. Guwahati, Dutta Baruah, p. 359.

30. Dutta, N.C. (1968). Land Problem and Land Reforms in Assam. Delhi, S. Chand & Co., pp. 1-5.

31. Elphinstone, M. (1987). History of India. Bombay. Orient Longman, p. 421.

32. Encyclopaedia Britannica, 15th ed. vol. 14. Chicago, Encyclopaedia Britanica, p. 208.

33. Encyclopaedia Britannica, 15th ed. Vol. 23. Chicago, Ency. Brit., 1985, pp. 86-87.

34. Gait, E. (1990). A History of Assam. 4th ed. Gauhati, Lawyer's Book Stall, pp. 327-336.

35. Ghosal, U.N. (1965). Studies in Indian History and Culture. 2nd ed. Bombay, Orient Longman, pp. 179-191.

36. Goswami, U. (1994). An Introduction to the Deori Language. 1st ed. Guwahati, ABILAC, pp. 1-3.

37. Griffith, R.T.H. (1995). The Hymns of the Rigveda. edited by J.L. Shastri. Delhi, Motilal Banarsidas, pp. 184-290.

38. Hazarika, R (1985). Morgol Kachari Gupta Itihash. 1st ed. Khowang, Doyal Saikiia, p. 340.

39. Hornby, A.S.ed. (1986). Oxford advanced Learner's Dictionary of Current English. 10th ed. Delhi, Oxford University Press, p. 476.

40. Hunter, B ed. (1998). The Stateman's Year Book. 134rd ed. pp. 656-657.

41. Inperial Gazetter of India (1909). Delhi, Eastern Bengal and Assam, p. 590.

42. India : A Reference Annual. (1996). edited by Research Reference and Training Division, Ministry of Information Broadcasting. Govt of India, New Delhi, p. 1.

43. Index India (1986). vol. 7 (1-2). Joipur, Rajas than University Library, pp. 273-274.

44. International Encyclopaedia of Indian Literature (1987). Vol III. Edited by Ganga Ram Garg. Delhi, Mittal Pubn, pp. i-xv.

45. Jain, M.P. (1981). Outlines of Indian Legal History. 4th ed., Bombay, Orient Longmen, pp. 1-10.

46. Jois, R. (1990). Seeds of Modern public Law in Ancient Indian Jurisprudence.1st ed. Lucknow, Eastern Book, pp. 1-2.

47. Kangle, R.P. (1997). The Kautilya Arthashastra, Part-II, Ch-I. 2nd ed. Delhi, Motilal Banarsidas, pp. 268-270.

48. Khanna, J.K. and Vashist, K.K. (1985). Knowledge Evolution, Structure & Research Methodology. New Delhi, Ess Ess Pubn, pp. 309-351.

49. Kirtan-Ghosa and Nama-Ghosa (1985). by Srimanta Sankardeva and Madhavdeva, 1st ed Dibrugarh, Basudev Chutiya, p. 21.

50. Kulashreshtha, V.D. (1995). Landmark in Indian Legal and Constitutional History. 7th ed. Lucknows Eastern Book, pp. 1-2.

51. Kumar, K. (1989). Reference service. 3rd rev. ed., Vikas Publishing house, pp. 110-117.

52. Mahajan, V.D. (1967). Ancient India. 4th ed. Delhi, S.Chand. pp. 126-127.

53. Maheswar, N. (1981). Tradition and Style. 1st ed. Jorhat, Assam Sahitya Sabha, pp. 105-111.

54. Maheswari, S. (1992). Information Sources in Law, their Role for the Legal Profession. Herald of library science. Vol. 31. (1-2) : 22-26.

55. Majumdar, R.C. (1977). A Brief History of India 34th ed., Calcutta, K.Roy Mukherjee, pp. 257-323.

56. Majumdar, R.C. ed. Age of Imperial Unity. Bombay, Vidya Bhawan, n.d., p. 356.

57. Marckward, A.H. and Classidy ed., (1997). Webster Comprehensive Dictionary. Vol. I Chicago,

58. Mathew, K.M. ed. (1993) Manorama Yearbook. Kochi, Malayala Manorama, p. 611.

59. Mathew, K.M. ed. (1995). Manorama Yearbook. Kochi, Malayala Manoram, p. 455.

60. Maurya, R.R. (1985). Hindu Laws. 3rd ed. Allahabad, Central Law, p. 20.

61. Mandelbum, D.G. (1972). Society of India. Vol. III. 1st ed. Bombay, Popular Prakashan, pp. 1-2.

62. Mills, A.J. (1984). Report on the Province of Assam. 2nd ed. Guwahati, Pubn Board, p. 113.

63. Misra, T. (1987). Literature and Society in Assam. 1st ed. Guwahati, Omsons Pubh pp. 23-58.

64. Moys, E. ed. (1976). Manual of law librarianship. 2nd ed. London, Andre Deutsch, pp. 12-15.

65. Mukherjee D.P. and Mukherjee S.K. (1982). Contemporary Cultural and Political Movement Among the Bodos of Assam. A Seminar paper Included in : Tribal Movement in India, Vol. 1 Ed by E.KS Singh and Published by Manohar, p. 235.

66. Mukherjee. R (1978). Local Government in Ancient India. 3rd ed. Delhi, Banarsidas, pp. 29-34.

67. Mulla, D.F. (1982). Principles of Hindu Law. 4th ed. Delhi, Oriental Research, p. 192.

68. Muller, F. Med (1998). The Sacred Books of the East. vol-25, trans by Various Oriental Scholars, Delhi, Motilal Banarsidas, pp. 253-277.

69. Marckward, A.H. and Classidy ed. (1997). Webster Comprehensive Dictionary. Vol. I. Chicago, J.G. Ferguson Publishing, p. 207.

70. Narzi, B. (1966). Bodo-Kachari Samaj Aru Sanskriti. 1st ed. Guwahati, Pubn Board, p. 139.

71. Nadbhi, J.A. Compilor (1995). Hadish Shangrahe. 2nd ed., Guwahati, Asomiya Islami Sahitya Prakashan Samity, pp. 45, 56, 143.

72. Paranjabe, N.V. (19940. Indian Legal and Constitutional History.4th ed. Allahabad, Central Law Agency, pp. 2-4.

73. Pilsk, S. (1991). Information Resource Centre and its Service. In: Herald of Library Science. Vol. 30 (1-2). Lucknow: 65-66.

74. Pound, (nd) An Introduction to the Philosophy of Law. n.p. , p. 243.

75. Puri, S.K. (n.d.) Indian Legal and Constitutional History. Allahabad, Law Agency, pp. 18-19.

76. Kulashreshtha, V.D. (1995). Landmark in Indian Legal and Constitutional History. Lucknows Eastern Book, pp. 1-2.

77. Radhakrishran, S. (1977). The Bhagavadgita. 2nd ed. New Delhi, Blakie & Son, p. 340.

78. Rafiqullah ed. (1979). The Hadis Sharif. 1st ed. Culcutta, Haraf Prakashani, pp. 60-184.

79. Rahim, A (n.d.). Muhammedan Jurisprudence. 1st ed. Allahabad, Law Agency, pp. 36-37.

80. Raychoudhury, S.C. (1988). History of Modern India. 3rd ed. Delhi, Surjeet Publications, pp. 264-289.

81. Saikia, N. (1993). Bharator Sanskritic Aitijya Aru Anyanya Rasana.1st ed. Guwahati, Banalata, pp. 25-28.

82. Saikia, N. ed. (1991). Assam and Assamese Mind. 2nd ed. Jorhat, Assam Sahitya Sabha, pp. 11-59.

83. Saraf, B.P. (1980). Law and Practice of Agricultural Income Tax in Assam. 2nd ed. Guwahati, Ashok Publishing House, pp. 1-12.

84. Saraf, B.P. (1977). Taxation Laws in Assam & Meghalaya Guwahati.1st ed. Ashok Publishing House, pp. 5-8.

85. Sarma, S.N. (1989). A Socio Economic and Cultural History of Medieval Assam (1200-1800 A.D.).1st ed. Guwahati, Govt of Assam, pp. 158-176.

86. Sen, S.P. ed. (1988). Sources of the History of India. Vol. III. 1st ed. Calcutta, Institute of Historical Studies, pp. 10-15.

87. Sharma, R.S. (1996). Aspects of Political Ideas and Institutions in Ancient India. 4th ed. Delhi, Motilal Banarsidas, p. 103.

88. Shastri, J.L. ed. (1996). Manusmriti. 1st ed., Delhi, Motilal Banarsidas, pp. 30, 329.

89. Sinha, B.S. (1987). Jurisprudence. 1st ed. Allahabad, Central Law Agency, pp. 54-55.

90. Singha. H.M. (1997). Legal Dictionary. 1st ed. Delhi, Pioneer Books, pp. 114-286.

91. Thakur, G.C.S. (1984). The Autochthones of the Brahmaputra Valley and their Contributions towards the cultural heritage of Assam. In : Bulletin of the Tribal Research Institute. Vol. 1 No.III, Guwahati, TRI, pp. 41.89. The Constitution of India (1988). 1st ed., Allahabad, Allahabad Law Agency, pp. 62-78.

92. Tripathi, R.S. (1960). History of Ancient India. 1st ed. Delhi, Motilal Banarsidas, p. 78.

Index

T

U

V

W

Y